The Builder's Secret

George Ehrenhaft

THE BUILDER'S SECRET

Learning the Art of Living

Through the Craft of Building

PRIMA PUBLISHING

PRIMA PUBLISHING and colophon are registered trademarks of Prima Communications, Inc.

Illustrations by George Ehrenhaft

Library of Congress Cataloging-in-Publication Data

Ehrenhaft, George.
    The builder's secret : learning the art of living through the craft of building / George Ehrenhaft.
      p. cm.
    Includes index.
    ISBN 0-7615-1607-7
    1. Dwellings—Remodeling popular works. 2. Buildings—Additions—Design and construction Popular works. I. Title.
TH4816.2.E3   1999
690'.8—dc21   99-15126
                                          CIP

99 00 01 02 HH 10 9 8 7 6 5 4 3 2 1
Printed in the United States of America

How to Order

Single copies may be ordered from Prima Publishing, P.O. Box 1260BK, Rocklin, CA 95677; telephone (916) 632-4400. Quantity discounts are also available. On your letterhead, include information concerning the intended use of the books and the number of books you wish to purchase.

Visit us online at www.primalifestyles.com

To all the men and women who start their weekends
with a trip to the hardware store

Contents

Acknowledgments

Special thanks to the owner-builders whose stories fill this book. Generous with their thoughts, their time, and their hospitality, they indulged me more than I had any right to expect.

I'm also grateful to the builders with whom I talked but whose stories could not be included in these pages—especially Bob Rasero, Patricia Liddle, Kirk Rankin, Norman Rinder, and Eric Statin.

Several good people encouraged me, advised me, held my hand—none more than Sherry Suib Cohen. Her counsel and unflagging optimism fueled my efforts from start to finish. I also thank Rose Scotch, Larry Cohen, Whitney Collins, Stedman Mays, the late Connie Clausen, my tireless agent Mary Tahan, and my editors at Prima Publishing—Julia McDonald and Andrew Mitchell.

Many thanks to Michele Beemer of the Heartwood School in Washington, Massachusetts. Also to John Esposito, Richard Polay, Marti Kirschbaum, and Glen Kitzenburger. All helped me locate owner-builders with interesting stories to tell.

By critiquing my manuscript—some of it more than once—Phil Restaino left a huge imprint. He has an unerring sense of language and logic, a discerning ear, and in me, a grateful friend.

Finally, I can't begin to count the ways in which my wife, Susan, supported and sustained me.

Introduction

Some years ago, as my fortieth birthday neared, I got it into my head to build an addition to my suburban house, though I'd never driven a nail in earnest or held a two-by-four in my hand. The decision to build was not made suddenly, but was hastened when Susan and I noticed we had a population problem at our house—too many people, not enough room. Our two children were practicing a domestic form of manifest destiny: They were staying up later, making more noise, and occupying more space. Moving about in our cramped six-room house, the four of us kept bumping into each other, as though caught in a perpetual game of musical chairs.

Our bank statement told us in an instant to forget about buying a roomier house, and my teacher's salary convincingly put to rest the idea of paying a builder to make our house roomier. So we turned to the drawing board and looked at ourselves, especially at me. Did I have the will to build? Yes. The stamina? Yes. The time to do the job? Yes. Did I have the know-how? No, but I could probably figure it out.

I laid out a do-it-myself curriculum. I studied the tools and asked lots of questions in the aisles of hardware stores and lumber yards. I crept into every corner of my attic and cellar to examine frame construction. I followed heating ducts and electric cables and measured everything. Books explained laying out a plot using batter boards. They told me about building foundation walls and showed me how to mix concrete, construct a frame, and shingle a roof. Months of research expanded my knowledge and added hundreds of words from the builder's lexicon to my vocabulary. (See the glossary at the back of this book for a selection of basic terms.) My course of study also included a practicum. Our house became my laboratory, and after a year of weekend experiments, every closet in the place had new shelves, our upstairs hall sported a partition it really didn't need, and a portico covered the front stoop of our house. Then, following Susan's sketch for a three-room, twenty-by-thirty-foot addition, I drew a set of plans to submit to the local building department. When I told the inspector I'd be building the addition myself, he frowned and warned me that I'd live to regret it.

Although it was the hardest, sweatiest physical work of my life, he was dead wrong. Seven days a week, often from dawn to dusk throughout a long summer, I surrendered myself to the project, exiled myself to a backyard island with stacks of lumber, boxes of nails, concrete blocks, shingles, bags of cement, plywood and Sheetrock in neat piles, doors, windows, drain pipes, and tools. As I worked, a structure grew out of this mass of material. And as I worked my own pieces came together, too, for during the solitary days of sweat, oblivious to the weather and to time and food, ignorant of my family's needs and the world's affairs, it came to me that I toiled not only to construct an addition to my house but to build a new foundation and frame for my life. Out in the backyard, propelled by a midlife craving for renewal, I had undertaken a defining test of endurance and will that would change my life forever.

One evening soon after I had begun to lay the foundation wall, I sat at the rim of the excavation and mused about some future archaeologist unearthing my rectangle of concrete and trying to make some intelligent guesses about the guy who built it. I decided to leave an account of myself, a personal Rosetta stone, sealed in a glass jar and embedded in the wall.

As I thought about what to say, it struck me that through the ages countless men who built structures of stone must have harbored thoughts like mine in the still of their evenings. The masons of Chartres, ancient Corinthian stone cutters, Indians sculpting houses in sandstone cliffs—all must have sat quietly after a day of toil and imagined a time a hundred or a thousand years hence when other men would walk among the ruins of their handiwork and contrive images of the original builders.

At that moment I felt a deep kinship with swarms of nameless builders whose lives had been occupied by the same rhythmic, body-honing construction work that I was doing. It felt as though I had suddenly broken through time and space and been engulfed—if you'll pardon the expression—by some sort of universal consciousness. The feeling was gone in a flash, but for that instant I saw myself as an essential bit of the mortar that binds man's dim past to his unknown future. Although my addition was but a pockmark on the Earth's face, it had granted me vision more often claimed by mystics than by amateur builders in the suburbs.

At first I thought I'd been too long in the sun that day. But several weeks later, after covering the frame of my addition with plywood, I stepped into the darkened shell for the first time and in the half-light was washed with a sense of expanded awareness, as though I had suddenly been freed from my ego and been allowed momentarily to merge with a power greater than myself. Again, the sensation dissipated swiftly and left me wondering whether the intensity of my work had either unhinged me or given me access to what is widely called a "spiritual experience." To be honest, though, the sound of that gave me the willies.

Those moments of heightened consciousness, along with others that hit me unexpectedly during subsequent construction projects (especially while building my own house in the country), continued to intrigue me. I carried them around for years, burning to know whether other amateur builders, self-styled do-it-yourselfers like me, ever had illuminating moments in their work, too. From time to time I met owner-builders and talked with them about materials and craftsmanship, but all on a purely practical level, the way men talk to each other around the counter at the lumber yard. During those conversations, I could never quite bring myself to ask casually, "Say, has your soul been stirred on the job site lately?" or, "By any chance, did you experience any enlightenment while you carried those roofing shingles up the ladder?"

No, I had to wait for a time when I could get past the small talk and seriously discuss the ins and outs of weekend building. That time didn't arrive until after I'd retired from teaching and couldn't think of a better way to occupy my days. So I began to seek out owner-builders who had completed major renovations, added rooms to their homes, or built their own houses from the ground up. From them I hoped to learn whether I was onto something big with my spiritual gigs or whether I was just a harmless old goose with a hyper-poetic disposition.

In all, I talked at length with fifteen owner-builders, most of them as avid as I about their avocation. This book grows out of my conversations with nine of them. In its pages you'll meet, among others, one ex-schoolteacher, a divorced mother of three, a writer, a big-city cop, an architect, a high school guidance counselor, an artist, and a member of the Boston Symphony Orchestra. Some have lived with tools and sawdust all their lives, while others didn't pick up a hammer until they were grown. Their one common trait is that they all earned a living in other fields when they undertook major building projects.

A group portrait of these folks would show a contingent of respectable, friendly, high-energy, adventurous men and women hailing from the cities, suburbs, and backwaters of seven different states. What makes them distinctive, of course, is that they are experienced owner-builders aching to tell their stories. Given that chance during my interviews, they adopted an almost reverent tone, as though they were reporting a miracle. Their eyes brightened with pleasure as they relived the experience in the telling of it, even though some of their accounts are filled with episodes of frustration and near despair. All had blissful moments—when the footings were done, when the ridge was raised into place, when the roof passed muster without a leak during a terrific downpour. But no event was quite as stunning as standing back for the first time and seeing their completed work occupying what had once been empty space.

Many of my respondents were prodded into a major building project by lack of space, lack of money, or both. Some needed a place to live, while others sought adventure. A few fell into weekend building because it was there. Now they all count the time they spent building among the most exhilarating months or years of their lives, on a par, perhaps, with falling in love. Not that every moment was sublime, but precious few of their previous endeavors had ever hooked them so completely. Predictably, all the builders remain passionately proud of their achievements even decades after they hammered the last nails.

Less obvious, and, therefore, more fascinating to me is the story of how they were drawn into building in the first place, how they went about it, and what the experience has meant to them. Did building stimulate their emotions? Alter their lives? Heighten self-awareness? Awaken their spirituality? During my interviews I tried to find out.

I met my respondents face to face in their workplaces and homes—once, twice, or three times. We also spoke on the telephone and communicated by e-mail. Some of my respondents readily laid their feelings on the table, speaking freely of their passion to build and the sensations they experienced on the job. Others hid their inner lives, leaving me to draw my own conclusions about how, or even whether, building had stirred them. One of them, Patricia Liddle, who built her own house in upstate New York, gave it to me straight after I endeavored to point out some evocative aspects of building, "That's not for me," she said, "but if you want to believe all that stuff, George, go right ahead." But Norman Rinder, a weekend builder in Vermont, told me, among other things, that some building projects, like his children, he'd love till he dies: "My backyard deck, for instance. It's four years old, and I still can't get over how gorgeous it is. I sit on it to read and before long I'm studying the design and thinking about the summer I built it. Some projects just won't leave you alone."

Although all the builders checked the accuracy of what I wrote about them, the margins of misinterpretation remain wide. Several of the building ventures described in these pages took place ten or more years ago. Having been filtered through layers of time and memory, then refiltered through my own understanding of what was told to me, they may not have happened precisely as presented. Regardless, the stories record experiences of nine resourceful men and women, all of whom seem to have learned something about the art of living though the craft of building.

Home Work

I began my search for owner-builders by picking up the phone and calling Pete Williams. He and I had been colleagues in the same high school for ten years. We crossed paths regularly—in the corridors, at meetings, and in the guidance office, where he was the head counselor—never failing to shake hands when we met. No one else did that, just Pete and I, as though by joining hands we acknowledged a powerful bond between us, doubtless born out of our mutual fascination with homebuilding. Pete's grip is surprisingly strong, his hand callused from swinging a hammer.

We could have discussed curriculum at our brief encounters, or traded school gossip, but Pete and I talked building, often to the disdain of others in our company who hadn't a clue as to what we were saying to each other. Our conversations usually picked up right where we'd left off: "What happened with that header that was giving you trouble?" he might ask. Or he would tell me about his new cordless half-inch drill with a keyless chuck—"a beauty, a real beauty!"

During the time we worked in the same school, Pete, at home, labored to complete a 2,400-square-foot, three-story addition to his house. I went over to admire it a few times. Twice I took my hammer with me. While helping him frame a wall and put up redwood siding, I observed Pete's knack for

1

growing rapturous about building. His fervor, bordering on the romantic, probably planted the idea in my head to write a book about amateur builders like us. In that sense, Pete has been my inspiration and my muse.

PETE GREW UP IN A SMALL house at the bottom of a hill in New Rochelle, New York. Whenever it rained a lot, the cellar turned into a puddle. One day when Pete was eight, a downpour created a pond deep enough for launching a toy boat. The flood also put the furnace out of commission. As Pete's dad, an industrial hygienist, went down to fix the boiler's firing mechanism, Pete followed, and asked him how he knew that he could repair the damage. "I don't," his father replied, "but I'm as smart as other guys who fix things. If they can do it, so can I."

Pete never forgot his father's words. They became a kind of creed, a can-do legacy that Pete says, "percolated inside me for years." But until 1979, when he and his wife Susan bought a world-class handyman special, Pete had few chances to fire up his fix-it spirit. The decrepitude of his newly acquired house changed that. Years of neglect made the place affordable and gave Pete a reason to tear holes in walls, bang boards together, and buy a Shopsmith, a high-end multipurpose power tool with which to make lots of noise and sawdust.

Had the house been anywhere except New Rochelle, Pete might not have bought it at all. But this one, on a sedate street with tall trees and well-kept properties, was just blocks from his childhood home. Occasionally, Pete drove past the house where he'd grown up and gave a wistful look at the bedroom wing his father had added for Pete's two younger brothers. He vividly remembers coming home from school one afternoon to find his father digging a hole next to the house. "I'm adding a couple of rooms," he told Pete. "Want to help?" And so, at age eleven, using a shovel that towered above his head and a wheelbarrow that almost outweighed him, Pete began to learn about building from the ground up.

Still another sentimental link attached Pete to his future home. The owner, an elderly widow, remembered Pete as a teenager bagging groceries at the A&P and wanted him to have her house, in which she had lived for more than fifty years. For him, she reduced the price from $72,000 to $68,000. Unable to resist the discount, he bought the house, delighted to discover that his $1.25 an hour after-school job at the supermarket included a belated $4,000 bonus.

As a new homeowner, Pete loved righting household wrongs. And with plenty of wrongs to right, Pete felt as though he'd arrived in handyman heaven. The house, built in 1921, had for more than half a century been ill treated and ill kept. Its condition was so poor, in fact, that for three months after the closing, Susan and Pete lived with Pete's mother. During that time, Pete, with zeal bordering on fury, brought the house up to move-in speed. Weekends and every night until he nearly dropped, he gave himself to home repair and renewal. With the help of an electrician, he updated the 80-amp service to 200 amps. With the help of a plumber he replaced the broken boiler in the basement. His first solo venture was the repair of a basement toilet. Next, he took on the only real bathroom in the house, a second-floor slum where water trickled through mineral-clogged pipes and the toilet could not be flushed. Only the shower, its head attached to the end of a rubber hose, functioned more or less as it should.

The room also contained an unusable claw-footed bathtub. Decades of drips had worn a hole through its floor. Pete attacked the tub with a sledge hammer. The first hits bounced off harmlessly. Then he wrapped the tub in a heavy blanket and let go with a crushing barrage of blows that in no time produced cast-iron shards small enough to throw out the bathroom window to the trash bin below. Next, he tore up the rotted floor, tiles and all, and suddenly found himself looking down past the joists into the kitchen below. It was a breakthrough in more than one sense. "I remember being startled," Pete says. "I remember thinking that, by God, I was beginning to be a real builder now. I had actually chopped the floor apart and had to put it together again."

If floors caved in so handily to assaults, Pete supposed that walls would too. So, he boldly resolved to relocate the bathroom's only window, originally situated above the sink. Thinking it preferable to look at his own face while shaving instead of at his neighbor's chimney, he planned to replace the window with a mirrored cabinet. With his brand-new reciprocating saw ("my wonderful Sawzall"), he dispatched the old window, leaving a large square hole in the side of his house. There he built a frame to hold the cabinet, then nailed a piece of plywood on the outside to cover the opening.

Installing a new window, however, was a more delicate operation. It required chopping a hole in the wall and removing a piece of framing—more specifically, extracting half a stud. Studs, Pete knew, held up the top plate—the pair of horizontal two-by-fours that form the top of the wall and help to carry the weight of the roof. Eliminating a stud might undermine the integrity of the roof, but probably not enough to worry about. Taking a chance, Pete sliced into the stud with his Sawzall. Nothing untoward happened. He made another cut. Still nothing—not a creak or a sign of strain. Then he pulled out the segment between the cuts and sawed a window-sized rectangle out of the sheathing. Except for daylight washing into the room, still nothing had changed. The wall appeared to be perfectly sound. But just in case he had somehow introduced a fatal debility into the structure of the wall, he framed the rough opening for the new window with twice the amount of lumber that the job required. On each side he inserted three studs, above which he mounted a double two-by-six header with a plywood spacer, an amalgam of solid lumber strong enough to hold up half a house.

When the bathroom walls and floor were whole again, Susan and Pete took up residence in their home for good. For good, perhaps, but not for gracious living. They showered in the half-finished bathroom on the second floor, brushed their teeth at the kitchen sink, and, to use the john, trotted down to the basement. Because their bedroom lacked a closet, they slept in one place and dressed in another. The dining room, desperate for a new decor, trapped them in the kitchen for meals. Every room in the house still cried out for help.

Inspired by the memory of his father, Pete tackled each renovation in turn, banking on a lot of faith and a little dumb luck to see him through. "Many people are too cautious," he says, "afraid that their house will fall down if they open a wall. My dad was the opposite." Pete believes that he and his father are part of what Herbert Hoover called "the American system of rugged individualism." While it's arguable that the gospel of the hardy individual is distinctively American, the qualities of do-it-yourselfism run deep in our culture and character. To his regret, Pete never talked man to man with his father about such ideas. The elder Williams died too soon, but, says Pete, "I'm sure that it would have been a kick for him to see me buy that old house. He would have been right there by my side as I worked on it." In a way, of course, his father has been there, ever since the day Pete tore into that old bathtub with a sledge hammer.

After seven years of repairs and home-improvement projects, Susan and Pete, now the parents of two children, developed the itch to do something with more cachet—in particular, to add an eating alcove to their kitchen. Susan had in mind a "bump-out" sort of structure, a small extension with lots of windows that Pete could build quickly and inexpensively. "Why not?" Pete thought. After all the remodeling he had done, a four-by-eight-foot cantilevered addition would be a cinch.

As Susan and Pete sketched a plan, the allure of more space caught their fancy. Since half the kitchen would be dismantled anyway, maybe they ought to tear down the whole back wall and add a large open area for cooking, for eating, and for looking after their children. The space underneath the expanded kitchen could then be combined with a basement storage area to make a one-bay garage. At the same time, by building on top of the enlarged kitchen, they could solve the problem of the cramped bedrooms and bath upstairs. Adding to the second story, of course, would also mean extending the attic and restructuring the roof. Like kids at play with Legos, Susan and Pete exulted in reshaping their house. "We didn't know exactly what we wanted," recalls Pete, "but Susan's plan for a 'bump-out' assumed a life of its own."

On a whim, they wrapped the new addition around a corner of the house, connecting it with the screened porch. "Yes, that's it," said Pete. "Let's turn the porch into a family room." (Finding the porch too flimsy to recycle, Pete later demolished it and built an entirely new room, from the foundation up.)

"Since we won't have a porch, let's add a deck," responded Susan, who preferred one that ran the length of the rear and would be accessible from both kitchen and living room.

"If we do that," Pete said, "we could support half the deck with a concrete wall rather than with posts. Then, we'd have enough space underneath for a two-car garage as well as a workshop."

How much their taste for expansion would cost, Susan and Pete didn't know. Nor did they have any idea when they finally asked an architect to draw up official plans for remodeling their house how completely their lives would be remodeled as well.

"THE MOST GUT-WRENCHING time of my life." That's how Pete describes the morning a backhoe clanked into his backyard, sank its giant claw into the grass, and started moving huge chunks of earth around. "On a par with getting married," he continues. "Maybe even worse. At the altar, at least, the ground didn't tremble."

It wasn't only the roar and unruliness of the backhoe that shook Pete's equilibrium. "I really didn't know what I was doing," he says. "I was about to take on a big building project, an addition that would double the size of my house, and I suddenly realized I had only the vaguest idea of how to go about it."

Twenty-four hours earlier he had had no such doubts. But his self-confidence had taken a plunge the previous afternoon, when he phoned the excavator to confirm his appointment.

"By the way," asked the owner of the backhoe, "where do you want me to dump the dirt?"

"Don't you have a dump truck? I thought that was part of the deal," insisted Pete.

"What dump truck?" responded the excavator. "No, you have to get the truck."

Caught off guard, Pete saw his excavation plans about to be unhinged. "For the first time I grasped the meaning of *novice*," Pete says, "and realized how ignorance can hurt you." He had scheduled the dig weeks before, and with groundbreaking just hours away, he needed to find a truck. Call after call led nowhere, until he located a landscaper with a five-ton truck and a day off.

"By the way," the driver asked, "where do you want me to dump the dirt?"

"Don't you have a place? I thought that was part of the deal," insisted Pete.

"No way, sorry. You get the place." Another unexpected snag.

Pete hurriedly erected a sign on his front lawn—"Clean Fill–Free"—but he doubted that any of his neighbors would soon be out looking for a hundred tons of dirt to cart home the next day. Then he remembered a nearby construction site where two homes were being built and tried to make a deal with the boss. "I have some good soil and can let you have it pretty cheap."

"No," said the man. "I don't need any at the moment."

"Would you take it, anyway, as a gift?"

"No, I really don't need it."

"You'd be doing me a favor," said Pete. He had visions of paying the man to accept his gift and was about to make an offer when the man agreed to take twenty truckloads, free.

To get himself ready for the next day's dig, Pete could think of nothing better to do than to worry. He paced around the house for a while trying to anticipate other crises, but none came to mind. What did occur to him, though, was that he might not be qualified to manage a construction project that surpassed in pith and moment anything that he'd ever attempted before. Although he'd done all in his power to prepare the site properly, the snafus of the day had intensified his pre-dig jitters.

Most of his preparatory work had consisted of measuring and marking the outline of the excavation. The area to be dug out would wrap around the rear and one side of the house. Part of the addition was to be built over a crawl space with four feet of headroom, the rest over a garage area with a standard eight-foot overhead. Pete computed the depth in each segment of the excavation. The architect had told him to dig at least to the frost line, forty-two inches below the surface. At that level, Pete's foundation would be immune to the swelling of soil that occurs when water turns to ice underground. A house sup-ported by a shallow foundation rises and falls with subter-ranean freezing and thawing. Such movement breaks footings, cracks walls, and over time, threatens the health of the whole building. Every new house is expected to settle while the foun-dation and the surrounding soil get to know each other, but no house—other than a quake-proof variety—can long stave off the motion sickness caused by frost heaves. To dig out a frost-free level area in Pete's backyard, where the ground fell steeply away from the house, half of a small mountain would have to be moved. Less than four feet of dirt would be scraped from the far edge of the excavation, but next to the house itself, the backhoe would have to gouge out more than fifteen feet of hard-packed rocky soil.

The topography of the site called for footings—the wide concrete platform underneath a foundation wall—to be built in steps ascending toward the house. On the footings, which were to be uniformly eight-by-sixteen inches, Pete planned to erect a foundation of concrete blocks, all of them seven-and-a-half inches high and cemented to each other by half-inch lay-ers of mortar. If Pete miscalculated or was unable to follow the specifications, the floor of his new addition would fail to match the existing floor of the house. "I was starting my build-ing career with one of the most difficult projects," Pete says. "Retrofitting can't be hit or miss," he explains. "You've got to be exact."

Late on the night before the dig, Pete recalculated the numbers one more time, and then slept fitfully while waiting for the backhoe to arrive. At eight the next morning Pete told the excavator where to dig the hole and just how deep to dig it. "I gave him the precise dimensions," Pete recalls, "but the whole time he was at my house—three full days—I had that awful knot in the gut that comes when you think you may have made an awful mistake."

To guide the backhoe operator through the dig, Pete had borrowed a surveyor's transit from a friend who also gave him a crash course on its use. A transit is basically a spirit level mounted on a tripod. By sighting through an eyepiece toward a vertical rod or rule, you can easily determine differences in elevation between any two points and track, to the width of a hair, the depth of an excavation. Because the transit that Pete used was old and shaky, the readings were a bit rougher than he would have liked. If he told the excavator to remove too much soil, Pete would be hauling gravel to refill the hole. Too little, and he'd be left digging the rest by hand. Neither prospect enthralled him.

The rudiments of house construction were not new to Pete. He had once taken a three-week homebuilding course at the Shelter Institute in Bath, Maine, where he learned how a house is put together and how its systems function. Still Pete suffered the uncertainties of a freshman builder, feeling like a stranger in a strange land where he spoke the language haltingly and didn't know the customs. In the distance, he envisioned a larger, more beautiful home for himself and his family, but the path to follow was dimly marked, and he hadn't the remotest idea of how long it would take to get there. As he watched his backyard being turned into a moonscape, his insides were in turmoil. He was excited by his venture into unfamiliar territory, but, as Pete readily admits, "That first step scared the hell out of me."

Frankly, that's hard to imagine. In his office, crowded with plaques, trophies, and mementos of his years as a coach, Pete projects the self-confidence of a man incapable of losing his cool, even while tottering at the rim of a huge crater being dug in his backyard. Ready with a smile and wearing the rugged good looks of a cowboy—tall, leggy, lean—he seems incapable of being frightened or flustered about anything. Over his desk he has push-pinned two-dozen yearbook portraits, some of the graduates he has helped navigate through high school. The school's grapevine says that he stands by kids when they fail, flounder, or do something ineffably "teenaged." Students think the world of him. They say he's well-informed, respectful, caring, and generous—in short, a mensch.

Pete marvels at how his simultaneous lives as builder, coach, and counselor began to intersect and collide when the work started. In his building mode, he frequently hired his school's varsity football players as helpers. As their coach, he knew which of them learned quickly and would give him an honest day's effort on the job. As someone with gaps in his knowledge of building techniques, he knew the frustration that a slow kid might feel in a fast class.

"I'm a better counselor and coach because of it," he comments. "I'm also more sensitive to kids in trouble. If the kid makes a mistake, OK, he's made a mistake. Without moralizing, I'll try to help him learn from it, and maybe he won't do it again."

Pete remembers a time when he himself had been the beneficiary of similar big-heartedness. Fresh out of college, he and a friend, Dave Hussel, apprenticed themselves to Dave's father, a professional builder in Cincinnati. "Mr. Hussel showed me how to cut and install baseboards," Pete remembers. "Then he handed me an old miter box and told me to go to it." Now, anyone who's tried it will tell you that good trim work takes skill and practice. Joints must be tight, so tight that seams should not admit the edge of a playing card. Cutting two perfect 45-degree miters won't guarantee a tight seam, because not every corner in a house is a true right angle. Experimentation, though, teaches you to tailor cuts that form perfect joints on imperfect walls. Mr. Hussel also advised Pete on forming inside corners: Don't miter both pieces. Instead, butt the end of one piece against the wall, and then, with a coping saw cut the end of the opposing piece in the profile of the baseboard.

The coped end placed snugly against the first piece will form a tight joint—provided, of course, that you cut the cope accurately, by no means a sure bet for a novice carpenter. "Fortunately," Pete says, "Mr. Hussel started me off installing baseboards inside closets, where mistakes would be hidden. He was willing to let me make errors without embarrassment or penalty. I've never forgotten that. He was the best teacher I ever had. I think of him a lot when I deal with kids."

As a guidance counselor, Pete guides dozens of kids through the labyrinthine college admissions process every year. With each student, he helps prepare a strategy and a winning admissions package. Leaving nothing to chance, he makes sure that kids attend unflaggingly to every detail. As Pete now knows, planning savvy is a basic tool for a builder, too. "When my architect kept telling me to plan out everything ahead of time," he says, "I heard myself talking to my own students," but, as a newcomer in major construction, Pete didn't always heed the advice, not because he wasn't listening but because planning is devilishly hard when you're a relative novice and don't know what lies around the bend.

Or, for that matter, on the other end of a telephone line. Pete likes to tell about the time he was just about to tear down his old porch. Needing a Dumpster for the debris, he called a carting company in the Bronx, five miles from the New Rochelle line.

"Who told you to call us?" asked the man who answered the phone.

"A friend of mine. Can you help me?"

"Who's your friend?"

Pete told him. Then silence on the line. After a minute, the man returned. "Look, pal, call someone else. We don't do business in New Rochelle."

Pete had apparently stumbled into the fine print of Dumpster etiquette. A neophyte, he didn't know the rules of the game. But the carters surely did. They were allowed to pick up refuse here but not there—and restraint of trade be damned. Pete surmised that the consequences of horning in on another's turf would not be pretty and so made several more calls before locating the carter assigned to his territory. Then, having no idea about Dumpster sizes, he ordered a thirty-cubic-yarder, the supertanker of refuse bins, with enough capacity to hold five demolished porches. "That'll be $631.25," he was told. "Pay on delivery, in cash, or the Dumpster won't come off the truck. Get it?" Pete got it.

His first brush with the carting crowd left a deep impression. He heard the message loud and clear, that as a beginner he shouldn't expect any favors. Rather, as a new kid he ought to be prepared for a few hard knocks. "If you're going to build," Pete says, "it helps to have thick skin."

It also helps to be prepared. On the day his footings were to be poured, Pete scheduled the delivery of concrete at twelve o'clock. Just before noon, with the ready-mix truck en route, he was still building forms. In his haste to bully the last planks into position, he got tripped up. In one spot he neglected to provide a step down between levels. Elsewhere, he set the forms two inches too high, an error that he failed to notice until he laid the last blocks of the foundation wall weeks later. "When I saw that the height of the new and old walls didn't match," Pete says, "I learned to use a mason's hammer." While chipping the tops and webs off twenty-eight feet of concrete block, he kept hearing echoes of his Shelter Institute instructor: "Get the footings right. If you start wrong at the bottom, you are going to fight it all the way to the roof."

For footings Pete ordered a ready-mix delivery of nine cubic yards. "I was clueless about what to expect when the concrete truck arrived," Pete tells me. "I had to trust the guy on the truck but I honestly hated being at his mercy." The driver, direct from Central Casting—beefy, tattooed, crewcut—drove his rig up Pete's driveway and waited for instructions. Unsure of what to tell the man, Pete said, "I'm Pete," and extended his hand, which the driver ignored.

"OK," the driver responded.

"How ya doin'?" asked Pete.

"OK," the driver responded.

"Glad you made it," Pete said.

"OK," said the driver.

This was going to be more difficult than he thought. "Listen," Pete blurted out, "I'm new at this."

"OK," the driver said.

"The job is sort of complicated, and I'd appreciate your help. And, by the way, here's something for your trouble," said Pete, handing the driver a twenty-dollar bill.

"OK," said the driver, suddenly interested, "I'll back up the truck as close as I can, but my chute goes only sixteen feet. Anything further, you'll need wheelbarrows." Pete was prepared for that. His crew of gridiron stars stood by with wheelbarrows, shovels, hoes, and rakes—implements with which to pull and push liquid stone into the waiting forms. One of the crew held an ordinary steel bar, a "vibrator" used to poke and stir the concrete in order to eliminate air pockets. "Fill the farthest forms first," continued the driver. "Then you won't have to work around concrete that's already been poured. It'll save you time, too. For nine yards you get one hour of truck time free. After that you pay eighty bucks an hour."

At that rate, speed counts. "But," says Pete, "you can pull concrete through those forms only so fast, and none of my crew had ever done it before. So we pulled and we pulled. And we sweated. It was ninety-five in the shade that day. It took us four hours to fill up those forms, but, by God, we got it done. At the end, I collapsed. I'd never been so tired in my life."

Before coffee the next morning Pete climbed onto his footings and marched back and forth. Yesterday's pudding felt solid and massive underfoot. "To say I had a feeling of accomplishment is an understatement," says Pete. "I was euphoric." The outline, the so-called "footprint" of his addition, was literally set in stone. Almost literally, that is. If his footings veered slightly off the mark—not unheard of in the annals of amateur building—he had four inches of wiggle room from side to side. That is, without fear of calamity he could erect the eight-inch-wide foundation wall anywhere on the sixteen-inch-wide footings, but not beyond either edge.

Completed footings mark a turning point in a construction project. Until the pour, Pete had focused his attention deep into the earth, calculating depths and distances downward. With the footings in place, however, he began to look up. From that day on, he would measure progress in ascending increments.

First to rise on the footings was the foundation wall (built with a mason's help) followed closely by the frame. The two jobs trapped Pete in a building blitz unlike anything he'd ever experienced. For sixty straight summer days Pete climbed unswervingly toward his goal, a weather-tight roof by Labor Day. At night, wrung out after sixteen hours in the sun and heat, he asked Susan to put his tools away. "I was usually so tired that I couldn't even roll up my extension cord," recalls Pete. If his addition had no roof when he returned to school, it surely wouldn't be for lack of trying.

An experienced carpenter and a helper might frame an addition the size of Pete's in two weeks. On Monday they'd attach the sill and install the floor joists. By Friday night most walls would be up, and by the end of the following week, the sheathed roof would be ready for shingling. But Pete painstakingly inched along: a whole day on the mudsill, two days on joists for the first floor, another day to nail down the plywood deck. He spent an entire afternoon framing a ten-foot segment of a bedroom wall, measuring every piece three, four, and five times. He cut the lumber with a surgeon's care and fitted the timbers together with the precision of a cabinetmaker.

Pete toiled ultra-cautiously in order to avoid mistakes—not that he was always successful. But whenever he miscut a board or nailed a stud incorrectly, he shrugged it off, remembering Mr. Hussel. "To err is human," his mentor of long ago had often told him. By chance, Pete had an opportunity to play Mr. Hussel to his friend Jim Ryan, who arrived from New Bedford, Massachusetts, for a weekend, ostensibly to help Pete frame his addition. Jim's real intent remains a mystery, however, because he'd never used a hammer before. "As Jim was growing up," Pete explains, "his dad discouraged him, told him over and over that he would make a mess of whatever he touched." Therefore, Jim, convinced of his own ineptitude, never made a thing, not even a mess, until the day he showed up on Pete's doorstep. "Jim was strong and willing to learn," Pete goes on, "and I was willing to let him try, even if he screwed up. He cut some boards too short—just as I sometimes did—but in most cases, I saved the short boards and used them elsewhere." Pete's indulgence paid off when Jim, who had come for two days, stayed for twenty. And every day he gave Pete twelve to fourteen hours of help. "He was a godsend," Pete says, "as crucial to my addition as the main girder."

On occasion, as the summer wore on, the momentum of the work slipped—even regressed now and then. After Pete put a window into its opening in the wall, for example, he and Susan would eye it suspiciously and sometimes find it wanting. "It's not right," Susan would say to Pete "it's got to be moved." One window looked too small, another not small enough. A third, located on the staircase landing, lined up perfectly with windows on the second floor, but it couldn't be reached by anyone under six-feet-nine. Undoing finished work is a price that beginners pay for being beginners. Pete says, "I couldn't tell how windows would look until I saw them in their openings." And when they looked bad Pete moved them. On paper he transplanted a window in seconds. But when the move required carpentry he'd be lucky to finish in half a day. Relocating the kitchen sink necessitated a ten-inch shift of the window above it, a task that also meant cutting and replacing vent and water pipes. On that job, Pete averaged about an inch an hour.

That fall, when Pete returned to school, he left behind a seriously unfinished addition. Wall-framing was done, but only a portion of the roof. Because half a roof keeps out only every other drop of rain, Pete almost hired a roofer to finish the job. But he didn't, and he beat the season's first snowfall by a whisker. Inside the addition that winter the climate was cold and barren, but thanks to Pete's assiduousness, bone dry.

Just how long Pete ultimately worked on the addition surprised everyone, including Pete. Four years after the studs went up Pete began to install the Sheetrock. ("A blessing in disguise," he calls it. "Because the foundation had settled and the lumber had dried, there'd be no cracks in my walls and ceilings.") Initially, he wrapped the exterior walls in Tyvek; six summers went by before he mounted redwood siding. His two children, Jenna and Mike, grew from infancy to school age in a construction zone. To them, home was a place with unfinished walls, dust, clutter, and a radial arm saw stationed between the dishwasher and the oven. Friends and family joked that when the job was done it would be time to begin remodeling again.

When the building project began, Pete and Susan had no sense of the beast they were unleashing in their home. They didn't know that it would color what they thought and govern what they talked about, not only to each other but to virtually anyone with ears. Just how completely the project shaped their lives for the next nine years is revealed by the annual letters that Susan sent with Christmas cards to far-off friends and relatives. Each year's news is dominated by a single theme, and the highlights of each month allude to siding, the delivery of double-hung windows, claw hammers, Japanese planers, and variable-speed reversible power drills. Some letters suggest that during the past year nothing but building the addition had occurred in the Williams household. Unless you read between the lines, you wouldn't know that two active kids were growing up there, nor that Susan had earned a master's degree, and that, by the way, Pete changed careers. No longer a math teacher, he'd taken up guidance counseling and switched from Eastchester to Mamaroneck High School.

Instead, the letters inform friends and kin from coast to coast that during the past twelve months:

". . . Pete and Susan take separate winter vacations. Pete goes to bank loan offices. Susan goes to mortgage companies.

". . . Pete works very hard on foundation and frame. Susan would love to help but is finishing her graduate work. Pete never questions that her courses run from 7:30 A.M. to midnight every day.

". . . Susan completes her coursework, spends one day at home and considers going for a doctorate.

"... Pete realizes that the new gray carpet in the living room is already a year old. Susan is sure she remembers buying a *blue* carpet.

"... Family goes to Camp Sloan for weekend of rustic surroundings, raw nature, no phones, no heat, no electricity, no indoor plumbing. Heck, we could have stayed home in the addition. Siding will go up next.

"... Susan plans to produce and market a video called *The Happy Homemakers*, the story of a fun-loving family with a dream to build an addition that costs more than they could ever hope to afford. Laugh with them and cry with them as they work to make their dream a reality. Sit on the edge of your seat to see if the building even remotely resembles the plan Susan designed. Feel their fear and frustration as they rebuild again and again the collapsed temporary roof of tarps and planks in torrential rain and freezing temperatures at 5:30 in the morning. See Susan, and feel the love she has for Pete. See Pete, and feel the love he has for his radial arm saw. Melt during tender bedroom scenes when Pete says, 'Susan, move over, the table saw has no covers.' Dare to guess what Susan means by 'My man carries a heavy hammer.' Finally, cheer, laugh, and cry with profound joy as their dream reaches the halfway point and they've run out of money.

"... The Thanksgiving turkey smells great in the oven, with the roof shingles right next to it warming up so they won't crack while being put on in freezing weather.

"... Plywood goes on the roof. Pete plans to make an instructional video called *The Addition*, starring himself. He will show homeowners how to build an addition for just under a million dollars. 'How can it be so affordable?' you ask. Just let Pete show you how to cut corners and save. Most people make the mistake of hiring experienced professionals. Not Pete. Learn how he builds with the help of high school and college kids, brothers, friends, neighbors, and colleagues from work. Discover how to estimate how many beers and sandwiches a day's work is worth. Let Pete show you the cost efficiency of leaving the entire inside unfinished.

". . . Window openings are boarded up and weatherproofed just in time for the delivery of the windows. Cold weather and Christmas preparations bring the addition to a halt. (OK, they *extend* the halt.) What can I say? Some gifts last a lifetime. Some gifts take a lifetime."

Lampooning life in a construction zone permitted Susan to blow off steam. She was entitled, for a work site is everything that a home isn't. Homes are filled with lots of soft, comfy stuff. Where hard hats roam, however, there are things that scratch, cut, splinter, and bruise, plus all sorts of hard objects to trip over and bump into. What's more, home renovation typically upsets family routines and confers refugee status on everyone in the house. There's no good time to be without a kitchen sink, but when the whole kitchen is out of commission for months, and the entire family competes for the same john, and a futile war on dust drags on and on, the mettle of a marriage can be tested. But Susan and Pete, both committed to the core, withstood pressures that break less steadfast couples apart. "We're both flexible," explains Pete, "and we were in this together from the first day." Readiness to forswear comfort ensured them, if not bliss, at least a measure of domestic tranquillity, although at times Pete thinks it might well have been therapeutic to be a little less saintly.

To the extent that Pete can be said to have started out with a distinctive building style, it was less as a long-term strategist than as a catch-as-catch-can solver of unforeseen problems. But by the fourth year of the project Pete had learned a thing or two about planning ahead. In due time, too, for he was about ready to cover ceilings and walls with Sheetrock. After mapping out a scheme for Sheetrocking each room, he ordered 160 pieces, from eight to fourteen feet in length. Most were half an inch thick, but he also needed some $5/8$-inch sheets to compensate for extra-wide window jambs, or frames. (The wall covering must be flush with the edge of the jamb to provide a flat surface for attaching the window trim.)

Although Sheetrock is not sold by the pound, weight may be its most memorable feature. At 1.75 pounds per square foot, a twelve-footer weighs nearly eighty-five pounds, about the same as a Cub Scout, but far more cumbersome to lift. One person carrying a piece of Sheetrock usually wishes he were two. One hundred and sixty pieces makes a stack almost ten feet tall. To move all that dead weight from his driveway to the rooms where it belonged, Pete needed more than a couple of halfbacks from his team. Even his whole defensive line couldn't lug the longer pieces up the stairs; there simply wasn't enough room. To complicate matters further, the dimensions of each room called for a different assortment of Sheetrock. Thinking ahead, Pete asked the supplier to organize the delivery according to a room-by-room distribution plan that he had masterminded. That way, the pieces designated for each room would be grouped on the truck and more easily dispersed upon arrival. Pete's plan worked: The truck came with a boom that could lift a load of Sheetrock to a large opening on the second floor where Pete had removed a window. It also came with two nimble guys who, as Pete puts it, "danced through the operation." Upstairs, they slid the Sheetrock off the boom and carried it to its proper destination. Down below, handling the Sheetrock like Sunday china, they stacked it neatly in the designated rooms. Mission accomplished, thought Pete. He had turned potential fiasco into logistical triumph.

"Days like that can make building addictive," Pete says. Acknowledging that he is hooked, he adds, "On days I'm planning to work, I usually can't wait to get started. I'm pulled out of bed, sort of like Christmas morning when you're young. Not everyone understands that but other builders can." The appeal of building for Pete lies partly in its palpability: "When it's time to quit," he says, "you can count the two-by-fours you've nailed into place. You can measure exactly how much the structure has grown that day." By contrast, Pete is never sure that he's earned the sunset when he leaves the counseling office. He says, "When I shut the door behind me, I often have a hard time seeing what I've accomplished."

Enamored of building now, he recalls a time when he was less sanguine about his part-time occupation: "At first I had trouble communicating with some of the people I met," he says. He'd like to forget chilly encounters with men in the trades who told him, not always in words, that they disapproved of his presence on their turf. In their faces and body language Pete read, "No trespassing." The message was anathema to Pete, who hangs on to the curious belief that people ought to be nice to each other. His school career is based on nothing except nurture and support, lending a hand and solving problems. Small wonder, then, that in the builders' domain Pete, at least in the early years, sometimes felt like a pariah.

PETE IS NOT THE SAME MAN who began adding rooms to his house late in the 1980s. He's changed his mind about builders. He no longer feels like an alien in their midst. "I sometimes visit construction sites and watch the show," he says. "It's very instructive." By observing two framing carpenters, he once learned the simple, labor-saving technique of marking the location of studs on the top and bottom plates at the same time. Before they drove a nail, he saw the carpenters lay one plate on top of the other and with a single stroke, pencil a line on both pieces. "And if the workers seem willing to talk," he goes on, "I ask questions. Most are proud of their work and happy to tell you about it." Just as Pete himself is. When he expounds on his own building projects, his face radiates.

Like a kid showing off his new toy, he delights in touring visitors around the addition he built: the sixteen-by-twenty-eight-foot cutting edge kitchen; the family room with a vaulted ceiling and a fireplace; the stairs to two bedrooms, a bath, and a full attic; an expansive redwood deck; and a cavernous workroom, housing practically every building tool known to man—not a bad crop for a builder with a full-time career on the side. "But," Pete admits, "at times it was not fun. I was always concerned about how much work I had and about not having enough time to do it. After an exhausting weekend on the job, I sometimes asked myself, 'Do I really want to continue doing this?'" Evidently he did, for he kept faith with the spirit of his father who would "try anything" and never regret it.

The two-story addition (left) and the family room with vaulted ceiling and fireplace (right) doubled the size of Pete's house.

"My beliefs have changed," Pete says. "I appreciate the effort it takes to build, and I recognize quality workmanship." Visiting a home for the first time, he is apt to scan the finished Sheetrock for seams and screw marks. He bounces on the floor checking for squeaks, and he studies the trim for telltale signs of a carpenter's indifference. Well-crafted handiwork of any kind moves him. Don't get him started on the bands of hand-cut dentil molding—each tiny block a perfect replica of every other—that he once saw in a 140-year-old whaler's house in Bedford, Massachusetts. "I marvel at it," he says. He's even been known to stop his car to gaze at wonderful roadside stone walls. "I admire the artists who built them and wonder who they were," he says.

Nine years after digging the excavation, Pete's addition is almost done, but not quite. A piece of molding is missing in the family room. A section of a wall needs a paint job. He and his family have settled comfortably into the rooms he built. The kids, who once thought that all fathers were supposed to beat on their houses with hammers on weekends, can hardly remember the pre-renovation house. Perhaps Pete will never finish his addition. It may be in his blood to keep tinkering, keep improving, keep striving for perfection, as though he subscribes to the Hindu notion that *becoming* is more precious than *being*. Don't do a task to get it over with; it's in the doing that fulfillment lies. "Part of relishing a place is changing it," he believes. That's why, for Pete, "finishing is never finished." True, the saws no longer scream in his addition, and his hammer is still. Someday Pete will turn to the work that remains to be done. In the meantime, procrastination is understandable. His long-lived building project stands as a defining experience in his life. Indeed, why would he want to end it by nailing that last piece of molding into place?

To Build a House

During the summer of 1997, while tracking down amateur builders, I spoke to Michele Beemer, the codirector (with her husband Will) of Heartwood, a home-building school in western Massachusetts. Michele told me that her students have included teachers, truck drivers, architects, social workers, retirees, and high school students, most with little or no previous construction experience. She also told me about Jennifer Lee, an alumna who, upon completing Heartwood's three-week program, built her own house in Plainfield, within commuting distance of the Heartwood campus.

On the phone Jennifer said, "I clean houses."

Wondering whether I had misunderstood Michele, I replied, "Oh, I thought you built them."

"Oh, yes, I do that too," Jennifer shot back instantly.

Two weeks later, I sat with Jennifer on the back porch of her home, which she shares with Glen, her younger son, now a teenager. The land behind the house drops steeply to a stand of tall maple trees, just turning to crimson. In spite of the first chill of autumn, she prefers to talk out of doors. "The birds can keep us company out here," she says, folding her legs beneath her, Indian-style. Her present house is five miles from the one she built mostly by herself nearly a decade ago. She leases that house now and counts on the income it generates.

Both houses are hidden behind trees along dirt roads in an area of Massachusetts called Pioneer Valley, an aptly named place for someone like Jennifer, whose life, I soon learn, has been a groundbreaking adventure in more ways than one.

"I'M LEAVING," said Jennifer after still another fight with her husband Alan. The discord that sent her packing that night was the last straw. It convinced her that it was time for a break in the marriage that had been foundering for years despite counseling and her best efforts to keep it afloat. Out in the dark, Jennifer took refuge in a small cabin a stone's throw from the front door. Hardly more than a cell, the cabin was empty except for a bunk bed, a wobbly rocking chair, a table with one leg missing, and a handful of resident spiders. It had no heat and no insulation. Wind rattled its windows. But its roof was sound, and Jennifer thought that with minor improvements her new lodgings could be made habitable, at least until she figured out whether her marriage could be saved. What's more, by staying close to home, she could continue to care for her three kids by day and stay out of Alan's way at night.

From the cabin's doorway, Jennifer could see their house, a sorry, broken-down affair that she and Alan had bought a year earlier as a "fixer-upper." They had dabbed it with paint and scrubbed it, but little more. "We didn't know much about fixing," says Jennifer, "but we didn't have very high standards, either. It was a place to keep us warm and dry."

Whatever its condition, though, the house, located in Worthington, Massachusetts, outclassed some of her previous dwelling places: a derelict trailer that cost her $400, and prior to that, a teepee in the Santa Cruz Mountains of California. Years earlier, swept up in the counterculture of the 1970s, Jennifer, not yet twenty, had fled New York's Westchester County in favor of the West. There she bought a horse and bartered caretaking chores on an estate for a small piece of grazing land and a clearing in the woods, where she set up a canvas-covered teepee. During the next four years, she moved her horse and teepee a handful of times in pursuit of winter

sunshine and summer shade. She also met Alan, another transplanted Easterner, married him, and had a baby girl, Jaylin.
Although Jaylin had no objection to a dirt floor or to wood
smoke in her diapers, over time her parents found a teepee's
appointments incompatible with childrearing. So, after their
son Timmy was born, they moved into cushier quarters—
a basement flat they rented from a local apple farmer. The
birth of another son, Glen, sent them three thousand miles
closer to their families, first to Charlottesville, Virginia, and
then to Worthington, in the Berkshires, where Jennifer, her
marriage *in extremis*, was about to make a small cabin her
new home.

The cabin had a solid foundation and floor. But its walls of
exposed studs and old rough-hewn planks begged for a facelift.
Horizontal strips of pine paneling was the concept Jennifer saw
her mind's eye, but "wood" was all she knew to describe it. "I
need some wood," she told the proprietor at a nearby sawmill.

The man smiled. "How much wood do you need?" he
asked.

"How do I tell you how much wood?" she responded. "I
want to cover the walls of a cabin."

"Well, OK, how big is the cabin?"

"I don't know."

"Well, go measure it," the man told her and held out a
twenty-five-foot Stanley measuring tape for her to borrow.

"Oh, I already have a ruler," she said. "It's three feet long."

The man laughed and said, "Suit yourself, but I'm tellin'
you—to do the job right, use tools that are right for the job."

Jennifer realized that the man was trying to help her and
took the tape. When she returned with the cabin's dimensions,
he asked what lengths of paneling she wanted. Again she was
stumped.

"Do you want all the boards to end at the same place? If so,
you'll have a seam running up the wall," he told her.

"No, I don't want a seam," she said.

"Then you want different lengths."

"Yes, that's right, I do," Jennifer said.

To this day Jennifer gives thanks that during her first foray into lumber-buying she met a man who made nice with her. Had he been a crank—who can say?—her building career might have ended before it began. But thanks to the kindness of a stranger, Jennifer was outfitted with the materials she needed to start. In addition, she found a hammer and circular saw in a tool chest that once belonged to Alan's father.

"Sawing was easy to learn," says Jennifer. "You just plug in the saw, push the button, and hold on, taking care not to cut off your fingers." As she practiced keeping her fingers intact while sawing scrap lumber, Jennifer took note of several fascinating phenomena: For one, the saw made an awful racket; it also spewed dust in all directions, from which Jennifer deduced that it might be prudent to keep her eye on her eyes as well as on her fingers. She also noticed that the cuts followed her penciled lines only when she guided the saw very slowly, no more than an inch every few seconds. In addition, she found that the blade removed about an eighth of an inch of wood in its passage across a board, a fact to keep in mind when measuring strips of paneling. She'd also have to remember to keep the good side of each board up when cutting because the blade left a smooth edge on the top, but a ragged, splintery one below. What perplexed her, though, was that her cuts were rarely perpendicular to the long edge of the board. Then, "by chance," she says, "I ran across this tool. It was a sliding ruler set at a right angle to the base, and if you put the base against the edge of a board, you could draw a perfect ninety-degree angle." Jennifer had discovered a combination square, one of a carpenter's essential tools.

The cabin's interior turned out well, far better, as it happens, than Jennifer's marital arrangement. For her, a fifty-foot separation from her husband proved light-years too short. Within months, she and Alan divorced, divided their earthly goods, and parted. With $14,000 in her pocket—half the proceeds from the sale of the house—she set out to reinvent her life.

The last time she had asked, "What do I want to do with my years on Earth?" she settled into a teepee in the woods. On her own, she might have done so again, but not now, not with three young children to raise. As Jennifer saw it, she owed Jaylin, Timmy, and Glen a happy childhood and a stable, loving home, especially on the heels of a divorce that had left them emotionally roughed up. At odds with her motherly instincts, though, lay a deep-seated impulse to take less-traveled roads. Soccer-momhood was an honor she would gladly do without.

Jennifer resolved the dilemma ingeniously: She made up her mind to buy a piece of land on which she and her kids would build a house that would serve as the centerpiece of a nourishing and durable family life. By doing much of the work herself, Jennifer would keep the faith with her individualistic spirit and need for adventure. Domesticity and derring-do— Jennifer would have them both.

TO EXPLAIN HOW SHE found her way into home building, Jennifer sketches a rough outline of her life since dropping out of high school at age eighteen: work in a Connecticut leather-goods shop, the only nine-to-five job of her life; a long spell in a West Coast teepee; three kids; a couple of years in Virginia; a marriage gone sour; browsing around in the Berkshires until— the final leg—she alighted here and planted roots on this sunny hillside.

An indifferent student, Jennifer had yawned her way through high school in suburban Harrison, New York. In her senior year she enrolled in Woodshop, a breakthrough of considerable note at the time. She not only crossed a gender barrier but changed the customary role of shop class as a dumping ground for wastrels. "As the only girl in the class, I felt very self-conscious," she recalls, "but I wanted to learn how to make things with wood." It was a vain hope. "The teacher spent most of his time trying to get the boys to behave themselves, and I wasn't learning enough about woodworking to make sticking out like a sore thumb worth it." So, Jennifer bolted from Woodshop and kept on going. "I was done with high school. I was eighteen and knew what I wanted. My parents were hoping I'd go to college," she says, shaking her head at the memory. "I still apologize to them." Now, at age forty-two, she's leavened a bit and admits how bullheaded she must have been. "I thought I knew everything," she says. "Today, I'm surprised at how little I know."

Hindsight suggests that Jennifer might have graduated had she told her teachers what she confides to me: "I love history," she says, but not, evidently, the variety taught in high school. She prefers to live history, or at least to pretend that she is living it. For years she has followed Native American powwows as devotedly as groupies once tagged after the Grateful Dead. A powwow—there are dozens held weekly in all corners of the country—attract devotees of Native American culture who camp in tents and teepees, dress in Indian garb, and take part in a potpourri of cultural events—dances, songfests, and recitations. Hoping to keep Native American traditions alive, both ersatz and ethnic Indians compete in contests of shooting, archery, tomahawk- and knife-throwing, fire-starting, and log-sawing. Costumed as an early Northeast Woodlands Indian woman, Jennifer concentrates on leathercrafts: fashioning headbands, moccasins, leather pouches, belts, leggings, and sheaths for knives. She also demonstrates tanning techniques and swaps her know-how in leatherwork for instruction in beading, dyeing, and decorating with porcupine quills. Lately, Jennifer has also begun to participate in reenactments—simulations of noteworthy events in Native American history, such as the signing of the tribal treaty that formed the Iroquois nation or battles in the French and Indian War.

Immersed in Indian history, she has absorbed some tenets of Indian thought, and while not a true believer herself, she radiates an inner quiet that is often associated with spiritual attainment. Around campfires at night, she talks with others about achieving personal serenity by being open to the harmony and unity in nature and by guiding one's life according to the cycles of the seasons.

How did a native of Harrison, New York, that quintessential corporate enclave (IBM, Texaco, Sprint, General Foods,

PepsiCo), wind up hunkering next to a fire pit week after week clad in deerskin and feathers?

"When I was little my family took many overnight camping trips," she explains. "Also, I had a book filled with Indian crafts and lore that I would read over and over. I followed the instructions and made every leather object in the book." Jennifer could as easily have taken up totem-pole carving or canoe building, but leather was her forte. "That's how I got a job in a leather shop," she adds. The book's treatise on Mohawk *haute couture* inspired her wardrobe, and another chapter told her about surviving on wild edible plants garnished with roots, nuts, and berries. What grabbed her attention, though, were the pages devoted to teepee construction. For years she longed to design and build a teepee of her own. "In California," Jennifer says, "I pulled out my book and finally got my wish."

Jennifer's lifelong devotion to all things Indian has intensified her devotion to all things natural. When streams and forests call, her heart responds. Years after she abandoned her teepee, her faith in nature helped prod her into home building. Providing a shelter for her brood fulfilled the demands of an elemental urge as basic as motherhood itself, and building a house became an act of preservation no different from lighting a fire to keep from freezing to death.

Her reverence for nature resounds through the house she came to build. Its interior is a paean to wood: Grand timbers frame the main room along with generous wooden baseboards and moldings that appear to pay homage to the spiritual ties between man and nature. Window and door frames, some with bark and the stumps of branches still attached, are the jewels of the house, all unique, all displayed against stark white walls that bring out the wood's rich umbers and siennas. Most of the frames are made of rough-cut pine—very rough—their texture and grainy trails swirling in lively contrast to the plain white surface behind them. But the *pièce de résistance* is the kitchen counter, a three-inch thick slab of wood, bark and all, cut diagonally from the trunk of a mammoth maple tree.

"The thing about wood," says Jennifer, "is that it's dependable. There are no unknowns when you build with wood. It's not complicated, like mechanics. When you open up an engine, you never know what you'll find. But with wood the only uncertainty is whether a piece will be twisted or bowed. If the piece is no good, you just burn it or use it where its flaws don't matter. It's all very basic." Jennifer puts in a good word for using rough-cut, true-dimensional framing lumber—that is, two-by-fours that literally measure two inches by four inches, available at sawmills but almost never sold off the shelf in a lumber yard. "You've got your exact dimensions," she says, "you've got your lumber, you cut it to length and hammer it in. If you make an error, you do it over or you live with it. With wood, everything is cut and dried," she says, ignoring her own pun. "That's what I like."

Jennifer's discourse on home construction carries the voice of authority. Having had a fling with almost all the building trades since paneling the walls of her Worthington cabin, she can hold forth on carpentry, excavation, masonry, roofing, and virtually everything else about the craft of home building. She can even tell you about zoning statutes and the price of land in this corner of the Bay State.

Her building education began as soon as her divorce proceedings ended, when she sought to buy a piece of Massachusetts on which to settle down. Figuring to save money by skirting the realty market, she studied tax maps at the town hall, then phoned property owners to ask whether they'd like to sell an undeveloped piece of their land. Moved by the power of suggestion, several said they were. As a result, Jennifer got to see a score of building lots, but not one of them excited her. Sometimes she never got out of the car. Finally, after weeks of searching, Jennifer saw a parcel with potential. The sticker price was $12,000. When she offered its owner only $6,000, he flew off the handle. "You've got balls!" he told her, apparently blinded by rage. Startled by the man's anger and shaky grasp of anatomy, Jennifer fled the scene and soon found a three-and-a-half acre lot that she agreed to buy for $10,000. "I was a nervous wreck over whether I'd made the right decision," she says. "The check sat in a stamped envelope for weeks before I mailed it."

While looking for land, Jennifer enrolled in Heartwood. The three-week home-building course she took there eliminated any doubts that she could build most of a house by herself. "It wasn't that I learned everything I needed to know," she says, "but I learned how I could figure it out." For one thing, she found that there is no shortage of user-friendly home-construction books to guide readers through every stage of home building. In Heartwood's library, she perused books devoted to roof and stairway construction, books on doors and floors and siding, on building decks and laying tile, even a monograph on how to draw a gorgeous house plan. What caught Jennifer's eye, however, were the charts that told her the dimensions of lumber required to span any given distance. By looking it up, she could find out, among other things, that a Douglas fir two-by-eight can be used to span twelve feet if she set the floor joists sixteen inches apart. But for a more solid feel underfoot, use two-by-tens. With information like that at her fingertips, Jennifer told herself, "Heck, I'm going to do it."

Home design was one of the topics covered in the course. After weeks of hunching over her kitchen table, Jennifer brought her teacher a sheaf of graph paper on which she had drawn an eighteen-foot by thirty-two-foot, two-story, shed-roofed house—in essence, an overgrown lean-to enclosed by four walls. On the south side, the tall side of the structure, she extended the roof five feet past the outside wall, hoping the overhang would block the summer sun and trap sun-warmed air during the winter. ("It's amazing," says Jennifer now. "With plenty of windows to let in sunshine, the house is remarkably warm, even when it's ten below outside.") On the windowless north side Jennifer drew a gabled extension to serve both as a vestibule and a place to stash sleds, skis, bicycles, and the other accoutrements of life with children.

Her drawings for the first floor showed a spacious main room adjoining a large kitchen and a full bathroom. Off a

On the south side of Jennifer's house, a wide overhang blocks the summer sun and traps warm air during the winter. Octagonal windows let daylight into the loft of each second-floor bedroom.

second-story hallway, she lined up three bedrooms against the south wall of the house. Each bedroom had a steeply pitched ceiling and one twelve-foot-high wall against which Jennifer planned to build a loft that her kids could use either as a play area or an upper bunk.

"This is a small house," said Jennifer's Heartwood teacher as he studied her plans, "but you've used the space well."

"He gave me an A," says Jennifer, grinning.

When she carried her drawings to the local building inspector and told him, "This is what I want to build, and this is how I plan to build it," he, too, approved. In retrospect, Jennifer counts the A from Heartwood the richer prize.

"Plainfield is a small mountain town," she explains, "where everything is informal. The building inspector—that's Ron. When I meet him on the street he gives me a hug and calls me Jen. It wasn't like going into the office of some big bureaucrat."

After paying for her land, Jennifer was left with a building fund of $4,000. The money ran out after she completed the shell, but the United States government rode to her rescue via a HUD-sponsored program that, according to its prospectus, "helps low-income families capture a piece of the American dream." Since HUD looked kindly on applicants who could cut costs by contributing their own labor, Jennifer was granted $12,000, a sum she spent on a drilled well, a septic system, and a new driveway. Finally, from her parents Jennifer borrowed $4,000, with which she completed the job.

To make ends meet during construction, Jennifer began to work as a part-time domestic, a position she holds to this day, although she's hardly wild about scrubbing other people's floors.

"Cleaning houses is not wonderful," she says, "but it's how I made my gambling money, so to speak. It's right for me: I work hard, can be my own boss, and come and go as I please. I know beforehand what has to be done, I do it, and I'm gone. Besides, I wouldn't want a regular job. Go to work at a certain time? I couldn't do that and wouldn't want to. I'll work my butt off, but don't tell me when I've got to start and stop."

Jennifer is truly a child of the do-your-own-thing era. "If I had gone to college or done the regular route, it wouldn't have worked," she says. "I feel that I could do something better than clean houses . . . and maybe I will someday," she adds wistfully. Her tone conveys the message that deep down she may regret her lifelong insurgency. Perhaps her trail of missteps—dropping out of school, years as a nomad, a failed marriage—weighs on her. Did she choose to build merely because she required shelter? Or was building a way to exorcise some private demons and fend off the fear of being something less than she could be? Could she have used building to prove both to herself and to the world that she's made of higher-grade stuff than her record showed?

Whatever the reason, Jennifer set her course toward home-building with the brio of a converted sinner, and once she got into the swing of it, couldn't have been happier. "Life was supposed to be that way," she notes. "I knew what I had to do, I knew how to do it, and I knew I was doing it. 'OK,' I said to myself, 'I'm a good girl now,' accomplishing what I want to accomplish, building the least expensive shelter possible for me and my kids. What could be better than that?" Now, when she goes back to visit her house, she's flooded with memories of who she had been at the time and what life had been like. "I was sort of scared then because I was fighting for my life," she remembers.

She fought indefatigably, but in fragments. In school, the kids were on different schedules. "Glen was in kindergarten," she recalls. "I'd put him on the school bus, run up to the site for a couple of hours, then run back to meet the other bus bringing Timmy home. Then back to work until the next pickup. At the work site my kids did their homework, played, and helped me in any way they could. Later we'd all go home and I'd cook dinner." On alternate weekends, the kids visited their father, granting Jennifer precious hours of uninterrupted time.

Thus, Jennifer toiled year-round except in deepest winter. But even then she couldn't stay away for long. On weekends when the cold showed signs of restraint, she donned boots and long johns and clocked another day on the job, often feeling caught in a classic kids-versus-house dilemma. The kids pressed their mother to take them ice skating or to a movie while the front wall cried out for only two more sheets of plywood. The kids needed help with homework, but Jennifer needed to puzzle out the assembly of a corner post before the next day. "Conflicts like those were hard to resolve," she says, "and it went on for two and a half years."

Although Jennifer's enthusiasm for building rarely faltered, there were times that she'd just as soon forget: when she prepared her site for the pouring of the footings, for example. "You should never have to be alone in a six-foot-deep trench," she says, alluding to the narrow pits dug by her excavator to accommodate the concrete footings and piers that one day

would support her house. Shovel in hand, Jennifer forced herself to climb to the base of each trench. There, mole-like between towering dirt walls, she scooped out a enough soil and
rock to make room for footings two-feet square and a foot high.
As she stooped at the bottom of each trench, visions of a sudden cave-in frightened her. Was this the place where three kids
would lose their mother? In spite of her dread, however, she resolved to finish the job herself. The night before the pour, a terrific rain washed a tide of mud to the bottom of the trenches,
obliging her to screw up her courage and descend once more
into the earth to dig out the sodden mess of dirt and rocks.

"That was the most nerve-wracking part," Jennifer recalls.
But having discarded other ways to build a foundation, she had
left herself no choice but to see the ordeal through. At first, she
had planned a foundation of poured concrete. Then she
switched to a wall made of concrete blocks. But either of these
methods would have left her deep in debt. What's more, she
had been scared off by the masonry contractor she had called
to assess the cost of a concrete wall. "He not only gave me an
estimate," Jennifer says, "he gave me an attitude. He tried to
scare the hell out of me by telling me everything I didn't
know." Rather than explain his services, the man frightened
her with tales of amateur builders whose plywood forms fell to
pieces under the first wave of wet concrete. He told her about
ill-prepared sites, cracked foundations, and improper ratios in
the mix, and he attempted to snow her with gibberish about
"set time," "snap-ties," and "psi's with a five- to seven-inch
slump."

"I hate when people do that to me," Jennifer says. "I'm not
afraid to be scared, but I don't need it. Basically, that man was
telling me 'Lady, you can't do this work; you need me.'" But
Jennifer refused to buckle, of course, and that's why she found
herself going from pit to pit, getting her site ready for the first
pour of her life.

When she ordered a batch of ready-mix from the concrete
plant, the dispatcher must have heard anxiety in her voice.
On the day of the pour, he sent over his two most courtly drivers. "They were wonderful—polite and very helpful," says

Jennifer. She toured them around her work site and pointed out that she had dug the trenches two feet below the standard forty-eight-inch frost line. She showed them her solidly staked forms, cut from lengths of two-by-twelve lumber.

Her two cavaliers were impressed. Clearly, she had gone the extra mile to do the job right. Many pier-builders go no deeper than the frost line, and some don't even bother to build footings. But Jennifer had seen unruly houses whose piers hadn't been sunk far enough into the earth. She had observed how frost heaves can throw a house off kilter. In such places, the floors squeaked, windows stuck, and doors wouldn't close properly, driving homeowners right up their cracked and crumbling walls. Jennifer had no interest in building a house she might want to murder in a couple of years.

Throughout the pour she questioned the drivers' every move. Unlike men finding themselves in similar circumstances, Jennifer had the self-confidence it takes to reveal her ignorance. Without embarrassment she asked elementary questions: What is a "yard" of concrete? How much does it weigh? Why does concrete solidify? Gentlemanly to a fault, her two gallants explained everything, and when they were done with the footings, helped Jennifer prepare for the next step, the pouring of the piers. They showed her how to insert vertical reinforcing bars into the still-wet concrete and guided her in placing heavy cardboard cylinders that would serve as the forms for nine concrete columns. These cylinders, which go by the name of Sonotubes, had to be stood as close to upright as she could get them. They all had to be cut precisely to the same height in order to give the sill (the main beam on which the house would stand) a level resting place.

Days later, her footings stone-solid, Jennifer backfilled the trenches, packing dirt and gravel around each Sonotube for support. The same drivers returned to pour the piers. They were again chivalrous, holding Jennifer's hand every step of the way. Jennifer was grateful. "You guys are my heroes," she wrote in a thank-you letter when the job was done.

While Jennifer's gender brought out the best in some men, it had the opposite effect on others. It seemed to her that some fellows bristled to find an amateur builder, and a woman at that, encroaching on their turf. She remembers in particular the man who had come to excavate her trenches. He was downright hostile. Before he arrived with his backhoe, Jennifer had drawn the footprint of her house on the ground with powdered lime. "When I asked him to dig on the outside of the line all around, he gave me a *who-do-you-think-you-are?* look." When the man drove off a few hours later, he left behind a series of trenches straddling the line that she had drawn. "He messed me up big time," Jennifer reports, "and I ended up digging a lot by hand."

Nor would the driver who brought a truckload of crushed stone to the site deign to take instruction from a woman. At the foot of Jennifer's driveway, he asked, "Where do you want me to dump the stone, Miss?"

"Up there," she said, pointing toward the construction site. "But you'd better look at the driveway, first."

"What's the matter with it?"

"It's muddy. It's got no gravel on it, just mud. Your truck might get stuck."

"No problem. You don't know this baby," he said, patting the side of his truck. "She'll make it, easy." When he gunned her engine, Baby inched backward, her tires sinking slowly into mud. When she had submerged to her wheel rims halfway up the drive, she stopped, her tires spinning helplessly.

After the truck from Bennie's towing service drove away, the delivery man dumped his cargo at the bottom of the driveway, leaving Jennifer to carry bucket after bucket of stone 150 feet, where she spread it for drainage all around the house.

Jennifer is philosophical about the incident: "I felt sorry for the guy," she says, "and the extra work—well, it wasn't so bad." In fact, she rather enjoyed the simple purity of repeatedly hauling single buckets full of stone from point A to point B and noting her headway with each trip. "I knew that every stone had to be moved eventually," she says, "so I just did it. Besides, there's something about physical labor I really like."

Schlepping tons of rocks wasn't the half of it. During the earliest stages of construction she worked without electricity.

In practical terms that means she used an ordinary cross-cut handsaw instead of a power saw to build the first floor deck, with its underpinning of sill beam, girder, headers, floor joists, and solid blocking—an altogether amazing feat of perversity, not to mention a prescription for blisters and sore muscles.

"It wasn't as hard as it sounds," Jennifer protests. The floor joists, which run the length of the house—thirty-two feet—required no cuts. They are eighteen-foot-long two-by-twelves that overlap atop a triple two-by-twelve girder that itself required lots of hammering to construct but not a single cut. Nearly every other member of the frame, however, including eighty-four pieces of two-by-twelve blocking, necessitated at least one application of Jennifer's handsaw.

By any measure, eighty-four pieces of blocking is a lot for a small house. "I wanted to build my house well," Jennifer explains. "I didn't want any insecurities about the house falling down on me or coming apart." Indeed, with pieces of solid lumber nailed at three-foot intervals between the joists in Jennifer's small house, the floor will never bounce or sag. The thing about bridging is that it's noticed only in absentia. Walk across a floor without it and the room vibrates. Even on floors reinforced with standard diagonal steel or wooden struts installed every four feet, a heavy footfall will rattle dishes in the china cabinet. Jennifer's floor feels like bedrock—perhaps her recompense for a long spell of brutally hard labor.

As much as she relished the work, Jennifer learned early on to get help—to get it free if she could but to pay if she had to. Jennifer's kids—nine, seven, and five at the start of the project—helped in their way. They nailed down much of the plywood subfloor, spacing the nails six inches around the edges of each piece, eight inches in the middle. "They practiced arithmetic by doing that and learned their times tables," Jennifer says. Later she asked her sister and brother-in-law to lift and install roof rafters with her. A friend donated most of the electrical work, but she paid a plumber to put in water pipes. "I had to have others do those things," Jennifer insists. "I couldn't learn plumbing and electricity at that point. I already

felt overextended—raising a family, cleaning homes, and building the house."

When courses end, Heartwood doesn't cut students loose
with a Godspeed and a handshake. Rather, instructors stand by
as consultants to help alumni work on their own houses.
Shortly after Jennifer graduated from Heartwood, Michele
Beemer, the school's codirector, instituted a one-week carpentry class for women only. Michele, attuned to the arguments
favoring single-sex education, believed that by letting the typically more aggressive men set the tone and pace of instruction,
women got shortchanged in coed classes. For women trying to
break into the carpentry brotherhood, the loss would be particularly acute. Michele, therefore, created a woman's course and
asked to use Jennifer's construction site as a lab. To Jennifer
the request was heaven-sent. "What, are you an angel?" she
said to Michele. "Of course you can."

Michele's offer came just in time because Jennifer hadn't
quite gotten the hang of wall-framing—"especially where two
walls meet at a right angle," she says. Michele's husband Will
set her straight. While preparing her site for the class, he
showed Jennifer how the top plates of intersecting walls overlap, forming a sturdy structural bond. Then, under Michele's
direction, the women in the class—novices all—fabricated,
lifted, and braced some of the longest walls in the house. "You
should have seen them," says Jennifer. "They were wet with
sweat and worked until they couldn't see straight. Yet they all
told me, 'Thanks for letting us work with you on this.'"

Knowing that Jennifer toiled alone to build a house, people
in the vicinity often stopped by to lend a hand. In the sparsely
inhabited area that was their community, to spend a few hours
with a neighbor was as natural as breathing. In tune with the
custom, Jennifer sometimes abandoned her own work to help
others. At times she bartered her time for theirs. Not far away,
a group of people calling themselves Earth Dance was erecting
a one-hundred-by-forty-foot, three-story behemoth of a building to serve as the main residence of a commune. "I worked
out a deal with them," Jennifer says. "I worked as a carpenter

for them twice a week, and for one or two days a month they sent a crew to my house. That's how I got Sheetrock up on the ceiling and the windows lifted in."

Jennifer sometimes got help from total strangers. "When it came time to lift a wall, I told the kids to wait on the road and ask the next passerby to lend a hand." Thus, tourists who sometimes wandered by in shorts and sandals were drafted. "I figured it was a way for them to get a taste of the Berkshires," she says. Recruits pitched in eagerly, happy to contribute their backs to the project and no doubt tickled to have something unusual to write about on their vacation postcards.

During the second summer of construction, Jennifer invited a corps of women friends to participate in a siding blitz. The women, mostly beginners but aching to learn, brought tools, ladders, extension cords, and a few extra saws. During a weekend of feverish work they covered most of the south wall with wood panels—known as board-and-batten siding—a job that would have taken Jennifer many weeks laboring alone. "By Sunday night they all felt high as kites," says Jennifer. "They could hardly believe what they had done." One of the group proposed leaving behind a record of their triumph on the inside of the plywood sheathing and wrote a letter to the future which everyone signed: "If you ever take this apart," a piece of the message read, "know that this siding was put up by twenty women whose lives were changed forever during one weekend in 1990 A.D."

Such moments reside in Jennifer's memory, not just because they move her, but because they were rare. The hard fact is that for most of two and a half years Jennifer worked by herself, putting in gruelingly long days that, in retrospect, blend into a miasma of unreality. Transfixed by the work, she behaved as though smitten by a mysterious force that wouldn't let go. "I'd get to a point where things would flow," Jennifer reports, "and I'd let myself ride that wave for all it was worth."

In spite of her passion for work, Jennifer arrived at the building site on some mornings unready to cope with the jobs that awaited her. She preferred to sit awhile, collect her thoughts, pull out her pennywhistle or guitar and make music. "I wanted to play before I got serious," she says, "or maybe listen to the birds for a while." She often used those tranquil moments to meditate on life's puzzlements, returning time and again to the obligations that pulled her in opposite directions simultaneously. One voice said to her, "Now, while your kids are growing up is the time they need you most. There will always be time to work later." But just as often she heard counterpoint that said, "Look, you're outside in the country doing something you adore. In the process, your mind and body are getting stronger, and you're making a real honest-to-goodness home for yourself and the kids. Stay cool, girl, you're doing the right thing."

Jennifer drew some of her energy to keep at it from the blizzard of building activity around her. "At one time," she says, "I had three next-door neighbors all building their own houses." From her site, she could hear the rap of hammers in all directions. Fellow builders often dropped in to borrow a tool, to kibitz, or to exchange shards of information about home building. In the boom-town climate of the neighborhood, Jennifer felt connected and supported and as happy as she'd ever been. But she also felt pressure to get the job done, to settle into her own house and stop paying rent for a farmhouse three miles down the road, where the well ran dry for months at a time and the windows let in more wind than light.

Two years, five months, and twenty-two days after Jennifer got her building permit, mail was delivered to her new home for the first time. The exterior was complete. Inside, the paint was dry, the floors sanded and sealed. Only some wooden trim remained to be done. While settling in, Jennifer filled the place with a mélange of furnishings. Each piece came with a story: "The kitchen cabinets I collected over the years, and a neighbor gave me some doors and windows," Jennifer tells me. The bathroom sink, an old-style pedestal beauty, she picked out of a heap of refuse by the side of a road in Westchester. The toilet, a ten-dollar item, she got in Maine, where she also bought the tub. Assorted light fixtures, doorknobs, switch plates, and a stained glass window came from tag sales, flea markets, "junque" shops, and salvage yards all over the East. The bathroom is clad in tiles of many colors. A tiling contractor, the father of a friend, had bins full of leftover tile and invited Jennifer to take whatever she wanted. *Funky* is the word that best describes the results. The entire decor is exuberant with the fantasy of Jennifer's rich imagination.

Jennifer revels in her accomplishment. While the house was going up, her children thought that home building is what mothers sometimes do. To them shingling a roof was as motherly a function as telling kids when to go to bed. It's unclear whether they ever saw fit to confide in their school chums that they had helped their mom with her j-bolts or joist hangers, but Timmy once gave a speech to his first-grade classmates, enlightening them on "The Ten Steps of Building a House." He knew them cold: First you build the first floor, then you build the second floor, then the third, and so forth right up to the roof. Jennifer's kids, unlike most of their peers, now know a j-bolt from a joist hanger and a great deal more. "I'm glad I taught them something about home building," she says. "But more than that, I taught them a lesson for life. I showed them you can have a dream that you can make a reality no matter what anybody else thinks."

SURELY, JENNIFER'S EXPERIENCE says something about her resilience. When, as a teenager, she quit school, conventional judgment would say she erred badly. Indeed, for some time afterward she drifted about in search of an anchorage. After her divorce, she took up home building, a measure born out of a desperate need for stability after several shaky years. "The divorce shattered my kids," she tells me. "It was a terrible hardship for them, but while building I gradually came to understand that my work on the house could make up for the devastation they suffered from our broken family. With every board I put up, I was really rebuilding my life." Hammer in one hand and three kids in tow, she discovered what she may have only sensed before: that, if you push hard enough, something good will happen, even when life tells you it may not be so. Fortune-cookie wisdom, perhaps, but one could do worse than live by such an insight.

Unhesitatingly, Jennifer counts her building adventure as one of the great successes of her life. "Right after it was done, I used the house as collateral for a loan to build another," she says. "The bank said it was worth $100,000. 'Wow!' I thought. That's a lot of money." She had tripled the value of her investment in two and a half years. "My guardian angel must have been watching over me," she adds, smiling. "Either that, or my mother was praying real hard."

Seven months after they moved into their home, Jennifer and the children moved out again and put the house on the rental market. Seven months! Less than a year in the house, and they took up residence in the nearby community home that Jennifer had helped to build. She explains why: "During the building, we all became good friends with the people down at the community, and as a single parent, I was getting kind of lonely." Understandably, Jennifer faced a big void in her life after she'd completed the house. For two and half years the project had been her companion day and night. What could take its place? "We had done the *house* thing," Jennifer says, "and so we wanted a community. We decided to try it for a year, or until my second house was built."

They stayed for less than that. The groupiness got to her. "I liked being with everybody, but not all the time," Jennifer told me. "I wanted more time alone with my kids. I saw no need to eat dinner with a crowd every night." So, they packed their things, parted amicably, and unpacked in the habitable half of Jennifer's second building project. This one was a clone of the first, only larger. Jennifer had designed it, but to build it she hadn't lifted a finger. Instead, she had hired a professional contractor whose charge was to construct a shell. It took him four months. Jennifer expected to finish the rest of the house on her own. Now, nine years later, her home verges on completion. Only the closets remain to be finished. "Compared to my first house," Jennifer exclaims, "this one was a joke." She knew the ropes and handled them like a trouper.

In this house, Jennifer's building finesse deprived her of the delights of discovery that had often sweetened her debut as a home builder. In exchange, however, she often felt another kind of rush—the thrill of being fully in control of her craft. Hardly anything swells her ego and soothes her soul like feeling competent. When you truly understand your tools, and every move you make on the job site is purposeful, your satisfaction knows no bounds. As Jennifer likes to say, "It puts you on top of the world." Once, she extended a hand to a nearby family rebuilding their house after a gutting fire. "It was the neighborly thing to do," she says, "but I was scared to death that I might not measure up." But when she drove onto the site, the foreman, a family elder, looked at her, looked at her tool belt, and told her to cut headers for the doors. "Make 'em just a wee bit short," he ordered. "I don't like to smush 'em in." Jennifer knew exactly what he meant, grabbed her saw and, giddy as a schoolgirl, started cutting two-by-six headers precisely a wee bit short.

Family Happiness

M y search for owner-builders led me to the Building Education Center, an evening continuing education school in Berkeley, California, staffed by professional contractors. Glen Kitzenberger, the instructor of a popular home-building course, referred me to Tom Brenner, a summa cum laude graduate of the BEC program.

Glen told me that Tom, a local resident and a schoolteacher, had built his own house in Covelo, California, about halfway up the road to Oregon from the Bay Area. Perfect, I thought. As someone intimate with building a house far from home, I was eager to interview and swap stories with Tom. That he had also been a teacher added to my incentive to look him up. We would have a lot to talk about.

More than I expected, as it turned out, while spending the day before Christmas with him in his home high on a Berkeley hill. Like me, he had retired eighteen months previously and has spent years at work on a country house three hours-plus from home. He told me that he'd begun to write a book (as I had) and that he paints watercolors in his spare time (as I do). That he also has grown children, a wife who continues to work, and an unflagging devotion to building struck me as more than mildly eerie. For years Tom's life and mine had been running parallel to each other, but on tracks three thousand miles apart.

TOM ADMITS THAT UNTIL HE bought his first house he
was a building illiterate. "My Dad had houses built—once in
Ohio and twice in Florida—but did none of the work himself,"
Tom says. "His forte was hiring good builders.

"As for taking care of the houses," Tom continues, "my
dad wanted no part of it. He owned a screwdriver, a pair of pli-
ers, and a brass-headed hammer that somebody once made for
him—and that's all."

Tom apparently inherited his father's aversion to building and home maintenance. But his resistance weakened in
1969 after he and his wife Nancy bought a house, situated on
one of the few level streets in the north end of Berkeley, California. "Suddenly it became important to learn how to do
stuff," Tom says, and in contrast to the mass of homeowners
who regard rank-and-file maintenance as an affliction, he discovered the promise of new beginnings in the routine stopping
of drips, mending of windows, and patching of potholes in the
driveway.

At first Tom leaned heavily on Hal Shepard for advice and
help. Hal ran the Regional Occupational Program for the area's
public schools and on weekends rented himself out as a carpenter. In 1970, Tom hired Hal to rebuild an extension at the
rear of his house. As Hal worked, Tom watched. A few years
later, Tom hired a neighbor with a wrecking bar and a taste for
dismemberment to demolish his run-down garage. Using the
heap of lumber the wrecker left behind, Tom set out to build a
new work shed in his backyard, methodically cutting the
boards and assembling them one by one. The work suited him.
He found the sweaty, physical stuff an invigorating mixture of
craft and athletics, even more agreeable than routine home repairs, and he yearned to do more.

Soon after the shed was finished, Tom's firstborn son, Sam,
then fifteen, took a fancy to the little building. He told his father that it would make a terrific getaway for a boy, a retreat, a
private bedroom in the backyard. And Tom, in a fit of generos-
ity, gave it to him—a gift—just like that, as though the shed
were Sam's birthright.

One might suspect that Tom had been far, far gone to hand his teenage son the keys to a personal hideaway behind the house. The truth, however, is that he knew exactly what he was doing. Within a week Tom was out in the backyard constructing another shed just like the first, relishing the process even more than the first time and being powerfully pleased with the results.

Tom's endeavor seemed to satisfy a deeply felt need to add to the world's supply of small wooden buildings, but for a long time the twin sheds stood as Tom's only contribution. In fact, more than ten years passed before he made another.

TOM CAN'T PINPOINT THE ORIGIN of his idea to build a house in the country. It came to him as an airy notion, something to daydream about—the way a man might think idly about someday having an affair or taking up golf. "During the 1970s," Tom explains, "I was quite taken by the back-to-the-land movement—you know, being close to nature, living off the land, that sort of thing." It was a time when stockbrokers cashed in their assets to buy vineyards in the valley, and corporate types opened bed-and-breakfasts along the coast. But Tom resisted the impulse to give up his career as an advertising copywriter in order to herd sheep or raise emus. Instead, he chucked the ad biz to take up teaching, a step that landed him in the schools of Piedmont, a community not far from his Berkeley home. For once, he had summers off to putter around his house and, coincidentally, to look for a piece of land on which to build another.

The land he found lay in Covelo at the edge of Round Valley in Mendocino County, 185 miles north of Berkeley. Tom explains that a neighbor with an appetite for remote, unspoiled areas of California bought a 450-acre ranch in Covelo and invited Tom up for a look. What Tom saw was an ex-lumber community, abandoned by the industry when the timber ran out. Left behind was a dusty little town at the edge of a dish-shaped valley and ringed by the peaks of the Coastal Range. Land in the area was cheap, but its price bound upward as city people with a yen for ranches and riding horses had started to move in. "Cowboy kinds of stuff," says Tom, "not eastern saddle riding." Tom and Nancy looked around, and just before the land rush began in earnest, bought sixty acres on the edge of the valley floor, most of it rocky and hilly, the rest meadowland dotted with valley oaks, madrones, and digger pines.

"At the time, we didn't know whether we'd eventually retire in our Covelo house or use it merely as a weekend getaway," Tom says. Because of their uncertainty, Tom and Nancy puzzled for months over the size and layout of their future house. How many rooms should it contain? One story or two? How many baths? What about a basement, a laundry room, an attic? Space for guests? The kitchen alone presented a formidable design challenge. Should it be a discrete space or an extension of a large family/living room? As a weekend retreat, their house would often be a meeting ground for family and friends. Wouldn't that dictate an open, informal floor plan? But in a year-round residence, mightn't the smells and sounds of food preparation often interfere with other activities going on nearby? All pressing questions—along with dozens more— that resisted intelligent answers until Tom and Nancy nailed down their long-range plans.

In the meantime, they also pondered matters of heat, waste, and water. A woodstove might suffice for brief holidays but not for a year-round home. Similarly, a small tank and leach fields instead of a full-sized septic system would do for weekend visits. As for water, they'd need a drilled well for permanent residency, but for occasional use they could probably depend on an underground spring they found on the ridge just above their building site. How they resolved such issues would not only shape the basic character of their house, but determine the spirit with which Tom undertook its construction.

"If it had been my choice alone," Tom says, "I would have planned a complete retirement home." He envisioned himself easily slipping into the role of a country squire—raising goats for their milk and fur, hiking the trails of the nearby national forest with Jack, his chocolate Labrador, at his heels. On rainy days he would write, paint a still life in watercolor, or tinker in his shop. He'd always have gardening to do and logs to split for the woodstove. When guests dropped in for a weekend, he'd rejoice at both their coming and their going.

Tom agrees, however, that his AARP idyll had little to do with reality. "It made no sense to pour time and money into a big house with lots of unused space," he says. "We needed only a one-bedroom house for the time being. I figured that I could add more later, if necessary."

To groom himself for the tasks of building, Tom enrolled in a home-building course at the Building Education Center. In one semester, the curriculum covered the how-tos of constructing everything from foundation to roof, plus the rudiments of home design. By the end, Tom had a couple of good textbooks, lots of notes, and a sketch of the house he intended to build on his Covelo hillside—a one-story, one-bedroom, one-bathroom lodge, thirty-by-thirty-five feet. The sketch also showed a large kitchen/living room/dining area all of a piece and all heated by a woodstove. A second stove stood in a brick-faced corner of the bedroom. (Later, Tom would discover that the house was more than amply heated. "We have to open the windows, even on the coldest nights," he reports.)

After conferring with experts in sewage, Tom added a full-scale septic system to his plans. Instead of drilling a well, Tom opted to tap his underground spring and then hope for the best. (It was an inspired choice; in five years the water supply system failed but once—when ice burst a pipe and his two 1,300-gallon storage tanks drained to the last drop.)

Because he expected to build the house himself, Tom excluded from his plans any materials that he couldn't handle alone: Instead of a plywood subfloor, he laid down two-by-six tongue and groove boards. On the walls and ceilings, rather than laying on giant pieces of drywall, he installed one-by-six pine paneling. Pricey stuff, Tom agrees, but with more money than muscle at his disposal—Tom, at five-feet-nine and 155 pounds, is no he-man—he preferred to pay the price rather than pack tons of material up the hill like a Sherpa. "It was hard enough carrying joists and rafters," he says.

As for sheathing the house, Tom couldn't avoid using heavy sheets of three-quarter-inch plywood. "I originally wanted to use one-by-six sheathing," Tom explains. "But the building inspector said no, not unless I stabilized the stud walls with diagonal braces running from corner to corner." Since Tom had already framed all the walls and windows, to "let-in" new braces involved notching nearly one-hundred studs, a job Tom declined to do. "So I had to do plywood," he says.

In Tom's house there would be no built-up beams or timbers that need a regiment to lift. Tom's BEC instructor, Glen, had recommended roof trusses—pre-assembled rafters and joists sometimes hoisted right off the truck and onto the walls—an instant roof frame that saves time and enormous wear and tear on a builder. "But," says Tom, "I could never get them up there alone. So I framed the roof, stick by stick. It was the only way."

Plans for the house also called for lots of glass, most of it in casement windows that open onto a wide deck that surrounds the central core of the building like the broad brim of a Stetson. "The deck is a thousand square feet," Tom says, "about the same as the interior space." That's a generous deck indeed and the most striking feature of the house when viewed from the bottom of the steep driveway. Because the pitch of the roof parallels almost exactly the slope of the site, the house and hill seem to "live together," to use Frank Lloyd Wright's phrase. "No house," said Wright, "should ever be *on* any hill or *on* anything. It should be *of* the hill, belonging to it, . . . each the happier for the other."

HAPPY THOUGHTS WERE FAR from Tom's mind when, in 1991, as a newcomer in Covelo, he set up a small tent near his future building site and moved in. Rather, his mind was on his body, which wasn't exactly old—Tom was on the far side of fifty at the time—but was working its way there. Would it con-

Casement windows in Tom's house open onto a wide deck that surrounds the central core of the building like the broad brim of a Stetson.

sent to nights encased in a mummy sleeping bag lying on a less than cushy tent floor? In short order, long bouts with insomnia gave him the answer: He was not cut out for roughing it week after week. Instead, he would pamper himself by putting up a small wooden shed like those he had once constructed in his backyard.

"I built it using parts prefabricated by students in my friend Hal Shepard's occupational-ed program," Tom explains. "I provided the materials and windows, and they built the panels. Then I hauled everything up to Covelo in a rented truck. The shed was ten-by-sixteen and set on prefabricated columns sunk two feet into the ground. In less than a day I had a permanent place to stay and a solid roof overhead. It was fast, efficient and, after the tent, pretty wonderful."

Then Tom was beset with doubt. The building authorities in Ukiah, the county seat, might take a dim view of this outlander putting up a shed without a permit, and he supposed that they could order him to take it down. So he hurriedly drew plans for the shed, drove sixty miles to Ukiah, and applied for a permit to build.

"The inspectors were very helpful," he recalls. "But they told me that concrete posts were OK for a storage shed but not for a habitable structure. If I intended to sleep there, I'd have to put in sixteen-inch footings and a solid foundation wall," a precaution taken by the county, Tom suspects, to avert lawsuits should a flimsy shed fall in on its soundly sleeping occupants. Lacking the stomach to dig a trench and build a foundation wall, Tom declined. The inspector, therefore, stamped the approved plans, "NOT FOR HUMAN HABITA-TION." "When I asked him about sleeping in the shed when it rained," Tom says, "the guy just shrugged," a gesture that told Tom to stop asking so many questions.

Back in Covelo he unrolled his sleeping bag inside the shed and went to work. He expected, by devoting himself entirely to building from late June to late August, to complete the house in three summers: the foundation and frame during the first year; roof, siding, deck and utilities the next; and the finishing touches during the final summer. By Labor Day of the third year, Tom estimated, the house would be ready for occupancy.

No sooner had the first summer begun, however, that Tom realized he might be about the worst estimator in the state of California. "I had no ability to judge how long everything took," he admits. "Just figuring out which materials to buy and the order in which I'd need them took forever," he says. He spent days surveying his land and picking the precise spot for the house. The excavation took nearly a week. Forms for footings swallowed up more weeks as did forms for a foundation wall which Tom built extra-wide in case he ever decided to add a second story to the house. After each pour, additional days slipped by as the concrete cured. Three summers? Not a chance. To complete the house in anything close to three years, Tom realized, would require lots of overtime—at least every weekend while the weather held.

In preparing forms for poured footings, Tom did all he could to level, square, and set them in the right place. It wasn't easy. The slope, full of rocks and steep as a ski run, banked twelve to fifteen feet from the front to the rear of the house. The foundation would be stepped, or built on six different levels from top to bottom and on four levels from side to side—a complex setup even for a professional builder. During his BEC course, Tom had been instructed to check squareness with diagonal measurements: If the distances between opposite corners are equal, the corners are square. But Tom hadn't learned what to do when each corner was on a different level. He tried story poles and strings and all manner of Pythagorean geometry to determine the angles, but the rugged terrain stood between him and exact readings. His insides churned with worry. "I had no idea whether I was close to square when I laid out the forms," Tom says. (Not until he reached the subfloor the following summer did he get finally the answer: The diagonals were one and a half inches apart. "Thank God," says Tom. Glen had cautioned him that only an inch or less was acceptable. But Tom managed to compensate for the discrepancy when he framed the walls. In the end, the diagonals between opposite corners of the house differed by three-fourths of an inch, to Tom an astonishing feat of engineering and a personal triumph.)

At the end of the first summer, Tom's house stood all of two feet high. Although the house had barely gotten off the ground, he was pleased with how he'd spent his vacation. "If I never did another thing," he boasts, "I had already contributed more to the construction of my own house than 95 percent of other homeowners." Indeed, he had completed roughly 160 feet of concrete wall, including a so-called "cripple wall," that bisected the rectangular foundation and would one day support the midsection of the house. He had also mixed and poured the concrete for a dozen piers—anchorages for posts that one day would hold up the deck. Before he returned to school, Tom wrapped his creation in a tarp, and twice during the off-season drove to Covelo to see whether it had blown off.

In June 1992, on the verge of an unusually productive summer, Tom started framing his house. By Labor Day, he had not only constructed the entire frame, but had sheathed the exterior walls, clad them in Tyvek for protection, and installed a watertight roof. How does Tom account for such industriousness? He holds his gas-driven Paslode Impulse nail gun partly responsible. When it functioned properly, his nail gun shot nails with astonishing power and speed, punching two three-and-a-half-inch nails per second into solid wood. Although Tom's model spent weeks in the repair shop that summer—its complicated internal combustion engine often went on the fritz—it both hastened the work and spared Tom's arm and elbow plenty of wear and tear. "It broke down after I had stopped using it for a few days," Tom says. "Like a spoiled brat, it seemed to resent being ignored, but it was there when I needed it most."

With or without his peevish nail gun, Tom also moved the work along by installing a galvanized metal roof. As Tom tells it, "I ran a plank up the side of the house as a ramp and carried the panels to the roof. Then I slid them into place and screwed them down." The process was quick and easy: Weighing in at less than a pound per square foot, galvanized roofing panels are one-third the weight of, say, asphalt shingles. Although flimsy and resistant to being installed in a brisk wind, panels are stiffened by V-shaped ridges, or ribs, along each side and down the middle. The ribs of one panel overlap the ribs of adjacent panels, creating a leakproof seam. Having had the panels cut to the size of his roof, Tom covered a swath roughly two by twenty-two feet with each piece. For expeditious installation, metal paneling was an inspired choice.

Most of all, though, Tom attributes his prolific output of work that summer to a procession of weekend helpers. Framing has a way of doing that. It attracts help. Unlike masonry, roofing, or any other grunt work, framing is a spectacle, the glamorous side of building. It is so seductive that even dyed-in-the-wool sluggards have been known to swath themselves in jeans and nailing aprons and appear at the work site bearing hammers. The reason? For a modest expenditure of effort and time, you get breathtaking results. A standard eight-foot wall with no doors or windows can be nailed together almost before you break a sweat. In hours a wall that reaches to the roof can be framed and stood in place, and in a matter of days, an efficient crew can fill an empty landscape with the skeleton of an entire house. It's intoxicating work, framing is. Nothing else that a builder does comes close to its dramatic effects.

The months that Tom devoted to framing left a particularly emotional afterglow in his memory, brought about, in the main, by his family's participation in the work. He remembers their vigor and enthusiasm. Nancy drove up from Berkeley every weekend to lend a hand. His children pitched in unreservedly. "Amanda, my oldest, gave her back—literally—trying to wrench form boards off the poured foundation," says Tom. "And Toby, the youngest, lugged four-by-eight beams up the hill for the wall that holds up the center of the house." Tom also mentions Sam's wife Jennifer, who doubled as gofer and holder of the other ends of boards. "But," says Tom, "Sam was the workhorse." He made weekly appearances, from Thursday to Sunday, during the long summer of framing.

As partners on the job, Tom and Sam blocked out a choreography: "Up early, work like hell until about one o'clock when it got too hot to continue, then start again at four." In the heat of the day, their "shade time," as Tom likes to call it, father and son played cribbage. Their games soon turned into a friendly rivalry. "It was addictive," Tom recalls. "Sam made a cribbage scoring board from scrap lumber. Whoever won would carve a notch on his side of the board—like gunslingers of old."

Although Sam came to Covelo with his own hunches and theories about building, he let his father make all the technical decisions. To frame an outside corner, for example, there are over half a dozen configurations: the traditional three-stud corner, a boxed corner, a one-stud corner with nailing blocks, and so on—all equally capable of holding intersecting walls together. Which of them to build depends on one's taste or one's budget. Corners with fewer pieces save money. Some corners contain more space for insulation, leading to lower heating costs. Says Tom, "Sam reminded me over and over that we were building my house and that, while he might not build it quite the way I chose, he'd go along with it." With a grin, Tom adds, "I've often told Sam that I can't wait for him to start building his own house. Then I'll do to him what he did to me." All told, however, Tom can't rave enough about his time with Sam. Working side by side, father and son forged an epoxy-like bond. Knowing that Sam's sweat is in the walls they built together adds immeasurably to Tom's affection for the house. While building walls, he and Sam also built what Tom calls the "foundation for a stronger adult relationship, not only father-son but man-and-man. And now that I think about it," Tom adds, "Covelo helped all of us grow together. It's true that the house was solely my project. But everyone contributed to it—Amanda, Sam, Toby. There's no longer a parent-child gap between us. We regard each other as equals. Building the house changed the family dynamics and created special relationships." The house has become the centerpiece of family life, a kind of magnet that Tom hopes will hold the generations together for a long time.

Between weekends, Tom saw almost no one. He spoke mainly to himself and to two canine companions—faithful Jack and a one-eared cattle dog named Dulcey that Tom adopted in Covelo. Working alone most of the time released Tom from the tyranny of the clock. He set his own pace, pausing often and laying his tools aside in order to decide his next moves. "I was glad not to have paid helpers standing around waiting for my instructions," he goes on. "That would have been very stressful." It was during precisely such a break that Tom, about to raise the last piece of wall, realized he'd better get his woodstoves inside the frame before the wall was finished. Otherwise, the stoves, too wide to fit through any opening, would be locked out. Off he went to Ukiah to buy two stoves, then waited for weekend help to move them into the house.

Being on his own also allowed Tom to get his bearings—to size up his undertaking and figure out what in God's name it all meant. He sometimes wondered how his ambition to build got diverted into this extraordinarily vexing activity, for he never lacked things to bitch about—if not the warped lumber, then the hidden nail that dulled his saw blade, the heat, or his own stupidity for leaving his tape measure in the basement when he needed it on the roof. Then there was his portable generator, a piece of equipment so loud and distracting that it had almost wiped rational thought from Tom's mind, leaving only the urge to hurry up, get the job done, and turn the damn thing off. Finally, while working fiendishly hard, he never stopped worrying that he was violating the building code at every turn.

While groping for a meaning, however, he realized that, despite the toilsomeness of it all, too many good things were happening for him to lose heart: A house was growing on his hillside and each nail he hammered brought his dream of a life in the country one nail closer.

BECAUSE THE RAINS CAME LATE in '92, Tom worked clear into the fall. He'd drive to Covelo on weekends to install windows and nail up one-by-eight cedar siding. "It was warm and pleasant to work outdoors," he recalls, and by Christmas he had a snug, waterproof, weather-tight shell of a house.

When he returned the next summer, he began to fill the shell with the accoutrements of a home. First came the electricity, via an underground hookup courtesy of the power company. The installation of two outlets at last silenced Tom's portable generator. What a relief, once and for all, to be rid of gasoline, exhaust fumes, and most of all, the engine's hateful din. To string wires and make the electrical connections throughout the house Tom hired a pro, a family friend named Chris Bratt. "I'm glad that I did," reports Tom. "I couldn't have done it as quickly and economically as he did. I would have strung much more cable and installed twice as many junction boxes." Tom estimated that wiring the house would take three days. It took eight. "By myself, it would have taken the whole summer," he says.

Having delegated the wiring to Chris, Tom took charge of the plumbing himself, although he knew precious little about it. His mentor, Glen, had done a show-and-tell on sweating copper pipes and had discoursed on "roughing-in," the plumber's term for installing drain pipes, supply lines, and vents inside walls, ceiling, and floors. Vertical pipes tend to run between the studs, horizontal pipes through notches cut into the wood. If the notches are deep or are cut into walls that carry structural weight—hence the name *bearing walls*—the weakened studs need to be fortified, usually with lengths of lumber, or cleats, nailed to both sides. The same is true of joists that have been attenuated to make room for pipes. According to Glen, roughing-in precedes installation of the subfloor. Otherwise, the floor will be a damn nuisance, always getting in the way and slowing you down. But Tom ignored the protocol. "I didn't know exactly where the walls would be," he explains, "so I installed the subfloor first, and afterward built the walls. Only then could I figure out where to cut the holes for pipes." Tom agrees that his inability to plan ahead prolonged the work, but it hardly mattered. "With or without a subfloor, I couldn't have worked any slower," he says.

Tom debuted as a pipe fitter at his water source high on the hill behind his house, where he directed the flow from his underground spring into twin 1,300-gallon storage tanks. With help from gravity and two feeder pipes, he guided the water straight into the house where it branched to several outlets in the kitchen and bathroom. The first time he opened the master control valve in the basement he got very, very wet. "Like the fountains of Rome," he says, "water shooting every which way." Almost every fitting in his maze of pipes leaked. In some places, lacy geysers arched into the air. Elsewhere, streams of water poured onto the basement floor. The deluge baffled Tom. What had gone wrong? He had sweated the pipes exactly as Glen had taught him: *Shine the fittings to remove impurities, dab on a small amount of flux, then apply solder and heat.* Damp but undeterred, Tom tore the pipes apart and tried again. And then once more, each time with the same soggy results.

One leaky line flowed into an Aqua-Star propane water heater mounted on the kitchen wall. While installing the unit, Tom called the Aqua-Star hotline in Vermont to ask about making the proper connections. On the phone, Tom intimated that he was something of a knucklehead when it came to plumbing. "The guy laughed and told me immediately how to improve my skills. He told me, 'Get yourself a Bernz-O-Matic torch.'" Tom's low-tech torch simply didn't have enough clout. Water inside the pipes prevented melted solder from sealing the joints. But with the hotter, more concentrated flame of a Bernz-O-Matic, Tom easily made watertight connections on all his pipes. "Afterward, I told Glen the story," Tom says. "In his classes from then on he used a Bernz-O-Matic just like mine."

Tom's goal during his fourth summer in Covelo was to finish the interior of the house. In turn, he insulated the walls and ceilings, then covered them with pine paneling. He dressed all the windows in cedar casings and built a mantel around the fireplace. In the kitchen he nailed down a hardwood floor and put in appliances. Then he filled the corner between the stove and sink with base cabinets made to order by Vern Bryant, a Covelo carpenter, and fastened on a thick cast-concrete countertop.

At once, the kitchen began to function as the heart of the house. Nancy held court there on weekends, gathering with friends and family to talk and relax—and cook. The tableau that for years Tom had held in his mind's eye—people he loved making themselves at home in the house that he built—suddenly sprang to life. His private vision of living in the country was quickly converging with reality.

But then, quite unexpectedly, Tom's plans hit a speed bump: Nancy, after ransacking her soul, declared that she wasn't cut out to be a full-time country girl after all. She adored the house and loved Covelo, but not enough to consider permanently abandoning Berkeley in order to settle there. Life in the city kept her refreshed. Besides, she fancied her job and was having too much fun to quit any time soon. Tom calls Nancy "a cross-breed mouse," torn between city and country.

Disappointed at first, Tom accepted Nancy's tidings stoically. (He isn't the sort to raise his voice or kick the dog to express his feelings.) In a way, he was relieved finally to have the issue resolved: The house would not be the villa of their golden years, but rather the family's vacation home for years to come. But he admits, "A lot of the momentum to get it finished just died when I realized that."

From then on, his life in Covelo assumed a different character. Without the pressure to get things done, he followed his preferences instead of his punch list. His tempo slowed. He sometimes ventured into the Covelo countryside for an afternoon or hiked in nearby Mendocino National Forest. In his garden he planted tomatoes and pansies. Sometimes he sat reading for hours on end without once thinking he ought to be tiling the bathroom floor or painting the front door.

Without a quota of work to fill or six things to do before sundown, Tom took pleasure in—no, *basked in* is more like it—the house he had wrought. Its light and air and informal personality possessed an irresistible power to draw the family together—three generations of kin enjoying each other's company, with Tom, the patriarch, presiding. "Nancy and I own the house," he says, "but it belongs to everyone in the family." He's thrilled when members of his clan use the house even when he's elsewhere. "My kids love it, Nancy loves it, the grandchildren love it, and I hope my great grandchildren will love it, too." Tom has often thought about carving initials and dates into the wooden mantel—a memento for Brenners of the future. "It would be neat for them to know that the house has a history and that the history is related to them," says Tom.

Eleven-year old Elizabeth, Tom and Nancy's first grandchild, doesn't need such a reminder. "She's been connected to the house since she learned to walk," says Tom. "It's part of her life. To her, it's a home." *Home.* Tom pronounces the word to suggest its succulence: "Where we love is home, / Home

that our feet may leave but not our hearts," wrote Oliver
Wendell Holmes, expressing a sentiment that Tom wears on
his sleeve while telling me all about his Covelo house.

IN HIS LIFE STORY, THE SEVEN years he labored in Covelo
will loom as a bright and shining chapter. To keep the memory
of it fresh, Tom photographed the process from start to finish.
Shuffling through his archives—stacks of photos and hundreds
of slides—he proclaims proudly, "Every phase of construction
is on record." Not only that, but twice a year he briefly relives
one of the most luminous times in his life. "Every semester,"
he says, "Glen invites me down to the Building Education
Center during their open houses to do a slide show on framing
a house."

That Tom has invested his spirit in the house is undeni-
able. But he's also invested time and over $120,000. "Would I
sell the place?" he asks, lobbing my question back at me.
"That's complicated. Money isn't the issue. Rather, Nancy
thinks it would be too hard for me to put the house on the
market. She says, 'Look, you nailed that board up, you installed those lights, you built that deck. You can't do it.'" But
Tom is not so sure. "Let's be realistic," he continues. "People
change. Right now, everybody loves it—even the kids. They
gather wildflowers in the spring, go to the river in the summer,
and hope for snow in the winter. They watch birds, track frogs,
look for bear scat, and are wary of rattlesnakes. It's a great
place for them now, but when they reach their teens it might
be harder to get them up there. The time may come when no
one will want to use the house, and then, who knows?"

In all likelihood, that time won't be soon. Tom is not rushing to complete the work that remains. During his most recent
visit—three or four solitary days in Covelo—he gardened a bit,
cleaned up some scrap lumber in the cellar, and took a run to
the town dump. He did no construction work, although the
closets beg for doors and pieces of baseboard are missing. He
says, "Glen was right when he told me that it's much harder to
finish a house than to start one." Why that might be so, why

builders often stop short inches from their goal raises intrigu-
ing questions. Is it that builders, sensing that realized dreams
rarely live up to their billing, don't want their projects to end?
Or are successful people, as Freud observed, subject to feelings
of unease over their own good fortune? Perhaps the completion
of a long building project casts builders adrift. They mourn the
sudden loss of a project that provided a focus and an outlet for
their energy and ambition. In other words, when life is orga-
nized around the pursuit of particular prey, the kill, as glorious
as it may seem, promotes disorientation.

Tom doesn't buy such exotic explanations. "No, it's much
simpler," he says. "It lies in the contrast between the early
stages of building a house and the last stages. At first, when
the frame and siding go up, it's exciting and dramatic. At
the end you're left with Mickey-Mouse stuff—piddling little
pieces of moldings and trim."

When it comes to the finishing touches, Tom admits to
being a shirker. "I'm not precision-oriented," he tells me. "I
don't have the patience to crawl into corners and make perfect
joints. I never feel compelled to run three flights down to my
workshop just to shave a hair off a piece of molding." To illustrate his failing, he points out an ill-fitting door on a kitchen
cabinet that he had recently moved. "The top touches the
frame, but the bottom doesn't. Something is out of joint," he
says, "but I haven't figured out what. You see this?" he goes
on, pointing to a spacer between two other cabinets. "I cut this
with a Skilsaw, holding the piece in my hand. To cut it square I
should have used my chopsaw," he says, "but I loaned it to
Sam." Tom's revelation is startling. Most builders would
weigh giving up their honor before giving up their tools. Yet,
halfway through a remodeling project, Tom loaned his chopsaw to his son—an awe-inspiring display of selflessness.

Tom has been at his kitchen renovation for about six
weeks, ever since he and Nancy moved into their house in the
Berkeley hills. "I'm using here what I learned to do in Covelo,"
Tom tells me, "but the difference is tremendous. Now I feel
confident. Up there I asked myself over and over, 'Will I be able

to build this?' There I did lots of things twice, even three times, learning from my screw-ups. Here, I hardly have to stop and think. I just do it. It's no longer a big deal to build a wall or seal up a doorway."

APPARENTLY, COVELO MADE A BUILDER out of Tom. Less obvious, unless you've had the chance to hear his excitement about his kinfolk, Covelo also cemented connections between him and his family in ways that even he doesn't fully grasp. He alludes repeatedly to Nancy and to his children and grandchildren—how their presence supported him, how their spirit resides in the Covelo house, how much they mean to him personally, how much he loves them all. Later, I realize that Tom's willingness to lend his chopsaw to Sam should not have been such a surprise. It merely proves that when he talks about love Tom means what he says.

When Tom began his Covelo house, he didn't understand that the act of building would channel warm feelings in so many directions. "It's been great," he crows, "just great." His satisfaction is understandable. Not often in life do men have the chance to spend weekends, vacations, and holidays doing precisely what they most want to do—or better, doing precisely what they have been called to do. For a long time now Tom has been following his own nature, which, it often seems, is hell-bent on trying new things, on taking calculated risks, and thereby courting some sort of failure. As a ex-teacher, a writer, and an artist, Tom knows about risk. The untried lesson, the blank page, the empty cold-press paper staring from his easel—all have dared him to hazard falling flat on his face. And if the new lesson bombed, the words were gibberish, or the watercolors ran wild on the paper, his innate tenacity compelled him to try again.

Tom brought that same irrepressibility to building a house, where the opportunities to err were legion, and some mistakes would take a bulldozer to correct. The foundation he eventually built is slightly trapezoidal but not enough to fret about. When Tom tried to strip the forms from the footings, some of the boards refused to budge because he hadn't oiled them properly. "I'm still drilling and chiseling and chipping them out," he says. Such missteps might have gnawed at a perfectionist, but not at Tom. "My biggest and most costly mistake," he says, "was ordering twenty-foot two-by-twelves for the roof frame. I quite forgot to account for the angle cuts to be made at the end of each rafter." Half the boards, therefore, were six inches too short, a discovery Tom made only after he'd sawed into them. Stuck with two dozen unusable rafters, he turned some of the lumber into two massive beds and constructed a sprawling picnic table for family outings on the deck. With other pieces he built what is doubtless one of the longest workbenches in Mendocino County. Tom viewed these oversights as random mishaps, events that, as a novice builder, he had to accept without regret or self-recrimination. Next time, if ever there was one, he'd know better.

Small House, Large Soul

Early in my search for owner-builders, a statement in an old issue of Fine Homebuilding *caught my eye: "In late 1985," it began, "my wife Julie and I began the first of 57 consecutive weekends building a house with our own hands." Eureka!—a fellow traveler in building country.*

The writer of those words, Allan Shope, an architect from Greenwich, Connecticut, was glad to hear about my book, and on three separate occasions—twice in his office and once at the country hunting cabin that Julie and he built together in 1995—indulged me with tales of his weekend building projects.

A Falstaffian fellow, Allan can talk inexhaustibly about land use, tools, types of lumber, home design, woodworking, and the two houses he built with his own beefy hands—one his present home in Greenwich and the other a mountainside hunting cabin near Amenia, New York. There's no stopping him either when he gets going on art, philosophy, architecture—even the human condition and the state of the world. He speaks rapidly and with the conviction of a man who has given every matter—including the spirituality of building—a great deal of thought.

TO ALLAN AND HIS WIFE JULIE, happiness is living in a tent on a piece of wooded land in Greenwich, Connecticut, and devoting a year of weekends to building a house. "We began in March," Allan says. "It was cold. There was snow. People felt sorry for us, but it was a wonderful twelve months."

Allan has probably had more comfortable years—or so one would infer from the offices of Shope Reno Wharton, Associates, one of the nation's more prestigious architectural firms, where he is a partner. In display cases everywhere are models of houses as graceful as cruise ships and so photogenic that they appear regularly in *Architectural Digest*. At computer terminals a dozen architects hunch over plans of multimillion-dollar structures for "people who run the world," as Allan calls some of his clients. But in his frumpy wool sweater and cranberry Keds, Allan, at age fortysomething, sends a strong message that he's not completely enthralled by big names, big money, and manorial homes. His taste, in fact, leans toward more modest structures and is embodied in the compact, light-filled home that he and Julie built for themselves during their second year of marriage.

In 1984, Allan had little money. "I was a young starving architect, didn't have a house, and needed one badly," he remembers. Although he calls building a house for himself "an act of desperation," he never doubted that someday he would do it. He had grown up in a family of architects and had been steeped in woodworking from the day he could lift a hammer. "I always liked doing things for myself," he adds. The thing he had in mind to do early that spring was to build a small house that, as he puts it, "integrated intellect and craft." Put another way, Allan intended his house to be a model of thoughtful design and excellent construction. As an architect specializing in custom houses that fit their owners like Armani suits, he wanted no part of a mass-produced low-grade tract house. Nor would he be content with a custom home built for someone else, even if he had had the money to buy one.

To build a house near his office in fourteen-carat Greenwich seemed out of the question. By chance, however, Allan stumbled across a piece of distressed local property that its owner was desperate to sell—virtually overnight. In a single day of scrounging, Allan and Julie combined their savings with money they borrowed from friends and family, and the following morning bought the land for a fraction of its market value. That weekend, feeling incredibly blessed by their good fortune, they pitched a tent, picked the best spot for a house, and started excavating with two shovels.

"We had never done anything like it," says Allan. "Julie is a city girl who'd never picked up a hammer and never slept in a tent. But she was a great sport about it and didn't complain, even when it rained. She thought it was an adventure in the wilderness."

Julie agrees that she had fun: "I loved getting away in the woods, and it was very good exercise." Monday through Friday, Julie commuted to a PBS job in New York City while Allan designed houses in his Greenwich office. "The whole experience was a little odd," adds Allan. "In the course of a day I would oversee tens of millions of dollars worth of very special construction, while at my own house I was counting nails." On weekends, to save money they turned fallen trees on their property into lumber with help from a portable chain saw mill, and they fished for dinner in a nearby stream. After coyotes stole their food once too often, they posted two sentinels on the site—Tito and Raoul, big black Labradors who kept at bay every beast on two or four legs. (Allan appended a small canine wing to the floor plan of his house. Later, the two hounds charmed their way inside Julie and Allan's more luxurious living quarters, leaving their former digs to a pet pig.) Occasionally, Allan knocked a goose out of the sky with a shotgun. "We'd cook him and ask nearby friends over for dinner," he reports. Neighbors reciprocated, promising not only a hot meal but a hot shower. "They were friendlier than most Greenwich people usually are," recalls Julie, "and they were extremely curious about what the two of us were doing." What they were doing, in effect, was violating Greenwich's unwritten laws of residency. In Greenwich, after all, people don't bivouac in tents and cook over an open fire. But Allan and Julie were having too good a time to worry about protocol.

Ordinarily, Allan was no rebel. On the contrary. He had spent his boyhood quietly in the farming community of Simsbury, Connecticut, where Shopes had been architects for seven generations. From his parents, he received what he calls "intuitive training in craft and architecture." His mother, a schoolteacher and weaver, taught him to respect fine craftsmanship. His father, who specialized in historical restorations, also kept a wood shop on the farm and apprenticed his son to local woodworkers. Right off, Allan says, he developed a reverence for wood. "I loved woodworking from the word *go*, particularly taking an unusual piece of wood and making something special out of it. Woodworking was spiritual. It felt good, smelled good, and filled my soul with good karma." Allan's ancestral home is filled with furnishings from the Shope wood shop: cabinets, tables, chairs, walnut paneling, as well as the wooden salad bowls that Allan at age twelve turned on his father's lathe. With that heritage, Allan's choice of career was virtually preordained. "I just had to be an architect," he says, "although at first I would tell people I was going to be a doctor."

Allan acknowledges that the progression from turning bowls to building a house is tenuous. "But there are obvious links between building furniture and building a house," he is quick to observe. "Both require special kinds of joinery and both are equally creative and fulfilling." Allan credits Tage Frid, a master woodworker at the Rhode Island School of Design, for showing him the beauty in building. "Frid, a Norwegian, taught me never look to tradition to solve a problem. He insisted I take a bigger look. There are forces at work beyond the mechanical, formulaic solution to problems— forces like the nature of the material, its density, its longevity. He told me not to let knowledge, or what passes for knowledge, hinder my creative thinking. He drilled into me to take a deep breath, pause, take a bigger look, and then act. That's the way to come up with fresh solutions to old problems. And that's what makes building such a pleasure for me." Indeed, Allan's account of building his house is laden with adjectives like *satisfying*, *joyful*, and *exhilarating*. He also gives his story a transcendent spin. Building, to Allan, has been more than just an ordinary, feel-good trip. Its rewards have been spiritually nourishing. Call it what you will—a mystical experience, ecstasy, rampaging endorphins—home building delivered spiritual payback with dazzling intensity. While he worked, he often rose above the material reality of nail, hammer, and wood and found himself in realms that he can't rationally define. "Everything is multilayered," Allan observes, and he regards it a blessing to have been granted access to levels of feeling not ordinarily associated with back-breaking construction work.

Even before he started building, Allan, being innately bouyant, expected that his time on the job would be sublime. "Life passes a lot of people by," Allan says knowingly. "I believe in the wonder of life. You're going to be here only for a short time, and you're going to be dead for a long time. So, why not have a little fun while you're here?"

Of course, not every one of the ten thousand steps of building a house gladdened Allan's heart. Shingling the roof did it better than painting the walls. Assembling leaded glass windows offered more magic than mixing concrete. Allan says of himself, "I'm highly craft-oriented at a fairly sophisticated level." It stands to reason, therefore, that he detests Sheetrocking. "It's almost Freudian how much I hate it," he exclaims. "I'm not a bad Sheetrocker, but I hate the mess. I hate the glop," referring to joint compound, the thick gray pudding that's smeared across wallboard to create a smooth surface. Because joint compound shrinks as it dries, it must be applied in layers until every seam, zit, or dimple is obliterated. Sheetrocking is everything that art isn't. In fact, it's the antithesis of art. Tolstoy wrote that art transmits to others the highest and best feelings. But it takes considerable self-delusion to feel anything but indifference toward a plain flat wall made of gypsum and fiberglass sandwiched between two layers of paper. The best Sheetrockers are those who eliminate any evidence that they had been there. Their success is measured in invisibility, an aesthetically nihilistic notion that turns the concept of beauty on its head. A perfectly Sheetrocked wall has height and width, but its allure lies in the absence of a third dimension. "Spiritually," Allan comments, "Sheetrock never did it for me."

On the other hand, he says, "Shingling feels very good to me," as well it might for someone in the throes of a lifelong romance with wood. Red cedar shingles are light in weight, easy to cut, very good-looking, and durable. Their main drawback as roofing material is that they are slow to install. With a three-tab asphalt shingle and a couple of swipes with a nailing gun, you can cover one and a half square feet of roof. To cover the same area in wood takes five or six shingles and a dozen "ringed" shake nails. (The rings keep the nails from popping out as the wood expands and contracts.) Also, cedar is not meant to be mounted on a plywood roof deck. Instead, it requires step-sheathing, pieces of one-by-three or one-by-four lumber that are nailed across the rafters one at a time and with small gaps between them, like the rungs of a ladder. Air circulates in the gaps, allowing the shingles to "breathe," or to swell quickly during a shower, and to resist water and damp rot. Adjacent shingles shouldn't touch. A one-eighth-inch separation lets them breathe more easily. Nor should the edges of overlapping shingles be less than two inches apart. Closer than that and the aligned seams will reduce the watertightness of the roof.

Roofing with cedar shakes is unusually slow work that quickly becomes routine. It tests a roofer's patience. But Allan, apparently born to shingle, tripped along at 150 square feet a day, ignoring oppressive sun, insects, and heat that would disenchant someone less smitten by the job. He was bothered only by the height and pitch of the roof. "It was twelve in twelve," the builder's term for a roof which rises twelve vertical inches for every twelve horizontal inches, or an angle of 45 degrees, far too steep to stand on without support. "It made me nervous to stand on a plank all day," Allan says. "I'm not well coordinated." But nervous or not, after three weekends on high, Allan had a tight roof over his head.

The chimney on the far end of Allan's house is balanced visually by the stairwell in the foreground. Note the built-in doghouse for Tito and Raoul.

Underneath stood a two-room house, sixteen by twenty-four feet, with a bedroom and dormered bath on the second floor and a living/dining room/kitchenette below. A glassed-in stairwell at one end of the house extended outside the basic rectangle of the first floor and was balanced visually at the other end by a massive fireplace and chimney. By keeping the house small, Allan fully expected to complete its construction in fifty-two weekends of work. The fact that he needed fifty-seven bothered him. "I don't like failing at goals as a builder," he says. Bad weather had slowed him down, but he refuses to use that as an excuse.

With only two of every seven days to devote to building, Allan rarely let discomfort—extreme cold, rain, the threat of a nor'easter—shut him down. "I'm pretty tenacious," he says. He set goals for each Saturday and Sunday, and by giving his all, staved off Monday-morning self-recrimination. "You have a lot of options when you're building your own house," he says, "everything from using tarps to working in the rain to packing it in. If you waver and begin to think about taking a day off, you'll grow resentful of the house. But if there's no question in your mind about how you'll spend the weekend, you won't become resentful, and you won't get discouraged. If you are serious about the job, you've got to make a punch list, finish the punch list, and be done with it. There's no satisfaction in 'almost' finishing."

Allan drove himself hard, as though something fateful hung in the balance. "Look," he explains, "you can't be overly fussy when you build a house. Careful, yes, but not meticulous. A house is not a chair or a fine cabinet. You can't take an inordinate amount of time to do a very small task. There are too many steps and the job is too big." Ever mindful of the clock, Allan chose time-saving methods whenever possible. For example, he once lacked a mortiser and a tenoner—power tools that would help him form tight joints on a door that he was building. Calculating how long it would take to rent the tools, he saw that he could do the job faster by hand. "I cut the tenons and mortises the old-fashioned way, using a hammer and chisel," he says. "It took much less time than it would have taken to pick up and return the rented tools."

Allan observes that not everyone has the temperament for do-it-yourself building. Anyone contemplating the construction of his own house must search his soul and ask why he wants to do such a thing. "If the answer doesn't come from the deepest part of their being," Allan says, "I'd advise them to turn around and walk away." Allan compares the decision to build with his choice of career. "I didn't choose to be an architect, I had to be one. There was nothing else I could do with my life. That's the kind of commitment it takes to build your own house. Once you've heard the call, you've got to be a zealot about it. If you're the kind of person who's going to do a half-assed job, you shouldn't build things for yourself. You have only a certain amount of time on Earth, and you want to feel that you've put it to good use."

Allan often specified "poured concrete foundation" on the architectural plans he drew in his office. But lettering the words on a blueprint is different from knowing how to mix the stuff and make the pour. To find out firsthand, he donned waterproof boots and joined a crew about to build a slab for a garage about the size of the house he and Julie had in mind. Amazed to have the architect of a project actually mucking about in wet concrete, the masons showed him exactly what to do, but as Allan reports it, "They also took it as a unique opportunity to rag on me just as I often ragged on them."

His one-day workshop in foundation basics emboldened him enough to pour a concrete slab of his own. He built the forms and laid in steel mesh for reinforcement. Using a portable mixer, he stirred up batches of cement, sand, gravel, and water. After the pour, he removed bumps from the surface of the condrete with a screed—a giant-size squeegee with a six-foot handle attached to a long wooden blade. When dry, the slab was mostly smooth, mostly horizontal, and as solid as a bunker. Allan says, "It was great."

Great or not, Allan admits to being an imperfect mason, especially when it comes to laying concrete blocks. "We built our chimney out of blocks," he says. "Julie hoisted them with a pulley and mixed the mortar while I stood on the scaffold piling them on top of one another. When it was done, the chimney was out of plumb and out of square, but not terribly out of either. It was good enough—not, however, what you'd call acceptable industry standards." If the guardians of Greenwich minded, they didn't say so. Mostly, they supported Allan's singular building practices. "When they came to do inspections," Allan remembers, "they brought sandwiches."

Since that time, Allan estimates, he and Julie have lit over a thousand fires in their fireplace. The chimney has never failed to carry the smoke away. "It works beautifully," Allan says. "Each time I light a fire is a special moment for me, and I suspect for Julie, too. It has an extra meaning because we built the chimney together."

Allan also prizes the custom-made, leaded cut-glass windows that adorn every room in his house. Fabricated from Allan's design by Tom Finsterwald, a master window craftsman, each window consists of 210 pieces of glass and 600 pieces of metal. With Allan lending a hand as an eager apprentice, Tom soldered crystal prisms in the corners of each window, an artful touch that has enthralled Allan on moonlit nights ever since he first caught sight of rainbow swatches gliding slowly up and down the walls. "As the moon rises and falls," he explains, "the colors of the spectrum float in the rooms and intersect magically on the floor or ceiling. It is very exciting."

Allan's awareness that the physiognomy of a house must be both physically and spiritually satisfying reaches far into his work as an architect. Buildings are "capable of touching our souls," he writes in "Humanism in Architecture," a one-page statement of his philosophy that he often hands to prospective clients. Comparing a great cathedral and a Connecticut tobacco barn, he says, "The rhythm of the sunlight filtering down through the long row of Gothic columns is emotionally similar to the pattern of light from the barn slats. The aisle of the cathedral is the same symbolic path as the aisle of the barn. The movement of the smoke from the memorial candles contrasts with the stillness of the great structure, creating the same sense of awe as the steam rising from the dirt floors of the barn."

At his own house, he experienced comparable awe on Gee Whiz weekend—when he suddenly realized that he had nothing left to do. On the fifty-eighth Saturday, his house complete, he sat back to admire his handiwork and thought, "Gee whiz, I did this whole job as well as anybody I could have hired to do it." That he had missed his self-imposed deadline by a whisper only slightly dimmed his inner glow of satisfaction.

HAVING BUILT ONE HOUSE BY THEMSELVES, Allan and Julie might easily have built another when, two years and two children later, they found themselves in need of more space.

But this time they had a different idea: to construct a separate 900-square-foot addition on a rock outcropping forty feet away from the original house and join the two buildings with a narrow corridor that would double as a fully equipped kitchen. And instead of assembling the new structure conventionally, stick by stick, they would hold a house-raising happening. They would invite friends, relatives, officemates, even Allan's clients, to bring tools, and during one day together, erect the entire house. All would be welcome, all would have a job to do, and all would take part in a vanishing ritual of communal life. Few turned down the opportunity.

The day he picked, August 6, marked the anniversary of the bombing of Hiroshima, but Allan concedes that planning for it was a logistical exploit more akin to D-Day. "It was important to think about the physical act of raising a house," he says. "I made lists of what sixty or eighty people could accomplish in a day and thought about what could go wrong." Because the roof design called for four dormers, framing the roof would be complex. In order to complete the job in a few hours, no time could be spared on that day figuring out how to cut odd-shaped polygons of plywood or rakish angles at the ends of valley jack rafters. Every joist and rafter, every collar tie and bit of blocking would have to be pre-cut, labeled, and stacked for quick and easy installation. Pre-assembled walls would be poised for lifting into position and every piece of sheathing trimmed to its proper size and shape. Allan also had to amass enough ladders, scaffolding, tape measures, levels, squares, and other tools to outfit dozens of workers. It would never do to have people queuing up to use a hammer.

For novice carpenters Allan prepared visual aids, drawings on plywood billboards detailing the steps of house construction. And to make the day productive for everyone who showed up, including those likely to mistake their thumb for a nailhead, he compiled lists of non-building jobs, from babysitter and paramedic to mayonnaise spreader on the sandwich assembly line. Sleepless, he anguished over interpersonal relations, trying to predict who would be a good foreman for work details and which people couldn't possibly work side by side. "My family, if anything, is less perfect than many," Allan says, "and when you get them all together, there are petty rivalries and emotional complications. You know how it is: Cousin Susie holds a grudge against such-and-such and would share a hammer with him only over her dead body."

By the eve of house-raising day, Allan had completed the preparations. Toe plates, to which the stud walls soon would be attached, were nailed to the perimeter of the first floor deck. Every piece of the frame had been cut to size, including a forty-foot prefabricated ridge beam of double two-by-twelves. In the yard stood a picnic table 120 feet long to accommodate hoards of guests. (Later, the table would be recycled as the frame and sheathing of the corridor that linked the addition to the original house.) Julie had stockpiled steaks, a full cord of bread, vegetables, drinks, and pies. No more could be done except wait for the next day. Allan was up at 2 A.M., worried that he'd forgotten something.

Before dawn, volunteers began to gather, some of them tycoons and socialites who, in Allan's words, "arrived in Bentleys and blue jeans." By mid-morning Allan's energetic helpers had erected the walls, and the ridge beam, which took fifteen people to lift, had been braced into position. When the work crews broke for lunch, the rafters and collar ties were in place and four sheathed dormers stood in a line along the front edge of the roof. Much of the afternoon was devoted to nailing four thousand feet of step sheathing to the rafters. By suppertime the workers had switched from soda to beer, and amid cheering and applause, nailed a small pine tree to the peak of the roof, signifying that the work was done.

From a distance the house-raising operation was smooth and efficient. Close up, it had its share of bumps. "Not everything was square, not everything was plumb, not everything was nailed quite right," says Allan. Although people got sunburned, wilted in the humid heat, and muttered expletives when a joist refused to drop neatly into place, none of that

dampened their spirits. "They felt immense exhilaration seeing it all happen," Allan recalls. "Even the children were
happy as they raced around and built little stick buildings in
the woods. It was an incredibly positive day." With framing
and sheathing complete, Allan's corps of volunteers, awed by
what they had accomplished, congratulated each other and sat
down for a celebratory dinner.

"How wonderful," people tell Allan, "you put up a whole
building in a day." But Allan demurs. "It was a feat that seems
miraculous for a group made up largely of amateurs, but the
fact is that it didn't actually save time. The planning and
preparation took longer than if I'd put that building together
myself as I cut the pieces."

In retrospect, though, he wouldn't have done it any differently. "Emotionally, it was very fulfilling. I still feel the friend-
ship and love that went on that day. Every part of the building
has friends or family members associated with it. And they, in
a sense, have become part of the building. Because willing
hands helped to raise the house, it is even more valuable to
Julie and me. It is a home," he says confidently, "that will always enrich our lives."

FIVE YEARS LATER, IN 1992, Allan bought land in Dutchess
County, near Amenia, New York, on which he intended one day
to build a small home where Julie and he could spend informal
summer weekends with their four young children. The house
would also serve as his own private getaway in the woods. He
planned to escape there occasionally with his son Ben, whom he
would teach to hunt partridge and catch trout. Or he'd invite his
cronies up for a "scratch-your-balls-and-belch weekend," as
likes to call a couple of days of male bonding in the country.
Above all, though, he anticipated building a house with his own
hands using materials that came from his property. He drew
plans for a thirty-foot square cabin that contained one large
room with an oversize fireplace, a sleeping loft with room for
six mattresses laid out on the floor, and a tiny kitchen and

bathroom. Allan says, "I wanted it to be plain but also quite spiritual and wonderful—very quiet as you approached it, but as you stepped inside I wanted it to lift your spirits."

A full year before turning the first spadeful of earth, Allan, chain saw in hand, strode into the woods with some friends and started to harvest lumber for the cabin. They practiced a form of triage, dismantling dead and dying trees first. None of the cedars, now part of the cabin's decor both inside and out, was alive when it was felled. "In Eastern forests aromatic cedars are an early-succession species," says Allan, shifting into an explicative mode. "That is, they start to grow before other trees. By coming up first, they provide cover for the hardwoods—birch, oak, maple—which eventually overtake and eclipse them. Having lost their sun, the cedars soon die. They seem to get a raw deal: By protecting other trees, they lose their lives. But because cedars don't rot, they remain standing in the woods. So, when we cut them down, we were basically cutting down skeletons."

Fir trees supplied the cabin's framing lumber, and white pines provided the planks for walls, floors, stairs, and trim. Except for shingles, all the wood for the cabin had grown within shouting distance of the building site. Allan and his crew cut most of the lumber with a Wood-Mizer, an 18-horsepower portable band saw mill. The biggest logs they fed into a Sperber chain saw mill, a hunk of machinery that requires at least two sets of hands to operate. "You need a person on each side," explains Allan. "In effect, you walk the mill through the log rather than vice versa."

In a nearby barn, Allan stacked most of his fresh-cut lumber with spacers (called stickers) between the layers to promote air-drying of the wood. The rest he stickered outdoors under sheets of plywood and tar paper. Allen took pains to dry the wood properly. A builder who ignores the moisture content of new lumber can end up with a mess on his hands, because wood shrinks profoundly as it dries. Framing a house with wood that is too green—say, with a moisture content of 25 percent or higher—spells trouble. Within six months walls begin to wave and buckle, nails pop, plaster cracks, and doors and windows won't open smoothly.

Allan has definite views on how dry lumber should be before you use it. He says, "The world thinks there's some kind of relationship between lower humidity and goodness, but there isn't." As the architect on residential projects he prescribes lumber with a 12 to 14 percent moisture content. He also prefers air-dried, as opposed to kiln-dried, wood. "Kiln-drying is a negative," he argues, "not a plus. It hurts wood. Eight percent kiln-dried wood is too brittle and dry. It wants to soak up moisture and expand in any kind of weather. It just doesn't behave." For his cabin, he brought the moisture content down to roughly 16 percent—a degree of wetness that he contends is just about right for a place without a heating system. With no hot, dry air to carry off its remaining water, wood with moisture content between 10 and 16 percent achieves a kind of equilibrium, expanding and contracting as all wood does whenever the ambient humidity rises and falls. "A wooden door is always going to be harder to pull open in August than in March," Allan notes.

Allan's place is not, by a long shot, your everyday cabin in the woods. It sits dramatically on a grassy windswept knoll overlooking a patchwork of low lying pastures and wooded hills. Catskill peaks rise faintly in a lavender haze, forty miles away. The building is essentially square with a striking pyramid roof topped by a tall copper finial, suggesting something churchly. Indeed, the cabin is almost monastic—simple and austere in its isolation, but nonetheless rather dignified. A Buddhist monk could find contentment in such a lair—close to the clouds and with an awesome view. Allan's description—"plain but also quite spiritual and wonderful"—seems right on the money.

The columns supporting the roof are the actual trunks of cedar trees, bark and branches intact. A robin nests on one of the upper limbs close to the ceiling. Even the porch's roof beams are pieces of cedar trees. Shelves just inside the front door hold snakeskins and the skulls of several small creatures,

also a display of arrowheads, ax-heads, and scraping tools—
artifacts left on the land by Lenape Indians who occupied
the surrounding hills centuries ago. A facing wall of books
shows titles on birds, guns, fishing, the history of art, and wildflowers. Allan's other interests are reflected in books on bee-
keeping, wood drying, cutting lumber, and making maple
syrup.

Allan set a cavernous fireplace against the cabin's back
wall. It is surrounded by three huge slabs of granite quarried in
Roxbury, Connecticut. Two young cedars stand astride the
fireplace, their upper boughs forming an arbor of intertwined
fingers above the granite lintel. On the opposite wall Allan
built twin staircases converging at the loft above the front
door. He cut the hand railings and newel posts from cedar
trees. Balusters, nailed to the side of each stringer and rail, are
tree branches that twist and curl like frozen flames.

But the cabin's crown jewel soars overhead. Allan has
intentionally left the skeleton of the roof exposed, creating
a geometric pattern of light and dark woods—rafters, step-
sheathing, and shingles. The effect is startling, for the pinnacle
of the building directly over the center of the room appears at
least half again as high as you'd expect. Suddenly, you're staring up into the lofty spire of a cathedral. "I told you it would be
uplifting," says Allan. "Everybody who comes in for the first
time sucks in their breath."

Denying any intent to provoke religiosity with a heaven-
cast roof, Allan says, "It's meant only to lift your spirits and
make you feel glad to be alive." He achieves the effect simply,
by using the architectural principle of forced perspective. "On
a slate roof," Allan explains, "you might graduate the
courses—large at the bottom, small at the top. That creates the
illusion of greater distance." The roof of Allan's cabin is
pitched at twelve in twelve. "When you're outside, it looks
like a regular forty-five-degree angle, but inside it looks much
steeper. It's an optical illusion."

If his cabin quickens emotions, Allan gives credit not to
the shape of the roof but to the setting—in particular the con-

trast between the enclosure and the vastness you face outside the front door. "The view really does it for my heart," he says. "You can sit on the porch at sunup and watch the light race down the valley, and in the evening you can see the darkness run back up. It's very dramatic."

In his aerie Allan feels doubly stirred knowing that much of the land spread out before him is in good hands, namely his own. Since 1993, he has increased his land holdings several times over. He considers his real estate more than just a nest egg. Rather, it's his attempt to keep the *wild* in wilderness. "People have a tendency to do the wrong thing with land," he asserts. "When you give a person a little chunk, they'll often take an acre and make a mess out of it." As an avowed conservationist, Allan is determined not to let that happen here. "The finest gift we can leave for future generations is open space," he says. Consequently, he's created "no-build" conservation easements to forever protect extensive tracts of woodland. Easement statutes, however, have permitted him to set aside four small building sites. On each site he hopes one day to erect a modest home for each of his children. He also has the right to build another residence on the hill above his cabin. After a fashion, the new house is already under construction. Allan has drawn preliminary plans for a structure similar to the cabin but with bedrooms for everyone. He's also cut and stickered most of the lumber.

When the subject is trees or land or even the great outdoors, Allan talks with the ardor of a lover—actually more like a bard waxing lyrical over his beloved. On weekends in the country, he routinely rises at 4 A.M. and walks to the top of the hill. "I sit quietly against a tree for two hours," he says, "and listen to the changes taking place as the nocturnal world turns into the daytime world. I just close my eyes and listen. It's a symphony, full of the fantastic sounds of nature coming awake. It's lovely. And as the light comes up you can feel the Earth just roll into the sun."

Allan's paean to daybreak explains why his shelves are crowded with nature books and why he still regards that year tenting in the wilds of Greenwich long ago among the best twelve months of his life. "Witnessing such beauty," he continues, "you've got to believe there's a bigger picture that we just don't understand. I'm not a religious person, but how can you not feel spiritual at times like that? You just feel the power of that beauty."

Allan believes that his design for the cabin may be one man's attempt to embody comparable beauty in a building. But he adds quickly that the thought must have been subconscious. "I didn't set out to make a big statement here. I just wanted a quiet little building, subservient to the hillside, that allowed me to walk out on the porch and look at the valley. Or, sometimes I'll sit here in the house with a little chardonnay and look up at the ceiling and feel good. I think that it turned out the way it did a little by accident and a little by not being able to do it any other way."

Once he broke ground for the cabin, Allan, typically, thrust himself headlong into the work, trying to get the cabin up and running as quickly as possible. "It took us twenty weekends," he says, "but I admit to cheating a little. Sometimes I started work on Friday afternoons." More than willing to have others participate in the cabin's construction, as often as not he brought helpers along. Recollecting his Greenwich house-raising, he knew the rewards—in speed, sociability, and personal satisfaction—of a group effort. "I had it in my heart to involve both family and friends," he says. Julie carried materials and cleared logs away. Even the children, who helped with painting, found decorative feathers and funky stones to dress up the inside. Allan says, "Whenever others have helped, I continue to find additional meaning in the things I've built."

Allan subcontracted the electricity ("I'm scared of it," he says), the plumbing ("I didn't have the time"), and some of the masonry ("I assisted the three guys who built the fireplace. One of them, Henrique, also did the chimney"). From a distance, the chimney, which stands prominently behind the cabin, appears to anchor the building to the hill. Allan thinks that he and Julie could have built the chimney themselves—

they already had one to their credit—but at thirty feet, this one may have been too high and maybe too demanding as well, for it is faced from top to toe with fieldstone, and it tapers inward as it rises from a four-by-six-foot base.

The weekend Allan framed the roof, using true-dimensional two-by-eights, each twenty to twenty-four feet long and weighing close to fifty pounds, he recruited three carpenter friends—Scott, Karl, and John—to help. Before they arrived, he built a tall scaffold on which to temporarily rest each rafter before nailing it into place, a technique he had often seen during the construction of his clients' homes. First, the four corner rafters of the pyramid were cut and nailed to each other at the peak, creating, in Allan's words, "a pretty stable form." Thereafter, the rafters were mounted halfway between those previously installed, until forty pieces of lumber spanned the space like the spokes of a wheel. Because forty two-by-eights cannot physically meet at a single point. Allan shortened all the intermediate rafters to fit into the increasingly narrow spaces near the hub of the roof, where he nailed them to the rafters already in place.

Not all of the cabin was engineered as meticulously as the roof. The balustrade on each staircase, for example, and the similarly quirky loft railing could not have been preplanned. Just the opposite. They are celebrations of spontaneity, each an improvised assemblage of random tree parts that Allan and his family picked up while roaming the woods. As he tells it, "We'd find a branch or a log that we liked, bring it back and try it out on the railing. If it didn't quite fit, we'd put it on the burn pile and look for another. After an hour's search we might find one that was perfect, or we might not. Overall, it was a subjective, trial-and-error kind of thing that the whole family enjoyed—a lot different from starting with a specific design in mind. All we had was the concept. The actual individual pieces were something we had to futz with as we went along."

Up on the hill, where his next do-it-yourself project is taking shape, Allan won't leave quite so much to chance. "This time I'm doing a serious design," he says about his four-year (thus far) effort to plan the next home he'll build on his property. He has collected "special pieces to build the house around, things that you can't get in a lumber yard"—for one, a huge piece of quartz that he describes by spreading his arms wide. "I'll put it in the foundation because it admits light like a block of solid glass," he says. "From inside, the house will almost appear to float above the ground." Only last week he trucked four flat stones onto his site, each at least the size of a flat-bed trailer. In his words, they are "beautiful reach-into-your-soul-and-make-you-feel-good stones," to be placed in front of the house to usher visitors to the front door. Allan has also cut and stacked oak rafters for the house. Now drying in a nearby barn, each one is sixty feet long, fourteen inches wide, and nearly three inches thick. "I needed a forklift to move them," he says.

ALLAN IS STILL COMING TO terms with the discrepancy between his private values and professional obligations. Off-stage he reveres the things of nature—its stones and trees, the land he intends to conserve forever. Yet, he is also an architect and a builder whose work unavoidably does violence to the very things he holds dear. (How many oak trees bit the dust to produce four dozen sixty-foot rafters?) Does he have qualms about that? "Yes and no," he answers. A diplomat's response.

Elaborating, he says, "In my personal life, no. I have no interest in being a tree-hugger, but I've been extremely gentle with the land. It would never enter my mind to allow clear-cutting on my property, but I'm very comfortable with forest management. The concept that every hundred years maybe ten percent of the eligible trees get taken down is fine with me. It's done in the wintertime when animals are not nesting and the ground is frozen so that mosses and other plants are not damaged.

"On the other hand, yes. Professionally, I've had to make a few compromises." Amenia, he explains, lies between Millbrook, New York, and Sharon, Connecticut—both high-development areas and current hotspots for yuppie weekenders—the Hamptons of the hills, so to speak. "As it happens," Allan goes on, "my job is to design houses for wealthy people, not all of them sensitive to the environment. Given the choice between cutting down a forest for a water view or preserving the trees, many of my clients will clear the land. I often try to persuade them not to. I tell them to prune the lower half of the tall trees and keep the top. That way they save the trees and have their view too." Allan adds that most of the time he gets his way.

"The truth is, I've spent much of my life trying to strike a healthy balance between these two competing forces. It's a real conflict for me. I have examples of houses I'm proud of architecturally but not proud of what the owners did to the site. I believe in my buildings. They are beautiful three-dimensional objects that people will like for many, many years. I'm not interested in putting scabs on the Earth. But I'm also sensitive to the siting of my buildings and how they're going to affect the land."

Because of the inevitable clash between two separate estates—the defenders of nature and wilderness, and their adversaries, the defenders of development—Allan's enthusiasm for architecture has limits. "Everybody has a few second thoughts about their careers," he notes. "I've often thought that I really ought to be running the National Park Service. I'm good with people and I'm passionate about the land. I'd be terrific at managing the largest land trust in America." Until Washington hears about him, however, Allan will remain in Greenwich doing his best to satisfy both his clients and his conscience. On weekends, though, he'll be found in jeans and boots, working on his next house and doing his damnedest to tap straight into the sources of delight that, for him, spring from building houses of his own.

The Prodigal Son

In Six Degrees of Separation, *playwright John Guare espouses the theory that everyone is connected to everyone else through a chain of no more than six people. When it comes to owner-builders, however, two or three degrees is more like it. Almost everyone knows someone, or at least knows someone else who knows an owner-builder.*

At the end of a chain that took me from a friend to a cousin to a brother-in-law, I found Richie Mueller (not his real name; he chose anonymity) an avid do-it-yourselfer from Closter, New Jersey. Richie, tall, blue-eyed, and restless, is a youthful-looking fortysomething, with plenty of light brown hair starting to pale around the edges. He's a talker as well as a pacer. During one interview in his home, he prowled the room, discoursing on building and what it has meant to him. Another time, in less than two hours, we migrated from kitchen to porch to dining room and back to the kitchen again. One afternoon we drove together, a ninety-mile trip, to look at the country house he restored in Pennsylvania. He talked nonstop. Every thirty minutes, however, he stopped chattering, pulled over, and strode briskly around the car three or four times.

"I'm not always so hyper," he told me as we took to the road again. "When I'm building or when I'm at my desk [he's a graphic artist], I can work for hours on the tiniest details.

*Then I'm like another person, sunk so deep into the work it
takes a crowbar to pull me out.*

*"To tell you the truth," he went on, "I start to pace only
when my hands and head are not doing something creative."
Then he added, "No offense intended, George. You're a nice
guy, but as you see, you just don't do it for me the way a chopsaw does."*

AS HE DIGS FOR CANS OF Diet Pepsi in the refrigerator,
Richie says, "My father was not a building guy." Flipping open
the top, he continues. "Just the opposite, I don't remember
him ever doing a lick of physical work. Maybe winding the
grandfather clock in the hall. That's about it. Our apartment
house had a crew of maintenance men. They did it all."

A tour of Richie's house makes patently clear that the son
is precisely what his father wasn't. At every turn, from back
porch to Jacuzzi, Richie points to what he himself has built,
installed, restored, repaired, altered, and serviced. "I made this,
too," he says, caressing the top of a long kitchen table with his
fingertips.

In the basement, surrounded by his woodworking tools,
Richie explains further what not being "a building guy" means:
Born in Amsterdam, Richie's father, Willard, at age eighteen, on
the eve of the Nazi invasion of Holland, had been sent by
his parents to live with relatives in America. In Manhattan,
Willard went to NYU, married, and found a career as an im-
porter of fine chocolates. Along the way he also began to gorge
himself on the cultural riches of New York City. He and
Marianne, Richie's mother, often went to the theater, to
Carnegie Hall, and to the Met. They frequented art museums
and galleries all over town. Barely a week passed without an
opening to attend. Willard also played the piano—"not at all
badly," according to Richie—while Marianne played the violin.
Once a month on a Sunday afternoon they invited friends to
their apartment on Riverside Drive for a chamber music recital.
When Richie's older sister Eva turned fourteen, she joined her
parents, playing the viola at the Muellers' musicales.

"You see what I'm driving at?" Richie asks. "Physical labor was not on my father's plate."

All in all, Willard was content with the life he had fashioned in New York and thought that Richie could hardly do better than to follow in his footsteps. As a boy, therefore, Richie was shown many of the city's cultural attractions: Saturday morning young people's concerts, *Carmen* and *Hansel and Gretl* at the Metropolitan Opera, children's art and music programs all around town. Willard also arranged piano and cello lessons for the boy and expected that Richie would one day turn the family trio into a family quartet.

Until age thirteen, Richie shared his father's aspirations. Then he began to think for himself. One day he stunned his father by announcing that he was through with music lessons. "I hate music," he said, a statement so subversive that Willard almost slapped his son's face. "He came *that* close," recalls Richie.

Today Richie admits to wounding his father wantonly. "I was crazy about music. I even composed some," he says. "I just wasn't crazy about taking lessons." His remark, however, signaled a turning point in the relationship between father and son. "After that," says Richie, "my father disapproved of almost everything I did, and I developed an aptitude for pissing him off."

Richie dropped his piano lessons but continued playing the cello, albeit under protest. "My father insisted that I practice an hour every day. I said no, half an hour. When I wanted to shoot baskets in the park, he said no, not until I had finished practicing. The truth is that he didn't want me to play basketball at all, or ride a bike, or roughhouse with my friends, or, for that matter, do anything athletic or physical. He was afraid I'd break an arm or a finger and never play the cello again."

As Richie talks about going to high school—Stuyvesant, the Harvard of New York's public high schools—his voice begins to crack ever so slightly, his blue eyes to pink around the edges. His shoulders have sagged noticeably.

But he goes on: In freshman year he fell in love with Rosa, a girl from Queens. "My father went ballistic," he says. "He didn't approve of boys my age having steady girlfriends. Her dad was a vocational high school teacher in Brooklyn and had a shop in his basement, sort of like this one." Richie surveys the room, crowded with woodworking equipment. "He had every-thing—table saw, a jointer and planer, a lathe, a router table— you name it. I owe my interest in building to him. Since I was always hanging around with Rosa—I practically boarded at her house—he showed me his shop and let me try out his tools." Richie remembers that Mr. Bondino called his shop his "house of magic" because that's where he transformed ordinary blocks of wood into beautiful museum-quality objects: cabinets, tables with inlaid tops, chairs. There he showed Richie the jointer he used to straighten and smooth edges and the planer that shaved the face of the wood. From Mr. Bondino Richie learned to push boards past the blade of a table saw, a tool that as eas-ily slices a paper-thin sliver from the edge of a massive timber as rip it down the middle. Richie was mad for Mr. Bondino's router, amazed that a small bit of spinning steel so quickly cut grooves and carved intricate designs into oak and mahogany. "I was in awe of the guy and his tools," Richie says. "He had the vision of an artist and the hands of a magician." Richie nods appreciatively as he thinks about his mentor of long ago.

"Rosa was a pretty decent carpenter, too," Richie contin-ues, "taught by her dad. We used to go down to the basement to fool around. With wood, I mean—well, sometimes in other ways, too. I remember that we made toys for her kid brother— little paddle-wheel boats powered by a wound-up rubber band and miniature cars with wooden wheels."

Richie recalls being "blown away" by yellow glue when Rosa spread a thin layer along the edge of two scraps of pine, clamped the pieces together, forging a bond stronger than the wood itself. When Richie tried it, Rosa cautioned him not to overtighten the clamps or he'd force all the glue out and weaken the bond. Later, when the glue dried, he sanded the two boards until the seam between them virtually disap-peared. "I couldn't believe it," Richie says. "I'd made one piece of wood out of two. I got more satisfaction out of that than I had ever found in playing the piano or cello. When you play

Chopin or Liszt, it's beautiful, but it's gone, vanished as soon as the music ends. In carpentry, though, you have something tangible to show for your effort. You can hold it, smell it, run your fingers over it, feel its texture. When I discussed this theory with my father, he said, 'Don't be ridiculous. You can't compare a polonaise to a piece of a dead tree.'"

Richie often arrived home from Rosa's redolent with wood and sweat, the detritus of the shop clinging to his clothes. His father's disapproving look said to him, "You should be making music, not sawdust." Nevertheless, when Richie and Rosa were high school juniors they decided to build something for Willard's fiftieth birthday, and in Mr. Bondino's files found plans for a piano bench. Perfect. A peace offering to Willard. They made it out of cherry and it took them three months.

Perhaps a kind of madness drove the teenagers to spend three months making a piano bench, but, as Richie puts it, "We wanted to knock my father's socks off." After they cut and glued the pieces, using wooden dowels to strengthen the joints, they started sanding, roughly at first with the belt sander, and then with a finishing sander using paper with increasingly finer grit. They sanded and sanded, until the surface of the bench fairly gleamed. "I really got into that bench," says Richie. "It was an emotional commitment, something I wanted desperately to do well, to prove to my father that I wasn't such a no-goodnik after all." Richie professes to carry a replica of the bench in his head. "Twenty-five years later I can draw its contours and grains on paper," he boasts.

To Richie the piano bench was a gorgeous *objet d'art*, well-balanced and set on slender legs. It had a rich, warm-bronze finish, hand rubbed with tung oil. Under its hinged seat Rosa and Richie had built a compartment for storing sheet music. "My heart was in that bench," Richie says. "It wasn't perfect. You could probably tell that it was made by two seventeen-year-olds, not mass-produced in a factory. But it had soul. You can't say that about furniture from Bloomingdale's."

Willard said he was thrilled with the bench, but Richie has his doubts. "He overdid it. It wasn't like him to go overboard.

Behind the effusion, he was probably thinking that I should have been making music, not benches. I read that in his eyes," Richie says.

The new bench was placed in front of the piano. It became a fixture in the Mueller home. Two years later, however, during his first visit home from college, Richie noticed that the bench had been shoved against the wall and had a plant on it. In front of the keyboard stood Willard's old mahogany piano stool.

As teenage ardor often will, Richie's and Rosa's cooled, and soon after Willard's birthday the sweethearts broke up. Calling it quits, Rosa alleged that Richie fancied her father's tools more than he fancied her. Today he doesn't deny it but is quick to add that not a woman he courted thereafter knew the first thing about gluing boards together.

In graduate school, Richie met Erica. She couldn't tell a bit from a band saw but had other virtues. In particular, she always kept her cool in trying circumstances—a good thing, too, because after she married Richie, bore a daughter they named Sara, and moved from Manhattan to a house in Closter, New Jersey, she had ample opportunities to complain, criticize, and cry. Out in the suburbs, she saw her husband immerse himself with piano-bench intensity into do-it-yourselfing. Even when he subjected their home to improvements she neither wanted nor completely understood, she never lost her humor.

She remained composed, for example, when Richie insisted on starting his quasi-career as a home handyman by installing dark-brown adjustable louvered shutters on every second-story window. Erica recalls, "I thought the house had more pressing needs—a functioning lock on the front door, for one, and a vent for the new clothes dryer." In time Richie got around to the door and to the dryer, but first he replaced treads on the back steps, hung new gutters, tiled the playroom ceiling, and built a toy chest for Sara and a vanity for the bathroom.

"Each project," Richie says, "required different techniques, which I learned by trial and error, although most of the time it seemed like error." When he bent a nail—"one out of three on average"—or drove one in the wrong place, he tried prying it out with the claw of his hammer. More often than not, however, the claw was too thick to reach under the nail-head. Using a chisel, therefore, he dug a shallow moat around the nail, removing just enough material to give the claw's two fingers purchase on the nailhead. If that didn't work, he tried using a crowbar to separate whatever he'd nailed together. Sometimes he simply cut the pieces apart with a saw, rendering perfectly good wood perfectly unusable. "Then," Richie says, "somebody told me about a cat's paw," a foot-long iron bar that's found in every carpenter's toolbox and with its rounded claw usually pulls out hard-to-reach nails.

In the backyard Richie built a brick patio, or, as he puts it, "It was supposed to be a patio, but it turned out to be a lemon." Richie's backyard flop began with a six-inch-deep, ten-foot-by-sixteen-foot excavation. So far, so good, but then he filled most of the cavity with four inches of fine, dry sand, a move that doomed the patio to a short life. In six months, with only a shifting layer of sand to support them, the bricks started to pitch and yaw. Had he known better, Richie might have set the bricks on a layer of quarter-inch gravel, or even better, stone-dust screening, a mix of small pebbles and fine powder, the stuff that's left over when stone is crushed. A four-inch base of hard-packed screening will keep a brick patio level and smooth for years. A still deeper layer will hold the bricks in place even longer, perhaps a decade or more. (Roman roads, still used in some parts of Europe, were built on a base six feet deep.)

On top of the sand, Richie laid nearly eight hundred bricks, herringbone-style—one piece placed on the diagonal, the next one perpendicular to the first, until the whole rectangle was clad in brick. Arranging the bricks at an angle left the patio with jagged edge, so Richie filled in the sawtooth spaces with fragments he fabricated by whacking whole bricks with a sledge hammer and chipping away lumpy spots with a hammer and cold chisel. (He hadn't yet heard of the more accurate and infinitely tidier technique of scoring the surface of a brick with the masonry blade of a circular saw and then breaking the brick apart with a hammer and wide chisel.) Then Richie swept sand into the chinks between the bricks. To frame the patio, he laid untreated two-by-sixes, edge up, into a furrow he had dug with a garden spade. For a year, the new patio served as a play area for Sara and a backyard retreat for Richie and Erica, but it soon began to show signs of premature aging. Grass and weeds sprouted between the bricks. The patio surface undulated like a choppy sea, and bricks grew slick with moss. In two years, when the frame no longer stood upright and wood rot had begun to set in, Richie saw that his patio was a colossal mess. Rather than dismantle and rebuild it properly, however, he let it be—a memorial to benighted effort. Soon after, though, he put his backyard eyesore out of both sight and mind under a smart-looking deck that he built quite correctly out of pressure-treated lumber.

"For a long time mistakes came naturally," Richie says, but they failed to deter him from trying new things. "Look," he says, "you aren't always going to make the right decisions, in building or otherwise. But the worst that can happen is that you look like a jerk. It's not fatal, and eventually, you'll get it right." A case in point is the Sunday afternoon when Richie determined to present Erica with a Valentine's Day surprise, a five-inch television set lodged above the counter next to the kitchen sink. With Erica out of the house for a few hours, he hurriedly screwed a clip to the underside of a cabinet and slipped the TV into place, noticing only then the dowdiness of having a black electrical cord plugged into the backsplash. He decided, therefore, to install a new outlet hidden from view between the top of the cabinet and the ceiling. "My plan was simple," Richie insists. "I'd tap into an existing circuit inside the kitchen wall and run a length of cable to the new receptacle. Then I'd thread the TV cord up through holes drilled in the cabinet shelves. I expected to finish the job with time to spare before Erica returned."

Since access to the wall's innards was blocked on the kitchen side by a tiled backsplash and a bank of cabinets,

Richie needed to gain entry from the dining room side, where only a massive oak breakfront full of dishes and tableware barred the way. After emptying its shelves and removing the drawers, he muscled the piece out of the way and found an un-used electrical outlet on the wall. "Voilà! Here was the power source I needed," recalls Richie. "I'd simply cut a hole in the Sheetrock, nail a junction box to the nearest stud, and make my connections." To open the wall in a hurry—Erica would soon be back—Richie grabbed his reciprocating saw, a tool more suited to dismembering a roof than cutting a square hole in wallboard. He punctured the surface, inserted the saw blade, and pulled the trigger. Seconds later, he nicked a water pipe that let out a geyser so fierce it knocked the cap right off of his head and began to flood the dining room. Soaked, he ran to the basement to shut the main valve and halt the deluge.

When she came home, Erica couldn't help being surprised: In her absence, Richie had apparently gone berserk. He had scattered her best china across the living room floor, punched a gaping hole in the wall behind the breakfront, and watered the dining room rug. Moreover, he had turned off the water throughout the house and now stood damp and disgruntled in the middle of the kitchen holding a propane torch in one hand and a guide to household plumbing in the other.

Trying to be helpful, Erica asked, "Would you like me to call a plumber?"

"No way," Richie responded. "I'll have this fixed in a jiffy." Had it been any day but Sunday, when the local hard-ware stores were closed, Richie might have kept his word. But it took an hour to find a store that sold the inch-long couplings with which to repair the damaged pipe and several more hours (while Erica watched *Sixty Minutes* and *Murder, She Wrote* on an old TV) to sweat the joint, wire the receptacle, and patch the wall.

Recalling the Valentine's Day fiasco and other ungraceful building ventures, Richie contends that he's been destined to "work uphill," or do things the hard way, a plight that he re-garded for years as penance for defying his father's wishes.

Although decades have passed since Willard Mueller died, Richie continued to be haunted by his father's admonition to make music, not sawdust. "I let him down," Richie admits, "in more ways than one." At the time Willard fell dead on the deck of an Amsterdam-bound KLM 747, Richie was a sophomore at Lafayette College in Pennsylvania. After his father's death, he switched his major from business administration to art, with a minor in education. "I thought about teaching art," Richie says. "My father wouldn't have approved, but frankly, I hated my business courses and partied more than I studied. Yet, I've always felt guilty that I waited until he died before changing majors. I betrayed him. He always wanted me to go into business and to do what he did."

Instead, Richie took the road to teaching, but was lured into graphic design after a two-year stint in the classroom. Richie is unsure whether "my son, the graphic artist" would have pleased his father any more than "my son, the schoolteacher," but he doesn't doubt that Willard would have taken a dim view of his son's weekend obsession with building. "Look at all these tools," Richie says, spreading his arms wide. "Look at this humongous table saw and this drill press. I have three different routers, for God's sake. Sometimes I come down here to admire all these tools. I shine them up like other people polish their cars. I just love this place, but I'm sure my father would be horrified."

SINCE HIS DISASTROUS VENTURE into patio building, Richie has made a point of talking with contractors and veteran builders before he starts a project. "There are lots of experts out there who have invaluable information," Richie says. "All you have to do is pick up the phone." Before applying brick facing to the concrete stoop at his front door, Richie called a mason in the yellow pages for a free estimate and pumped him for free information instead: "What is a good mix for mortar?" "How do you cut a brick in half?" "Which kind of brick is best for this job?" Richie concedes that it may not be cricket to use contractors as unpaid consultants, but he justifies his ruse: "It comes with the territory," he says. "Contractors expect to run into dead-end customers like me, but they hike their fees to make up for their lost time. Besides," Richie adds, "even professionals give you bad advice sometimes," alluding to the counsel of a certain Vince, whose idea of a screened porch was so far off the mark that Richie refers to the monstrosity he built under Vince's watchful eyes as "damaged goods, the worst thing I ever did to my house." After Vince, he adds, "I always get two or even three opinions."

Vince appeared on Richie's doorstep a day after Richie had spread the word that he planned to add a screened porch to the side of his house. Erica and Richie had in mind a modest structure, just nine feet by thirteen feet, but spacious enough for a barbecue, a small table and chairs. As Erica describes it, "We thought it would be lovely to sit outside on warm evenings and listen to the sounds of summer." Richie drew plans and, true to form, phoned a handful of contractors to discuss porch construction. Except for Vince, they gave Richie short shrift after learning that he expected to do the work himself. Vince dropped by to talk Richie out of it.

He tore into Richie's plans. For one thing, Vince told him that he had broken a cardinal rule of construction by choosing odd dimensions. "The way to go is always even," Vince insisted. To save money and cut waste, "the way to go should always be divisible by four." Vince had a point. Plywood, as well as Sheetrock, comes in four-by-eight-foot pieces that can be mounted whole onto studs set at the customary sixteen-inch intervals. Cutting material to uneven dimensions takes time and produces waste. Vince made a persuasive case, but it didn't occur to Richie until later that, except for the porch roof, his specifications didn't call for any plywood.

Other "ways to go" that Vince advanced were less compelling, but Richie listened like a lad at his father's knee. "The way to go is a poured concrete foundation," he told Richie, "and the way to go on the porch floor is masonry. It keeps out the bugs and won't rot on you." For posts to hold up the roof, "the way to go is solid four-by-fours," Vince advised, and "the way to go on screens is aluminum." About the roof, which Richie planned to cover with shingles that matched the house, Vince declared, "Too dark! The way to go is FRP," referring to fiber-reinforced plastic panels, a translucent material that bathes a space in incandescence.

Vince spoke with such authority that Richie began to harbor second thoughts about his own design for the porch. Before acceding to Vince's ways to go, however, Richie took himself to the lumber yard where a cadre of contractors used the counter as a hangout and might love to have their brains picked on matters they certainly knew a great deal about. But when Richie disclosed he was an owner-builder, they shrugged and suddenly grew too busy to talk. One loudmouth, however, took time out to rail against cocky amateur builders who, he opined, couldn't discern the difference between an ass and an elbow. Another told his cohorts at the counter that building porch screens was a bitch and intimated that he wouldn't bet a dime on Richie making a watertight seam where the porch and house intersected.

It dawned on Richie that he was as welcome as a virus in this company. He was competitor, a weekend dabbler who eroded their brotherhood and took their trade. Although he didn't like it, Richie understood. As a graphic artist, he too worked in a field perpetually wary of interlopers. Innumerable know-it-alls practiced graphic design. Desktop publishing made every computer hack a potential rival. Other professionals—in the law, business, government, medicine—excluded untrained wannabes from their fold. Why should contractors be any different?

But one of them—Howie—was different. He pulled Richie aside after his chums had exhausted the subject of smart-ass amateurs to talk about building forms for a poured concrete foundation. "They gotta be strong," he told Richie. "Use three-quarter-inch plywood for your walls and oil them up good so the concrete won't stick." He also cautioned Richie not to skimp on two-by-four braces to hold the walls in place. "It's better to overbuild," he said, "because wet concrete weighs

160 pounds a cubic foot and will knock down forms like ten pins if they're not secure." Then Howie added, "Don't forget your snap ties," meaning slender metal rods that hold opposing walls of a form together and keep them uniformly apart at the same time. Howie's concern so stunned Richie that he suspected an ulterior motive. "I thought he was trying to scare me into subbing the foundation to him," Richie recalls, "or maybe he hoped I'd call him for help in a pinch." It also occurred to Richie that Howie might be setting him up. The specter of the gang around the counter enjoying a good howl at his expense flicked across his mind. "But Howie never gave me his card," says Richie. "We shook hands and he wished me luck." While driving home, Richie thought, maybe there's goodness in contractors, after all.

And that included Vince, who lavished building tips on Richie and explained himself by declaring, "I'm only trying to help. I just want you to do a good job." Richie, however, couldn't shake his sense that Vince was a vulture in-mufti.

Regardless of his suspicion, though, he let Vince's words sway him to try Vince's ways, a wish-come-true for Vince, who then doubled his attentiveness to Richie's project. He phoned to ask how things were going and stalked the site in Richie's absence leaving notes behind like "Lookin' good, kid" and "Footings are out of sight!" After he began to frame the porch, Richie found "Way to go!" written on an index card tacked to a corner post.

Erica's views on Vince ran the gamut from "strange" to "downright creepy," and late one evening, after Vince had come by "to make a pit stop," she and Richie decided that Vince had become a household pest. "I told him that I wanted the porch to be my project, not his," says Richie, "and that I wouldn't mind if he didn't come around as often." But Vince wouldn't be jettisoned diplomatically. Even after Richie said to him, "I don't need your help any more," his visits and his *billets-doux* continued unabated. Only after Richie's hints grew less subtle—in the style of *Don't come back or I'll call the police*—did Vince finally catch Richie's drift.

Vince faded away, but to Richie's regret his legacy lived on. Richie followed Vince's ways far too often, and realized far too late that he'd been led astray. The porch was a catalog of blunders. The change from odd to even measurements brought one of the porch's side walls smack into a dining room window. "Don't shrink the porch; remove the window," Vince had said, an alteration that halved the natural light in the dining room. The porch's foundation, a concrete monolith, looked, from Richie's steeply inclined backyard, like the prow of a battleship. For a lighter, sleeker aspect Richie ought to have used concrete piers or wooden posts. Richie also chafed at the cold and gritty masonry floor that Vince had persuaded him to build. A wooden floor of pressure-treated decking lumber would have been cozier and far more attractive. Solid wood posts to hold up the roof also proved to be a mistake. They offered no channels to conceal the electrical wiring, and worse, the wood began to split as it aged. Hollow posts of clear fir joined with waterproof resorcinol glue, the kind used in boat building, would have been a better choice. To Vince's credit, however, the space was bright and cheerful under the translucent roof he recommended, but Richie had to devise an elaborate fascia to conceal the unsightly edges of corrugated panels that better suited a chicken coop than a Closter porch.

Once he was finished, Richie surveyed the damage he had wrought and decided almost at once to tear it down and start over with a pre-Vince design. Erica, however, calmly squelched the idea. "It's not so bad," she said. "Besides, we can't afford to build another one right now." In time, they adapted to their ill-contrived porch, used it as a place to eat, talk, and entertain, but on warm summer nights it never gave them the heart's ease they had hoped it would.

Ten years later Richie still puzzles over Vince's hold on him: "I don't know why I caved in so easily, why I used his plan instead of mine. Maybe because Vince was older and more experienced. I don't know. Somehow, I needed to satisfy him more than I needed to satisfy myself." Richie's shakes his head and takes time out ponder the implications of his own words.

He struggles to grasp why long ago he defied his father only to defer to someone who presumed to be his guardian. Then he asks, "Don't you think that a shrink would have a field day with me?"

As part of his legacy, Vince also left behind a smarter, more savvy Richie. "When it came to building and home improvement matters, I decided to trust my own instincts more fully," Richie recalls, "unless it was clear that I was being a damn fool." The strength of this resolve was unexpectedly put to the test within months after the porch was completed, when Richie came into a modest inheritance. With the after-tax balance, he and Erica bought a down-and-out vacation home on a Pocono Mountain lakeshore ninety miles from Closter. The decision to buy almost tore Richie apart. The money had once belonged to his father, who, Richie asserts, would have been dead-set against squandering it on a waterside shanty.

A debate raged in Richie's mind between himself, the vagabond son, and his dour father. "'Invest it in blue chips or bank it for college expenses.' That's what he would have told me," Richie declares. "But I also think that deep down he would have wanted me be to be happy." And since nothing would gladden Richie more than fixing up a jalopy of a house in the country, he decided once again to defy his father. It seemed like the right thing to do.

The house that he and Erica bought was a mess, but it had possibilities. Evidently someone else had thought so, too, because a not very meticulous home improver had already raised the roof over the main room, leaving behind a cathedral ceiling of knotty-pine, V-groove paneling that spanned the greater part of the interior. Fiberglass insulation had been stuffed into the cavities between the paneling and the roof but without the customary air space to carry away moisture. Consequently, trapped condensation had begun to nibble away at the underside of the roof deck and sometimes trickled through the insulation, leaving dark brown stains on the pine boards. Fixing the roof already ranked near the top of Richie's list of things to do to the house, but when water soaked through the bedroom ceiling during a heavy rain, it leaped into first place.

Hurriedly, he sought a way to keep his pillow dry, and his interest in meteorology took another giant leap after shoveling drifts of wet muddy leaves off the roof and uncorking a number of new holes. Every day he scanned the sky for dark clouds. His radio was locked on a station that forecast the weather five times an hour. The old saw about waiting a few minutes if you don't like Pocono weather no longer amused him. He draped big blue tarps over the roof and began to study literature devoted to the plugging of roof leaks.

A reference to a "cold roof" caught his eye. A cold roof, he read, is a second roof installed above the first. The two roofs are separated by a few inches, roughly the width of two-by-three or two-by-four "sleepers" nailed onto the first roof. Properly shingled, a cold roof serves as a kind of passive air-circulation system that prevents condensation from forming on the inside of a vaulted ceiling the way condensation often forms on the inside of window panes in the winter. Theoretically, with a cold roof overhead, water vapor produced by cooking, washing, and day-to-day life inside Richie's heated house would flow benignly up through the airspace between the two roofs and out a vent he could easily install on the ridge of the house.

Richie tried to validate the theory by surveying a handful of professional roofers. Three respondents told him, in essence, "Cold roof? Sorry, don't know what you're talkin' about." A fourth had once heard of a such a thing in Minnesota as a way to prevent ice dams, and a fifth actually had a cousin who installed one years ago but now worked in insurance. Meager evidence to be sure, but not flimsy enough for Richie to call the whole thing off. "At least no one told me I was nuts," he recalls.

Off came the curled and broken shingles from the old roof. Some he pried with a crowbar. Others he lifted by hand, their underpinning eaten by dry-rot. He stripped the roof one section at a time, removing no more than he could replace in a day. Once a swath of roof deck had been laid bare from eaves to

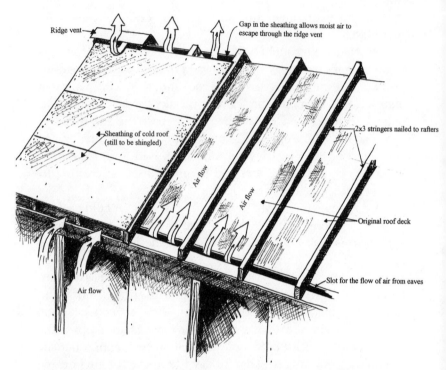

A cold roof installation prevents ice dams and condensation damage.

ridge, he nailed down sleepers and then attached sheets of half-inch plywood. He left a two-inch gap at the peak where he would later attach a ridge vent, and extended the roofline past the edge of the house, once and for all putting a stop to rain and snowmelt cascading down the side walls into the cellar.

Roofing, Richie quickly realized, takes youth, muscle, the balance of an acrobat, and a healthy streak of masochism. It also helps to be tolerant of repetitive, mind-numbing work. On all counts, Richie failed to qualify. "My legs could take only so much straining, kneeling, and stretching," says Richie. "And I couldn't work on bright sunny days when the surface of the roof grew literally too hot to touch. Neither could I easily hoist those eighty-pound bundles of shingles onto my shoulder and climb the ladder, so I split open the package and took the shingles up a few at a time." Moreover, the pitch of Richie's roof was more than 45 degrees, too steep to stand on without something to grab on to. On a roof pitched less than 35 degrees, you can stand, walk, kneel, sit—navigate as on level ground. A roof pitched 35 to 40 degrees is unfit for human habitation. Standing upright is unthinkable. At best, you can crawl upward on all fours and skitter down on your backside, but to stay up there without support is a nothing short of theatrical. On a roof steeper than 40 degrees, you need footholds—strips of wood nailed to the roof surface or a ladder fitted with hooks that reach over the ridge. Or, as Richie did, you can construct a platform with triangular brackets that may be adjusted for the pitch of the roof. The two-by-ten shelf that Richie devised kept his tools, lumber, plywood, new shingles, and most of all, himself from sliding to the ground.

Aside from staggering up ladders with stacks of shingles hoisted on his shoulder, Richie's most formidable task was covering the roof with asphalt-saturated felt, a.k.a. tar paper or building paper, a heavy, black, oily material that comes in rolls of nearly 150 feet. Spreading felt on a steep roof is a job for two. Alone, an installer pits himself against gravity, expecting against all common sense to hold in place a long horizontal piece of unfurled felt that is hell-bent on recoiling itself or sliding out of position. "At first," Richie recalls, "I carried a full roll of felt to the roof. When I attempted to uncoil it, the entire roll spun away, skidded down the plywood roofdeck, and thudded to earth. One lesson learned. Back on the grass, I rolled out and cut a piece to stretch from one edge of the roof to the other, about ten yards. I stapled one end of the piece securely to the roof. When I pulled the felt across to the other end, the staples held fast, but the material didn't. It tore away and was left dotted with holes the size of a nickel. A second lesson learned." A hole of any dimension, of course, misses the whole point of roofing felt, which is to keep rain out of the house before applying shingles, so Richie discarded the ten-yarder and wrestled instead with a shorter piece, about twenty feet long, which also refused to be pinned down. During Richie's bout with the building paper, the material tore, got spindled and far too mutilated to be of much use. "I finally got wise," Richie says, "and gave up trying to do the work of two people." He cut the roofing felt into manageable pieces, six to eight feet long, and installed them, carefully overlapping the vertical edges by six to ten inches.

On overcast days, Richie camped on the roof, descending to earth only to pick up more materials and to stand back from the house to make sure that he had laid the shingles in straight, even rows, or "courses," as they are known in roofing circles. Perched high, he enjoyed the panorama of his property, the nearby apple orchard, and the majestic mountains beyond. "Boaters passing by on the lake waved at me," he says.

Shingling the roof tested Richie's patience more than his prowess as a builder. "I just followed the instructions printed on the wrapper of every bundle," he says. "Each shingle is a yard long and divided into three tabs. Alternate courses had to be offset by six inches. Although the package said to use four nails per shingle, two or three seemed enough to me."

As with any routine work, the novelty of roof installation wears off quickly. Among builders, roofing has a reputation as the dullest, most God-awful work. It has few moments of high drama and enlightenment. But Richie was never bored. How could he suffer from boredom when his life hung perpetually in the balance? Mindful that a misstep could send him tumbling, he found matters of foot placement endlessly absorbing. He was astonished at how rapidly he used up stacks of shingles and was unprepared for the ease with which shingles could be bent and broken. Up on high, Richie had his share of low moments, brought on by piles of shingles sliding out of his reach, soakings by sudden summer storms, and running out of nails at the wrong time (although on the job is there ever a *right* time to find the nail bin empty?).

In retrospect, Richie thinks that ultimately the most enervating part of the job was psychological. Anxiety and self-doubt plagued him. At no time, from the moment he tore out the first rotten shingle until he hammered the ridge vent into place weeks later, had he felt confident that a new cold roof would noticeably improve the house. Ultimately, it did. "If I had to do it over again, I wouldn't fret so much," Richie says. "I should have been my biggest fan." Indeed, he ought to have been a cheerleader.

RICHIE NOW UNDERSTANDS what years of being a one-man, do-it-yourself construction crew has meant to him. For most builders, the daily grunt and grind is not a means of personal self-expression. Ask a roofer on a blazing summer day how he likes expressing himself with asphalt shingles so hot they scorch his fingertips. Tell a Sheetrocker that his mudwork clearly conveys an angst about the human condition. Talk to a backhoe operator about the emotional color of his excavation. A mason mixing concrete in a wheelbarrow mixes concrete in a wheelbarrow; he's not unleashing bottled up feelings or creatively working out subconscious longings. Unless he's neurotic, he works to collect a paycheck and looks for emotional release in another venue.

For Richie the story is different. The house was his loft, laboratory, and studio, and each construction project was an endeavor not far removed from designing a corporate logo in his office or composing a piano sonata. While reclaiming the house from squalor, Richie became a planner, an architect, an engineer, a physicist, and a craftsman. "It was probably the most creative time in my life," Richie says, "being preoccupied with problems of form, proportion, scale, even the color and the texture of the materials I was using." No less fiercely than an artist at work on the masterpiece of his life, he poured himself into constructing a breakfast nook in the kitchen, adding a new half-bath, paneling the bedrooms. He spent three weekends on his knees scraping black paint off the living room floor with a belt sander until beautiful honey-colored pine appeared. "Turning a frog into a princess," he calls it. Later, he pulled layers of old shingles from the outside of his house, replacing them with cedar clapboards that he treated with pickling oil until

While reclaiming his lakeside house from squalor, Richie freed himself from the oppression of his father's spirit.

they shone silver-gray. Throughout, he savored the long spells of hard labor that strained every ounce of his ingenuity and pushed his body to the limits of its endurance.

It may defy logic to find such punishing work so blissful, but Richie has no thirst for whys and wherefores. He chalks up his good fortune to blind luck and enjoys his gift quietly, as one might accept one's own good looks. Out in the promised land west of New Jersey, Richie seems to have found himself. He thinks often of Mr. Bondino and his magician's hands. "I understand him better now than when I knew him," he remarks. "I appreciate good, professional-looking work, the way he did. I respect tools and what they can do."

Does he ever think about Vince? Richie laughs aloud at the question. "Hardly ever. I don't brood about him. He probably meant well, but he came into my life at the wrong time. Back then, I was gullible and inexperienced. Now, I could probably teach him a few things, or at least know when he was giving me a bum steer."

With regard to his father, Richie can't say for sure that he has done the right thing. "I don't think he'd approve of what I've done with my life, but it's no longer a moral issue." In fact, Richie believes that restoring his Pennsylvania house has, in effect, sprung him from the oppression of his father's spirit. He says, "Basically, I don't let him bother me anymore."

Adagio

When I asked Michele Beemer, the codirector of Heart-wood, the home-building school in Washington, Massa-chusetts, for the name of an owner-builder who successfully balanced home construction with a career in an altogether different line of work, she immediately thought of Fenwick Smith, second flutist of the Boston Symphony Orchestra.

As it turned out, Fenwick, harking to the demands of a thriving career in music, had dropped out partway through Heartwood's three-week program. But he returned the follow-ing summer to finish the course, and upon graduation, set out to build a house just as he'd been taught.

I sat with Fenwick on the deck of the cedar-clad hideaway that he built near Tanglewood, the BSO's summer home in the Berkshires. On this August morning, it is a quiet place, ex-cept for the hum of distant airplanes and the occasional flut-ter of a ruffed grouse who's taken up residence on the west slope of the property. Fenwick's unhurried, laid-back manner gives no clue that he is about to decamp his summer lodgings for a year or more. In a few hours he'll be in Tanglewood's Music Shed rehearsing for that evening's Boston Pops concert, the finale of the '97 summer season. Tomorrow he will start a sabbatical from the BSO. In the morning, he'll pack his things, drain the water pipes, and lock up the house. By the

time he returns, he'll have spent most of a year commuting
between Boston and the University of Michigan at Ann Arbor,
where he'll join the faculty as a visiting professor of flute.

"I DIDN'T HAVE A LIFELONG DREAM to build my own
house," Fenwick begins. "And it didn't happen with a bang. It
just evolved slowly."

The choice of words suits him. When it comes to building,
Fenwick is not one to rush. His home-building project began
more than a dozen years ago and isn't over yet. During that
time he designed and built roughly 90 percent of a one-and-a-
half story saltbox-style house perched atop a limestone bluff,
ringed thickly by hemlocks and tall hickory, maple, and iron-
wood trees. "I've let building my house take however long it
wanted," he says with pride. "My taking on the project was
completely predicated on enjoying the process."

For the past two years Fenwick has done literally nothing
to complete the work that remains. "I don't know whether I'll
ever finish it," he says, noting that the house has recently re-
ceded into the middle distance of his life. "I'm teaching more
flute than I used to, and I'm in the process of refurbishing a
16,000-square-foot, turn-of-the-century commercial building
in a neighborhood of Boston." He bought the building to convert the third floor, a former Masonic temple, into a state-of-
the-art recording studio. "That's something Boston needs
badly," he adds. "I started out wanting to be directly involved,
but it was soon apparent that I'd be better off serving as general
contractor." As the work progresses, Fenwick plays the flute
and gives lessons—earning money to pay carpenters, electricians, and a host of other subcontractors.

Meanwhile, with no urgency to finish his house in the
woods, Fenwick is perfectly content to let it languish. He's already lived there for ten summers, during the annual music
festival at Tanglewood, and could contentedly live in it for
ten more without door and window trim or a handrail on the
staircase. That he has no deadline is a relief to Fenwick because his non-building life is driven by a breathtaking schedule

of rehearsals, concerts, classes at the New England Conservatory, recording sessions, travel, and recitals. During each summer, his putative off-season, Fenwick is obligated, as a member of the BSO, to rehearse six times and play in three concerts—a "nine-service week" in musicians' parlance. On his days off, he coaches chamber music groups at the Tanglewood Music Center and drives to Boston to keep his eye on the progress of the studio renovation.

The house, far from the road, is reached via a serpentine drive consisting of two dirt ruts separated by a grassy median that brushes the undercarriage of low-slung cars. It is a well-proportioned retreat for a man living alone. Its 700-square-foot ground floor leaves little room to rattle around, but its overall design creates the illusion of spaciousness. The vaulted ceiling of the central room follows the peaked contour of the roof. Skylights frame a canopy of trees far overhead, and banks of large windows admit views of the surrounding forest. Front and back doors open to a wide wooden deck wrapped around three sides of the house. On the partial second floor Fenwick has framed a sleeping area, a study, and a full bath. The loft is now stacked high with aging Sheetrock destined for the walls and ceiling if Fenwick ever decides to pick up the work where he left off. A garage attached to the north side of the house holds Fenwick's pickup truck, a large workbench, tool cabinets, and a radial-arm saw. He tells me that he built the garage first. "I wanted a commodious space to work out of as I proceeded to the house itself," he explains. Now the garage and its loft serve as Fenwick's basement and attic.

BUILDING IN ONE FORM or other has taken up an impressively hefty piece of Fenwick's life. "I always liked doing things with my hands," he explains, alluding to his boyhood passion for model railroading. Young Fenwick, aiming for the greatest possible realism, built Lilliputian towns, landscapes, and stations for a whole freightyard full of electric trains. He contrived switches and laid tracks on tiny wooden ties across the miniature countryside that covered the attic alcove of the

Smiths' two-family house in Medford, Massachusetts. The hobby, he asserts, gave him "some sense of what looks right," an aesthetic that he pressed into service when it came time to choose the site, shape, and size of his country house. While developing his eye, model railroading also put tools in his hands and early on exposed him to the pleasures of puttering.

At eighteen Fenwick graduated from both model building and high school. During his pre-college summer in Boston he worked in the shop of one of the world's leading flute makers, to which he returned year after year during holiday breaks from the Eastman School of Music in Rochester, New York. Before long, he had learned how to fabricate the intricate mechanism of a flute. Crafting a flute is an exacting procedure. Dozens of sterling silver pieces must be formed, filed to precise dimensions, bent, fitted, and soldered correctly. To do it right takes a sharp eye, deft fingers, and the capacity to do exceptionally meticulous work. Fenwick says, "I was always interested in seeing how much I could refine the process." He figured out ways to eliminate wasted motion by placing his tools where he could reach them most easily and by aligning them in the sequence they were to be used. In time, he became a first-rate flute builder. The instrument he plays in concerts and recitals worldwide is one that he made himself.

Building a house, while a slightly more strenuous enterprise than building a flute, calls for comparable dexterity. There are scores of techniques to master, from selecting materials to choosing the proper tools for every operation. Each piece of a house, like the components of a flute, must be cut precisely, fitted, and firmly anchored. Home building, like flute manufacturing, follows an orderly process consisting of numerous steps. Therein lay the attraction to Fenwick. "I built the house partly because I was interested in the process," he says.

Still, it's a long way from flute making to home construction, a leap that Fenwick was stirred to make only after he'd completed a ten-year stay in a '60s-vintage collective residence in Boston where he had learned a lot from a more experienced housemate who was doing his utmost to keep the building, an antiquated Victorian mansion, from falling into ruin. Around the place Fenwick learned to fix whatever broke. Working with his mentor, he also added a back porch to the building and refurbished an old bathroom, taking a swipe at carpentry, plumbing, electricity, and tiling in the process. On the job, he gradually acquired a taste for new construction—as opposed to repairing and retrofitting, which he calls "fixing other people's mistakes"—and became acquainted with the basics of building a house.

Just because one knows the rudiments of construction, however, is not ordinarily a reason to build unless a shaky hold on reality compels you to try it just for fun. In Fenwick's case, the notion remained dormant for years because he'd been focusing his attention on building a career in music rather than building a home in the country. After college he had tried to land a permanent position in an orchestra in Germany, which Fenwick estimates "has eight times as many orchestras per capita as the United States." Following a fruitless three-year search, a job offer from a stateside contemporary music group, the Boston Musica Viva, lured him home again and pushed him a tad closer to a seat with the Boston Symphony Orchestra, which he joined as a substitute in 1978 after one of its regular flutists fell ill.

During his first summer with the BSO, he lodged on the Tanglewood grounds in a tent, but tone-deaf to the call of the wild, he thirsted for a solid roof over his head. The next year, having achieved card-carrying status in the BSO, he rented a house but recoiled at the toll exacted just for a place to lay his head. The following year, still renting a house for the summer, he began to flirt with home buying. He read realty ads and bought a sheaf of topographical maps, the kind that hikers use to navigate the woods. "I spread them on the kitchen table," he says. "Using Tanglewood's Music Shed as the center, I drew a circle with a ten-mile radius." Within this eighty-square-mile area of farmland, ski slopes, historic sites, colonial towns—places that Edith Wharton once called "derelict mountain villages" but that now contain some of the priciest country property in the East—he hoped to find a house. "Then I mounted my ten-speed bike and systematically began exploring, choosing a new route every day." Cruising the roads and byways of the Berkshires, he kept his eyes peeled for a "For Sale" sign in front of a small, affordable, and private place well off the beaten path, either an old farmhouse or an interesting contemporary.

His house-hunting forays soon told him, however, that his was a fool's mission. He'd be more likely to find the Northwest Passage than the house of his dreams in western Massachusetts. His requirements—*small, affordable, and private*—contained a contradiction in terms. Old houses stood close to the road, and the newer houses, with multiple bedrooms, breezeways, and three-car garages, were far too baronial for Fenwick's taste. "In time, I concluded that I'd own a dream house only if I built it myself," he says.

Initially, he thought to hire an architect and contractor. But, in 1981, after he purchased a sixty-two-acre parcel situated on a dirt road with no electricity, no other houses, and no snow-plowing service (a feature he didn't need anyway), a conspiracy of forces largely unrelated to building pushed him toward owner-buildership. Because of the quirky schedule of BSO musicians, he could count on the better part of four months every year—from June through September—to devote to building. (Typically, after the BSO season, members play with the Boston Pops for six weeks, but leaves of absence without pay are freely granted. Prior to the season at Tanglewood everyone gets two weeks' vacation, and afterward, four additional weeks.)

While know-how and time rank high on a list of prerequisites for building your own house, they are not enough. You also need the inclination, and, because solo building tries both body and soul, the temperament. On both counts, Fenwick was qualified. He is methodical and thorough. The details of house construction are endlessly absorbing to him. He's energized by the most mundane tasks, even such repetitive tasks as nailing beveled cedar shingles one by one onto a wall. "To me shingling is not at all mind-numbing," he says. "I enjoy the rhythm of it and love the sweet smell of the wood. The shingles feel good in your hands. And the best part is that, as the finished walls emerge course by course, you finally see how your house will look when it's done." Amply endowed with patience, Fenwick set a glacial pace from the outset. He approached the project like a scholar, versing himself in every step of the process. "I'm lucky," he claims. "I've never fallen to the temptations of instant gratification. The length of time it has taken me to build my house has never frustrated me at all." Only once did he watch the calendar—during the summer he framed the house. That year he pushed to get the shell closed in by the fall. "I never put a deadline on anything else," he says. Nor has the town pressured him to finish. The plumbing and wiring remain uninspected. Maybe next year he'll apply for a certificate of occupancy, the town's official imprimatur that the house has been properly built, or, if not, maybe the year after that.

Just before he began what has now lapsed into a moribund building project, Fenwick enrolled in a three-week home-building course and a one-week post-and-beam workshop at Heartwood, a forty-five minute drive from his property. He also studied guides and how-to handbooks, concentrating on materials and methods, never quite envisioning the intuitive, mysterious, and sometimes problematic home-building experience that lay in store. Like others who've built their houses, though, he soon realized that construction is far more creative than checking off items on a to-do list.

While inhabiting a used trailer that he had parked on his land, for instance, he pondered two problems for which there were no answers in the back of his books: First, what sort of house to build, and second, where to build it. The second question needed an answer before the first, because he had long before resolved that the building site would govern the size, configuration, and look of the house as intimately as the weather determines the clothes one wears. He strongly believed that the peculiar genius of a house lay in its fitting in.

"I had no intention to pick a boilerplate house plan from a magazine and just plop it onto the land," he asserts.

The site for his house seemed almost to choose itself. An overgrown logging road that would save Fenwick the trouble of building a new driveway led directly to a south-facing limestone bluff near the center of his tract. Once he discovered the bluff, so hidden by trees and brush that he passed it repeatedly without seeing it, there was no question that it was the most advantageous spot. It stood high over the rest of his land, and the limestone outcropping provided a sturdy, ready-made pedestal on which to build a small house. (Fenwick didn't know it then, but a geological fault runs though his property. But he's unfazed; for eons there's been no subterranean restlessness in the Berkshires.)

In truth, Fenwick's decision to build directly on the bluff was partly intuitive and partly a conclusion based on empirical observations. "At the time," he reports, "I couldn't tell whether the spot I'd chosen was solid bedrock or just loose boulders, and I didn't ask anyone." Instead, he performed a crude experiment to test the stone's mettle. "It worked this way," he says. "I stood on a section of stone and dropped a heavy iron pike beside my foot. If I felt vibration through my foot and heard a dull *thunk*, it was a loose boulder. If I felt virtually no vibration and heard a bright *ping* from the stone and the iron, it was bedrock. The presence of sufficient bedrock gave me confidence that the bluff was structurally solid."

Fenwick also saw that rainwater rolled off the sides of the bluff in all directions. With no possibility of water standing under the house or rising from the ground, Fenwick took it on faith that the limestone was strong and deep enough to carry a foundation even without footings sunk below the frost line.

When the time came to put his faith on the line, he bought a truckload of bank-run gravel, so called because it is dredged from a swift-flowing river. Because bank-run gravel is washed free of organic matter, when compacted it forms a mass almost as dense as concrete. Fenwick spread the gravel over the limestone, creating a surface as flat as a table top. Then he compressed it by watering it heavily with a sprinkler for two days. Fenwick explains, "Before the soaking, you leave footprints as you would on a sandy beach. Afterward, your feet leave no impression."

With a solid layer of gravel underfoot, he prepared the site for a concrete slab foundation. Using two-by-twelve lumber, he built a rectangular form the size of his future house and lined it with three inches of foam insulation. Before ordering a truckload of ready-mix concrete, he also laid a three-foot-wide band of insulation around the outer edges of the floor area.

Fenwick didn't sail through these arcane procedures on inspiration alone. To a point, he trusted his instincts, but he also got coaching from Will Beemer, codirector of Heartwood. Among other things, Will checked Fenwick's forms to ensure that they would stand up to tons of wet concrete pressing against them, and he directed the pouring operation. Formerly a teacher of design at Cornell University, Will uses nearby sites as labs for his Heartwood students. After morning classroom instruction in renovation, carpentry, masonry, design, and other subjects, he takes his students out for hands-on practice in the afternoon. On the day the slab was to be poured, Will arranged with Fenwick to bring over a platoon of novices eager to learn by doing. Equipped with work gloves, rakes, shovels, and rubber boots, the class pitched in under Will's watchful eye. "Considering that any mistakes would have to be exploded with dynamite," Fenwick says, "it was great to have an experienced guy like Will Beemer to supervise the pour, which was a pretty formidable undertaking—twenty-two by thirty-two feet and up to nine inches thick."

On his foundation Fenwick was to build a house that had taken him two years to plan. Crucial to the overall design was not just that the house fit comfortably on its site, but that it faced south and was solar-friendly—in all ways the antithesis of the drafty Boston house in which he had lived for years. "That old Victorian exemplifies the Industrial Revolution in America," Fenwick says, "a time when we ignored nature, paid no attention to the environment, and boasted, 'We can build anything anywhere.'" In contrast, Fenwick's more thoughtful, up-to-date view was that his country home must be energy-efficient and insulated well enough to stay cool on hot summer days and retain heat in the winter. It was not altogether accidental that the top of a limestone bluff caught his eye. The stone augments the thermal mass of the foundation slab to fend off rapid fluctuations in outside temperature.

Fenwick owes his interest in energy conservation largely to Heartwood, which, according to Will Beemer, aims to help builders "design houses that are affordable, efficient in the use of energy and materials, and beautiful and healthy to live in." Fenwick made Heartwood's aim his own aim too, and at his drawing board referred consistently to his class notes. By his elbow he also kept the course textbook, *A Pattern Language* by Christopher Alexander, et al. "The book changed my life," Fenwick says. "It opened my eyes and helped me to see." The text, used widely to train architects, makes the case for using age-old design ideas to make houses comfortable and nurturing. Alexander argues that the design of every component of a house—from alcoves to ceiling heights, from staircases to window placement—can be reduced to a few essential principles—a "pattern"—that holds true through all architectural styles, through all periods of history, and through all cultures of the globe. Furthermore, each design decision touches a dozen others and affects one's emotional response to the house. Convinced by Alexander's logic, Fenwick pored over concepts for making living rooms sociable, bedrooms restful, and kitchens and baths user-friendly. "The book became my bible," he reports.

Without necessarily following its teachings chapter and verse, Fenwick incorporated many Alexandrine principles into his plans. The concept of "entrance transitions," for one. "Entrances create a transition between the 'outside'—the public world—and some less public inner world," writes Alexander. "The experience of entering a building [i.e., house] influences the way you feel inside the building. If the transition is too abrupt there is no feeling of arrival, and the inside of the building fails to be an inner sanctum." In sum, the

arrangement of the entryway helps to define visitors' expecta-
tions for the rest of the house. If, from one place, they catch a
glimpse of another, they will be filled with anticipation. What's
more, when their glimpse tells just a little but not everything
about the space beyond, their imagination is awakened.

Intrigued by that notion, Fenwick built a partition to form
an entryway inside his front door. "In my small house there's
not a lot of leeway, so I just imply an entrance hall with one
wall. When you step across the threshold, you don't see the
whole interior. You have to come in a little farther to see the
living room and farther still to see the kitchen." This concept of
gradual revelation is echoed in the approach to the house itself.
Trees create a visual barrier along Fenwick's sinuous driveway.
"You don't come around the corner and, Bang!, see the house in
front of you," he says. "It reveals itself a little at a time."

Such visual subtleties "took quite a while to evolve," says
Fenwick. "One of the trickiest steps was fitting my house to
the site I chose. Some people have the capacity to visualize a
house on its site. I don't. But Heartwood showed me a technique to see just how the house would look here." All
Heartwood students are taught to build scale-model mock-ups
of their houses using foam board. When Fenwick had set up his
foundation forms, he walked down the driveway to a point
where he could hold the model a foot or so in front of him,
align the base of the model with the line of the foundation,
squint a little, and see exactly how the house would "sit."

He didn't like what he saw. "Too austere and forbidding,"
he says. "It turned a cold shoulder." As a result, he softened
the facade with a curved top on the garage door, a half-round
window on the gable, and another on the attached garage.
He also attached corner braces to suggest a rounded arch on
the square-cut front-door canopy. For still more visual interest,
he added a bump-out storage shed that breaks the monot-
ony of a fourteen-foot-high expanse of side wall that runs
length of house. Altogether, the simple foam board model was
an indispensable tool for giving the house a look that says
"Welcome."

To cement the union between the house and its woody site, Fenwick chose timber-frame construction for part of the house. Timber framing, often called "post-and-beam," is a timeless house-framing technique that probably originated with a Stone Ager who figured out how to fashion a shelter made of tree parts. In fact, until the mid-1800s almost every wood-framed house in creation was fabricated with posts and beams. The invention of power tools during the Industrial Revolution simultaneously made short work of sawing trees into strips of lumber and sired the so-called "stick-built" construction of today. Once the components of a house frame became light enough for one person to lift ("sticks" rather than timbers), solo home building began to be much more practical. Anybody with a hammer, some nails, and a supply of ordinary lumber could construct a standard wall in a fraction of the time that a crew of timber framers needed to cut and join two posts and a beam.

Fenwick's house is a hybrid. Its exterior walls are stick-built, its interior structure—partly for aesthetic reasons—is post and beam. Ordinarily, timber framing calls for bevies of workers gathering at a site to lift and hold weighty members that a builder can't handle alone. A house- or barn-raising can be the social event of the season. "But," Fenwick explains, "I read an article in *Fine Homebuilding* about one-man post-and-beam buildings," and after completing the timber-framing course at Heartwood, he was convinced that he could assemble posts and beams by himself. He ordered from a local lumber mill the equivalent of a small grove of fir trees—beams and posts, three-by-five, five-by-seven, and seven-by-seven inches—and with the care of a woodcarver began to shape the pieces of the frame. Hours at a time, he applied his razor-sharp chisels—one with a blade an inch and a half wide, the other slightly broader—to each bulky timber. To master the technique, he focused on the point where the blade incised the wood fibers and learned to adjust both the angle of his chisel and the force of his mallet's blow to slice off a sliver of wood with a single tap. Before long, the process became unconscious

and automatic, as though the chisel had become an extension of his hands and he had become part of the chisel.
Understandably, Fenwick now claims a "sentimental attachment" to those tools.

Each of the tenons, the stubby, tongue-like protuberances
that Fenwick carved at the ends of each beam, slipped snugly
into the pockets, or mortises, that he had chiseled into the
posts. True to traditional joinery, he used no steel braces, no
nails, bolts, screws, or any other hardware—just solid oak pegs
to secure each joint. Framing in this manner ate up the better
part of his fourth summer on the job. With the pieces
assembled and laid out, Fenwick recruited help from Tom
Morse, a neighbor's teenage son who hung around a lot watching Fenwick at work and lending a hand when he could.
Together, they raised the components of the frame in a few
hours. Fenwick never regretted his decision to use post-and-
beam construction. In fact, he asserts that crafting the frame of
his house yielded more pleasure than almost any other part of
the house-building process.

Despite the satisfactions of timber framing, practitioners
of the craft are becoming an endangered species. Most homes
today are stick-built. To save time, in fact, builders often buy
entire walls prefabricated on assembly lines. Only for the
traditional look of a rustic home, in which the framing members remain exposed, is post-and-beam construction still *de
rigueur*. The thick posts suggest tree trunks, the horizontal
beams, a tree's branches—conspicuous reminders that a house
owes its existence to the forest outside. To some, a timber-
framed house seems less an imposition on the land than an extension of its surroundings. It dominates nature while also
being part of it.

In that respect, Fenwick kept his vow to build a home in
harmony with its site. The house spiritually communes with
its leafy setting. Its crisscrossing timbers are obviously hewn
from the woods. A natural stone ledge serves as the first tread
on the front stoop. The siding of the house wears the silvery
gray patina of weathered cedar and is trimmed in rich russet

The rising sweep of the shingles at the end of each course brings to mind the tips of a hemlock's boughs.

that calls autumn foliage to mind. On the gable ends of his house Fenwick applied an eye-catching decorative flourish: From every shingle abutting the rakeboard—the trim that runs along the roofline—the corner has been nipped off, giving the ends of each row a slight upward thrust that vaguely suggests the rising sweep of a hemlock's boughs.

Although he accepted help from time to time, Fenwick preferred to build alone, at least at the start of the project. On his own, he could depend on A-1 workmanship no less fastidious than that which he'd employed while building flutes in Boston. Using only high-end materials and the best tools, he had made up his mind to construct a house that would look good and last indefinitely. Each piece of it had to evince Fenwick's superior skill and a high degree of care. "I was a control freak when it came to building," he admits. He seldom sought help or advice, even when it might have been foolhardy not to. Brandishing a chain saw for the first time soon after he bought the property, Fenwick felled literally hundreds of trees—some eighteen inches in diameter—to widen his 1,200-foot driveway for a well-drilling rig and to clear a parking space for his used house trailer. "I was lucky to have gotten away with all my limbs," he now concedes. "I must have been driven by a macho, Wild West, pioneer kind of fantasy that I could do everything myself and it would be fine. It's the same kind of impulse that causes men never to ask for directions when they're lost." (Fenwick actually considered drilling his own well, too.)

He now grants that he had suffered from a chronic case of self-reliance, a condition that helped to prod him into do-it-yourself building in the first place. Owner-builders, as a genre, are stalwart nonconformists, loath to let others do what they can do themselves. Fenwick regards himself as an individualist who has often followed an unconventional path through life. "I'm gay," he tells me, "which explains partially why I live here by myself. In my generation being gay had no precedents. You had to create your own life and figure out what it meant because you didn't get any help from anywhere else." In short, since his youth Fenwick has been obliged to find his own way. In fact, he claims to be an incipient hermit who's led a decidedly un-hermitlike life. "For better or worse," he adds, "my self-reliance has enabled me to accomplish a lot in my forty-nine years. Designing and building a custom house, for one."

After weeks of solitude on the work site, however, his isolation intermittently got the better of him. He says, "I found out early on that building a house alone wasn't the most mentally healthy way to go about it. At times, I found myself going stir crazy out here and had to drop everything and go back to my group house to recharge my batteries."

Once his wall of seclusion began to crumble, Fenwick began to welcome a parade of willing helpers. They came singly or in groups, bearing assorted curriculum vitae and various levels of skill. The season that Fenwick framed the house, Evan Hirsch, a friend with good carpentry skills, drove out from Boston on weekends to lend a hand. Colleagues from the string and woodwind sections of the Boston Symphony Orchestra showed up, too, some merely to gawk at their eccentric associate at work, others to be of use. Onstage, they extracted exquisite sounds from their instruments; on the building site, many barely knew which end of a hammer to hold. But reluctant to turn away volunteer help no matter how raw, Fenwick did his best to find useful jobs for every-one. He allowed some to sweep the work site, some to haul waste to the dump, others to stack lumber. Leone Buyse, a fellow flutist, held windows straight in their rough openings while Fenwick leveled and plumbed them. A whole crew from the BSO came to lift the north wall, a stick-built behemoth thirty-two feet long and fourteen feet high that Fenwick had framed with two-by-ten plates and two separate stud systems (two-by-four and two-by-six) for thermal separation. "I assembled this wall on the slab," he says, "then insulated and sheathed it. A dozen BSO members were barely able to raise this monster."

To other volunteers, such as his good friend Janet Corpus, he assigned more exalted tasks. Janet, who had dug a vegetable garden during a previous visit, this time came prepared to build. Having just finished framing the joists for the loft of the garage, Fenwick put Janet to work nailing down one-by-eight floorboards. She had never before done anything like it but was game to try, and turned to the task with a hammer, nails, and gusto. For most of a day she labored on her lofty perch, ten feet up, having the time of her life. The day was sunny and the shadows of magnificent trees danced on her workspace. She was thrilled, not just to see a permanent floor taking shape beneath her feet, but to leave a personal mark on the project. Fenwick says, "At the end of the afternoon, her hands were blistered, and she was exhausted, but she was all aglow. She talks about it to this day."

After Fenwick observed Janet's joy and the elation in the faces of other friends, his resistance to ask for help virtually dissolved. "My thinking about sharing the process of building the house changed," he says. It occurred to him that building one's own house was more than mastery of technique and a

triumph of will. There was a humanizing aspect to it as well.
Therefore, when he noticed Janet's nailheads in less-than-per-
fect alignment, he bit his tongue. At one time he might have
grabbed her hammer to demonstrate the way nails ought to be
placed. But with his fussiness fading, he let Janet do it her own
way. As a result, Fenwick cherishes Janet's work in the loft.
"There is a piece of her in the house," he says. "I look at the
nails up there, think of her, and smile."

Of all his home's features, Fenwick especially favors its expansive, wraparound deck. At first glance, it's an ordinary deck,
made of pressure-treated decking lumber nailed diagonally
across its joists, and enclosed by a railing mounted on two-by-
two balusters. At the back of the house the deck measures perhaps ten feet across at its widest and stands roughly eight feet
above the ground. "After the foundation slab for the house
and garage, this deck was the first thing I built on the site,"
Fenwick recalls. "The site slopes away so sharply on all sides, it
gave me a flat area on which to stand and set up a ladder."

But Fenwick's fondness for the deck is rooted in something
deeper and more abstract than its use as a handy platform. By
design, the deck conforms to patterns of successful outdoor
spaces propounded by Fenwick's architectural guru, Christopher Alexander. Fenwick took to heart Alexander's admonition to give a deck "a distinct and definite shape," a quality
that invites people to behave there as they would in an indoor
room. The deck faces south rather than north because people
seek the sun and, according to Alexander, find north sides
"dead and dank, gloomy and useless." Also, two walls of the
house offer the deck "some degree of enclosure," for comfort
and a feeling of security.

But while adhering to Alexander's precepts for siting the
deck, Fenwick relied on his own aesthetic sense to build it. "I
like the way the deck looks," he declares, pointing out noteworthy features: The deck functions like a catwalk between
the front entrance and the rear of the house. Its irregular angles
come from the placement of its supporting pillars. "I put posts
where I found solid rock," explains Fenwick, "which, in turn,

defined the shape of the deck." Rubbing his hands over the rounded corners of the satin-smooth railing, he says, "It's very inviting—nice to touch. Notice there are no nailheads on top. It's fastened from underneath, which makes the wood weather-tight." Fenwick's deck has been built with painstaking care. Boards are evenly spaced, and every mitered joint is tight. "I'm particularly pleased with the built-in benches," he says. "I looked and looked through the literature on bench construction and couldn't find anything about the proper angle for a backrest or the height of the seat. So I figured the dimensions out myself by trial and error. You should try sitting on one." I stand up, wiggle onto the bench at the end of the table, and lean back. Indeed, the bench is comfortable, as comfortable as any wooden seat is likely to be. "Did you notice that there are no table legs?" he asks, "nothing for your feet to bump into or trip over? The table stands on two posts braced underneath the floor of the deck."

I can't help thinking that Fenwick's house is a metaphor for himself. He's designed it humanely, with its occupants' physical and emotional comfort in mind. Its modest size, simplicity, and tranquil setting bid you to enter and invite you to put your feet up. It is obvious that its builder thought tirelessly about every detail of construction, which also explains his leisurely pace of building. With no time clock to punch, he allowed himself to contemplate the ways a person works, relaxes, moves about, and rests both inside and outside the house, then rendered spaces to accommodate each function. He fussed endlessly over matters as minuscule as the way a vestibule makes visitors feel welcome and how one seats himself on an outdoor bench. Lacking a deadline, he could quit when he tired, come and go as he pleased, and take time-outs whenever his mind wandered. He talks about the morning he slipped off the roof and landed on the wooden deck. "I was unhurt," he says, "but I took the rest of the day off, anyway."

Fenwick agrees that had he been a clockwatcher while building not only the deck but the whole house, he would have hurried needlessly, loathed the work, and made mistakes. "I could earn a living as a builder, but I wouldn't want to," he declares. "I'd take risks to speed the work along, and I certainly wouldn't enjoy the process." Indeed, the one summer he cranked up the tempo of the work, he fell prey to a wasteful blunder. In his haste to close up the house before autumn, he neglected to nail the floor onto the joists of the loft—as Janet had done in the garage—and had overlooked the fact that green timbers, unless they are firmly braced, tend to warp and bend as they cure. "During the winter, the joists twisted and curled," he says. "When I returned in the spring, they looked like the rolling sea. They were completely unsalvageable."

Fenwick's oversight led him directly into a structural conundrum: how to replace the useless joists without laying waste to his house. The joists, crucial pieces of the frame, spanned the width of the interior and kept the side walls from being pushed apart by the crushing weight of the roof. Removing them could splay the walls, depress the rafters, and send the house to the brink of collapse. To solve the problem, he installed a pair of turnbuckles. Theoretically, turnbuckles, each consisting of two steel rods screwed into the opposite ends of a threaded connector called the "buckle," would hold the imperiled walls in place while he cut and yanked out the defective joists. Even though he'd seen turnbuckles successfully stiffen sagging houses before, when it came time to sick a chain saw on his own joists, he nearly faltered. He remembers, "It was a nervous moment."

But it also proved an elegant solution, although marred by a single blemish: It violated the spirit of traditional post-and-beam framing. "Metal fasteners of any kind are a no-no," Fenwick says. But with his house in dire straits, he had to compromise. As soon as the substitute joists were installed, he laid a floor but left the turnbuckles in place to continue carrying the structural tension created by the roof pressing against the walls. He had no other option. Try as he might to transfer the load back to the new joists he couldn't find a structurally sound way to do it. The original connection between joists and the top plate had been made with one-inch diameter oak pegs.

Fenwick used a turnbuckle, consisting of two steel rods screwed into opposite ends of a threaded connector called a "buckle" to hold the imperiled walls in place while he yanked out the defective joists.

As Fenwick explains, "When the old joists were removed and the new ones put in place, the old peg holes in the plate were inaccessible from below because of Sheetrock and other details." As a result, Fenwick couldn't find a way to align holes drilled in the new joists with the existing holes in the plate. So the turnbuckles remain, a perpetual reminder to Fenwick of the price he paid for exceeding his congenital speed limit. But, he says, "I hardly notice them anymore."

In the long run, Fenwick's steel reinforcements will probably add years to the longevity of the structure. Knowing that he will be extinct long before his house, with or without turnbuckles, he's taken a stab at preserving his legacy. On the wood trim near the gabled peak he's carved his initials and the date in six-inch-high letters. He tells me, "A hundred years from now people will see 'F.S. 1987' up there and remember that this house was built by a guy who played in the BSO." By then, the particulars of Fenwick's life will have faded, but not the fact that a musician built the house. Fenwick suspects that his tale will long survive as a tidbit of local lore because "the surrounding hills will continue to be an enclave of BSO-connected people."

Yet, Fenwick denies that his house has given him a measure of immortality. "That's just a romantic notion," he says, "although I have had such thoughts about the recordings I've made. If I am remembered at all it will be through my flute playing." He deems the half-dozen albums of flute music he's recorded his most significant accomplishment bar none. As a performer, he's steered clear of Bach and Mozart, the warhorses of the flute repertoire, in favor of lesser known, even obscure, composers. His preference for less-traveled roads has led him to the likes of Carl Reinecke, a German romantic composer of the late 1800s, and to a twentieth-century Frenchman, Charles Koechlin, whose *Sonata for Piano and Flute* Fenwick made the world-premiere recording. Once a CD is cut and on the market, Fenwick seldom listens to it. But others are listening. A Japanese flutist from Osaka, after hearing a CD of Fenwick's, came halfway around the world to study with him.

Although Fenwick claims to be basically blasé—"I'm not very excitable about most things"—he's not immune to getting a charge out of such compliments. "I like hearing back from people I don't know," he says. "When word comes to me from people who have enjoyed my recordings, I have the same feeling as when I have guests in my house. I love it when they come through the front door for the first time and look around. Their jaws drop." Visitors hail Fenwick's work and praise everything from the portico to the paint job. Their reactions remind Fenwick of the magnitude of his achievement as a builder. "I forget sometimes. I stop seeing my house day to day, but when someone else sees it for the first time, I see it again." At those moments, the pride returns.

Smiling like a first-time father, Fenwick glances at the walls around us. Nodding his approval, he states, "Without being a trained architect I think I did at least as well as most professionals would have done."

THE OBVIOUS JOY WITH which Fenwick talks about his achievement makes me wonder whether his professed nonchalance masks greater emotional friskiness than he cares to admit. With relish, he recalls for me the "single most memorable and wonderful moment of the whole project." It occurred just after he had closed in the house. The walls were weathertight, and the roof, not yet clad in Vermont slate, was sheathed and tarpapered. One afternoon it started to rain—not a riproaring Berkshire thunderstorm, but a gentle shower. Fenwick recounts what happened next: "I lay on my back on the floor looking up at the big pair of roof windows, watching the raindrops falling straight out of the sky at me, and stopping suddenly at the surface of the glass. I recall the sensation of feeling protected in a previously undefined volume in the middle of the forest and being filled with a thrilling and joyous sense of Shelter—with a capital S." So much for Fenwick's insouciance.

Ordinarily a paragon of reason and self-restraint, Fenwick, it seems, behaved on occasion like someone on a creative binge while he built his house. He tells about the time he was installing two-by-ten joists for the garage loft: "I was excited because the joists were the first horizontal, overhead elements I put in. They were not part of the roof, but they symbolized *shelter* more vividly than anything so far. I had a pattern going, nailing them into a header on one end, and then going boom, boom, boom down the line on the other." All of a sudden he awoke as if from a trance, shocked to discover that he hadn't left an opening for the stairwell. Swept along in the flow of the work, he had attached four joists too many. "If you look carefully, you'll see nail holes where I had to pull out the extra joists," he says, pointing to a pockmarked two-by-eight.

It's difficult to imagine that Fenwick's current venture, the refurbishment of a commercial building in the city, will grant him the same manner of reward he's received in the country. Yet, he supervises the renovation assiduously. Considering that the building needs a new roof, a new boiler, new paint, and new mortar between the bricks, it's small wonder that he's put his country house on hold indefinitely. Soundproofing the studio, vast electrical work, and catching up with twenty years of deferred building maintenance absorb him more than the need to hang a few pieces of drywall on the ceiling of the house. "It's a very tall order to retrofit an air-conditioning, heating/venti-lating, and humidification system in an old building and have it run silently," he says, and because he's invested his life's sav-ings in the project, it's no surprise that his concerns have wan-dered from his *dacha* in the woods.

As though to emphasize the point, he discloses, "I've even let my subscription to *Fine Homebuilding* lapse."

Risky Business

D ave Daniel was an officer in his fifth year with the District of Columbia Police Department when he bought and almost single-handedly restored to life an abandoned fire-ravaged three-bedroom house in the extreme southeast corner of Washington, down where the city narrows to a bull's nose between the Maryland line and the Potomac River.

To pay for his venture in rebuilding, Dave sought help from investors, chief among them his sister-in-law, Marti Kirschbaum (a long-time friend of mine) from Falls Church, Virginia. Marti and her husband Ira, an attorney in the U.S. Bureau of Prisons, invited Ira's boss to join them in backing Dave's project. In a period of robust realty sales, they all expected within a year to reap a substantial return on their investment.

Until Marti introduced me to Dave, I had talked only with owner-builders in the suburbs and out in the country. Dave's house, which offered someone standing on its roof an unobstructed view of the United States Capitol dome, was a few minutes from downtown Washington. Therefore, I assumed that Dave's story would be different from the others. It was—but not in the ways that I expected.

WHEN I ARRIVE ON A November day, Dave, with a leaf blower strapped to his back, is clearing drifts of oak and poplar

131

leaves from the grass of his bowl-shaped yard in Dunkirk, Maryland, forty-five minutes from Washington. He knows I've come to talk building and immediately steers me down the hill toward his shop, a barn-like structure clad in gray board-and-batten siding. "I built the main part of this shop soon after we came here," he begins, "about nine years ago, after I retired from the D.C. Police Department." Indeed, Dave wears the expression of an ex-cop, perpetually grave and imperturbable. "Beth and I have 7.2 acres," he continues. "We love it out here in Calvert County. You know, we're only ten minutes from Chesapeake Bay."

Dave raises an overhead door, revealing a warehouse of space crammed with every manner of appurtenance for gardening, engine maintenance, and building. In case I hadn't noticed, he says, "This is where I keep things." Garden hoses curl over a table saw. Pieces of a dismantled lawnmower lie on top of fertilizer bags and grass-seed boxes. A jerry can of gasoline sits on the table next to a radial-arm saw. Lengths of plastic drain pipe stand in a corner. Threading his way through the jumble, Dave points out a cache of walnut boards piled high on a rack. "Someday I'll use those for making furniture," he says. Pointing to one area free of clutter, he says, "That's where Beth sometimes parks her car," he says. "That floor is made of pressure-treated two-by-twelves and two layers of three-quarter-inch plywood. It's strong enough to hold a tank."

On a wall of shelves Dave has lined up a collection of red, white, and blue boxes. "I'm an Amsoil dealer," he explains, "an entrepreneur. I sell these products to auto-supply stores, service stations, a mower company, and to boatyards along the Bay. Amsoil makes synthetic oils, greases, lubricants, and filters. Their oil is the best motor oil money can buy. It's so good that every jet engine in the world uses it." Dave continues to pitch his product, listing Amsoil's salutary effect on cars: It prevents slow starts in cold weather, improves gas mileage, provides more power, and emits cleaner exhaust. "What's more," he adds, "it prolongs engine life."

"Sounds magical," I remark, "like an automotive steroid."

He shows no sign of having heard my lame attempt at wit. "You hardly ever have to change your oil," he goes on. "The record for a car going without an oil change is 409,000 miles."

The tour of his shop concludes with look-see visits to three add-ons to the original structure. Two of them are storage sheds. The third Dave uses as an auto-repair center. "I plan to dig a pit pretty soon," he says. "I'm too old to keep crawling underneath cars." Dave is in his mid-fifties, judging from his lined forehead and expansive midsection. The pit he has in mind will be six feet deep and lined with concrete block. To dig it, he'll draw an outline on the floor using the wheelbase of Beth's Miata as a guide. Then he'll cut along the line with a masonry saw and fiber blade. "I've got four inches of concrete and steel mesh to remove," he says. "On one end of the pit I'll build steps to get in and out. Excavating the pit by hand won't be too bad. There are no rocks around here. The soil is sandy because this used to be the bottom of the Bay. When I dug five feet down for the foundation of the shop, I came across only two rocks, each about this size." His hands shape something like a cantaloupe.

Altogether, Dave's shop exceeds 1,700 square feet. It looks almost as big as his house. When I observe, "You've turned your shop into a mansion," he looks at me stonily.

At the bottom of his property a creek winds past a small oval pond, perhaps five yards wide. Leaves float on the pond's black glassy surface. Across the creek the woods rise steeply to a ridge, the rim of the surrounding bowl. "I built the pond last spring," he says. "I dug out the hole and put in a rubber liner. Then I got two pallets of fieldstone for the border and built up this rock for a waterfall." He places his hand on a waist-high pile of stone at the near end of the pond. "Here, let me show you how it works." He lifts a fieldstone plug from the ground, revealing a cylindrical hole about four feet deep. "I glued plastic buckets together to make this shaft," he says. At the bottom there is a pump submerged in water from the creek. When he flicks a switch on a nearby post the pump begins to throb, and in seconds water splashes out of the stone piling and falls into the pond. When I compliment Dave on his ingenuity, he responds, "That's a one-third-horsepower pump that draws 5.2 amps and delivers 3.6 gallons per minute."

Next stop—a footbridge over the creek. "Since I built this bridge, floods have washed it away three times. To tow it back I used a come-along," he says, referring to an ingenious device of steel cables, hooks, and slings that allows one person to use the mechanical advantage of a lever and a gear to exert the pulling power of half a horse. "It was slow work, pulling the bridge along a few inches at a time," he recalls. Turning back toward the house, Dave points out his homemade picnic tables and a bevy of Adirondack chairs he made in his shop. He also gives an account of the garden sprinkler system that he installed and the canopy he erected over the front door. Entering the screened porch, he says that he built that too. "Beth and I eat breakfast out here in the summer."

If nothing else, Dave has proved in spades his fecundity as a builder. Over coffee in his kitchen, he describes additional building projects that could keep him occupied until he's too feeble to lift a hammer: a new garage and a two-story addition to his house; he'd like to fix up a bungalow by the Bay and dreams of one day restoring a gone-to-seed restaurant overlooking the water.

PEERING PAST HIS MUG Dave begins to talk about his "D.C. house," as he likes to call the burnt-out house in town. "I never should have taken on that job. It wasn't a brilliant move. I'd never done any building before, except for stuff like that," he says, pointing to a short pine cabinet mottled with dark-brown stain squatting near the kitchen door. "The only reason I took it on was that George said he knew what he was doing." George, he explains, is George Reeder, more an acquaintance than a friend, who boasted lots of building experience. He agreed to work alongside Dave and show him the ropes in return for $10 an hour. "He gave me confidence," Dave continues. "I would be his helper, and together we would rebuild the house in one year."

The house, a 1920s Cape in a working-class area of well-kept single-family homes along a tree-lined street in southeast Washington, had suffered a major fire in 1976. The fire inspector declared that old aluminum wiring sparked the blaze, which destroyed some of the first floor, most of the second floor, and all of the roof, except for a handful of severely charred rafters. Miraculously, the exterior walls remained largely intact, although the windows were smashed and the doors torn from their hinges.

Neighbors, ignoring "Keep out" signs posted when the owner packed a suitcase and left, picked through the debris. They walked off with small pieces of furniture, bric-a-brac, cast-off clothes, and the few unbroken dishes. When Dave saw the house for the first time, it was like a body from which the life had departed. Abandoned for over a year, it had begun to decompose. Water dripped through its timbers and collected in the basement. Its floors were buckled. The plaster walls had turned to mush. Mildew had spread everywhere. George told Dave that the interior would have to be stripped to the studs. Together they filled three large Dumpsters with soggy refuse.

"No," Dave reiterates, "it wasn't a brilliant move to take on that D.C. job under the circumstances." What those circumstances are he reveals moments later: "I found out about a year and half ago that I have attention deficit disorder. "When I was young, I was hyperactive and always had problems. People used to think you outgrew them, but you don't. I outgrew hyperactivity but not the other problems. So I take Ritalin every day, and that helps a lot."

Dave pauses, leaving a silence between us. "Millions of adults have ADD," he informs me. "Before Ritalin, I'd go down to the shop to get something. On the way I'd get distracted and forget completely what I went for. I also had trouble staying with one project for long. I'd work on one thing but soon grow bored and then work on something else. That explains why I have so many unfinished projects around.

"Before taking Ritalin," he continues, "I'd get up in the morning and watch dumb TV talk shows that I had no interest in. But I don't do that any more. I wasn't on medication when I rebuilt the D.C. house, which probably played a big part in why it took me two years instead of one."

Precisely how his disorder doubled his time on the job remains unclear, but throughout the rebuilding process Dave probably fell short of the very qualities that ADD tends to undermine and diminish: focus, long-term attention to details, patience, skill at planning and sequencing, ability to tolerate frustration, and above all, doggedness. That Dave completed the house and afterward became a prolific builder, in spite of his disorder, is astounding—a heroic feat on the order of an artist defying color blindness or a high-wire performer ignoring a fear of heights.

On a construction site, it is complex work to organize time, material, and people. In fact, professional contractors pay supervisors high wages to assure that the proper materials are on hand in the proper amounts at the proper time. At Dave's D.C. house, those duties rested on Dave. To rebuild the roof, he needed rafters and plywood; also building paper, aluminum flashing, metal drip edges, shingles, roofing cement, plenty of nails, and a good ladder. When he faltered or forgot to bring an item at the time he needed it, the project stood still. A minor oversight, in fact, sometimes cost a whole day's work.

Despite his sincerest efforts, conditions beyond Dave's control caused other delays. Without a truck of his own—he drove a '70 Ford coupe at the time—Dave depended on building suppliers to bring materials to the site. Because unguarded materials tended to walk away in Dave's D.C. neighborhood, he requested deliveries only when he could be there to receive them. And since delivery schedules often lack precision, he suffered through what he calls "a logistical nightmare," missing some shipments altogether and impatiently waiting for hours for others to arrive.

"In D.C. you can't leave a site unattended for long," Dave says. "If I had to go to court or down to the store for something, I'd have to pack up everything and take it with me." For many months, or until the house was secure, Dave kept no more than a day's worth of material on hand. If he misjudged the amount, he carted away the leftovers when his workday ended. All his tools, manna to thieves, Dave kept safely by his side or locked in the trunk of his car.

Although dead-bolted, the doors of the house failed to keep intruders out. "One night after the framing was done," Dave recalls, "some kids broke in and burned up the basement stairs." Dave suspects that the arsonists started the blaze under the steps, hoping that the fire would shoot up the stairwell to the second floor. Before that happened, though, a passerby saw smoke and called the fire department.

Had Dave been forewarned of such perils, he might have thought twice about rebuilding a house in the city. On the other hand, people like Dave—that is, men with ADD—habitually drift into shark-filled waters. According to psychologist Thom Hartmann, author of *Focus Your Energy: Hunting for Success in Business with Attention Deficit Disorder*, many adults with ADD possess traits akin to those needed to survive in a primitive hunting society. They act impulsively and often take risks that other, more circumspect people, don't. In short, they act like Dave. "I tend to take on jobs that I shouldn't," Dave acknowledges, "but I don't know any better." In Hartmann's view, people with ADD crave constant stimulation from the world—some intoxicating activity to distract them from the mental storms raging inside their heads. Thus, they seek thrills, which relieve frustration and keep them focused. So, Hartmann concludes, ADD sufferers often favor high-risk, fast-paced occupations such as sales, advertising, and creative arts. One might wonder why he didn't include police work and part-time home building on his list. Dave confirms that he is a risk taker: "I don't know that I can't do something unless I go ahead and do it," he says. Perhaps that's why he chose to become a cop. On the police force, Dave had a knack for defusing potentially nasty situations. When restless young toughs hung out on street corners, Dave, equally adept at playing the heavyweight or mister nice guy, maintained law and order by routinely walking into their midst for a chat.

Dave's beat was the northeast quadrant of Washington, one of the more felonious sections of the city. On patrol he wore a bullet-proof Kevlar vest and never left the station house without a nightstick, a gun, extra ammunition, two pairs of handcuffs, pepper spray, and a two-way radio. For most of his time on the force, he did "midnights," the only shift that starts on one date and ends on the next. Between 11 P.M. and 7 A.M. Dave listened to his police radio and responded to the situations that crackled over the airwaves—a collision at New York Avenue near P Street, reports of broken glass or a stolen car, a bunch of guys shouting in the street. Whatever came up, he investigated. The nights were often manic—moments of intense activity followed by lulls. On a quiet night, Dave might pick up a couple of domestic disputes or assist in an emergency medical evacuation. Then there were nights the city convulsed, and Dave, by the time the morning came, might have had his health and safety—if not his life—on the line more than once.

At the end of his shift Dave donned jeans and work boots, strapped on his tool belt and straightaway reported for duty at his D.C. house. Typically, he worked there for three or four hours. By early afternoon, he was on the road to his home in Bowie, Maryland, for a shower and sleep before returning to his post on the streets of Washington. On days off, he toiled at the house until dusk.

"That was my schedule for two years," he says. "But I was an aggressive police officer and made plenty of arrests, which meant I had to go to court during the day. Of course, that kept me away from the house a lot." To make up for lost time, Dave sometimes brought in adjunct builders. One of them was a teenager he arrested late one night after receiving a complaint that the boy refused to leave his girlfriend's apartment. Dave charged the youth with disorderly conduct, worth a ten-dollar fine in the District of Columbia. "At the station the kid couldn't raise the ten dollars," Dave says, "so I paid his fine and told him to meet me at my house in the morning to work off his debt. He showed up and worked all day. I paid him a day's wages minus the ten dollars he owed me. Then he left and I never saw him again."

The kid was but one of many transient helpers. A long line of volunteers passed through the house to lend Dave a hand for an hour, a day, a week, whatever they could spare. They donated whatever talents they had—cleaning up, hauling materials, standing watch for would-be pillagers. Dave wasn't picky. His teenage son Mark came with chums to help shingle the roof. Beth and his sister-in-law Marti painted walls and ceilings. When he needed extra muscle to carry drywall from the street to the second floor, he called on brother officers from his precinct.

Most of the time, however, Dave toiled alone. George, who had vowed to steer Dave through the project, jumped ship after two months, pleading overextension. "He had a full-time job in D.C. and commuted seventy-five miles each way," Dave explains. "He couldn't do it all. From the start I told him so, but he didn't hear. He apologized all over the place when he bailed out." Did Dave feel jilted? "No," he says. "I don't blame him for leaving. He had no choice."

Before George walked off the job, he and Dave had cleared the house of rubbish and had framed new walls for the second story. The rest—the roof, the windows, siding, doors, plumbing, electricity, and finishing work both inside and out—was up to Dave. With no tools, no experience, and now no teacher, he had only a seat-of-the-pants instinct for the way pieces of a house are meant to go together.

When I ask him where he acquired such a gift, Dave hesitates, as though it had never occurred to him to wonder about its origins. Finally he says, "I guess that I learned to do things by myself because in Ohio, where I grew up, we were too poor to have someone else do them for us. Anyway, I've always been good with my hands."

Indeed, since childhood Dave has hung out under the raised hood of somebody's car. At age fifteen he was given a '47

Studebaker coupe equipped with a shattered engine. In a junk yard, he paid $35 for a whole one and figured out how to put it in. Mechanical work fascinated him. Where others found dirt, grease, and a maze of metal, he saw a living thing rich with possibility. Two engines might look alike but they never act alike. To Dave, a car's engine is an organism with a distinctive personality and way of behaving. At present he drives a '91 Buick with a special filtration system to keep the oil clean. "Oil changes are virtually eliminated with this system," he says. "You send in a specimen of oil every few months for a spectrograph analysis that checks for copper, iron, bearing wear, and ring wear. I've changed oil only four times in 155,000 miles." Like a parent gloating over his kid's SAT score, Dave seems genuinely proud of his engine's achievement.

In 1970, Dave switched his métier from autos to airplanes. In Columbus, he signed up for a two-year course in aviation mechanics. But afterward, he couldn't find a job. In fact, airlines were laying off both pilots and ground crews. As Dave tells it, "There were mechanics with twenty years' experience begging to work for minimum wage at small airports. With that going on, I didn't stand a chance." Instead, he got work as a line mechanic at a Chevy dealership in Bowie, Maryland, twenty-five miles east of Washington. Within months, however, President Nixon authorized the expansion of the District of Columbia Police Department from 3,000 to 5,200 officers. "I went right down and took the test," Dave says, and weeks later he took his oath as a rookie cop. Dave was thirty years old. At thirty-four, with two kids, a Bowie home, and a wife about to return to college for a degree in social work, Dave thought about taking a whack at building. Along came George, and when the inexpensive fire-ridden house in need of a rehabber turned up, he grabbed it. As a whiz with mechanical things, he figured that a house—with no moving parts—had to be simpler to rebuild than an internal combustion engine, and before long, he felt in his bones that, George or no George, he could do the job.

Originally, a two-story foyer projected from the front of the house. Before the fire, it had served as the main entrance and added visual interest to the facade. Dave intended to restore that feature, despite his uncertainty about framing the tricky intersection, or valley, between the foyer's roof and the main roof. Common sense told him to build the foyer roof as though he were building a dormer, that is, to mount it directly onto the main roof. It was a shrewd idea, for the alternate method required truncating several roof-rafters to make room for the dormer. But it also called for a great variety of exotic cuts with a circular saw. Framing two intersecting roofs, each with a different pitch always requires cutting across the lumber at a bias and tilting the saw blade to cut through the piece obliquely. Such compound miter cuts pose problems of geometry and spatial relations that drive carpenters nuts. Beginners are especially baffled. They spend lots of time staring at the boards, rotating them in space, drawing cut lines that rarely turn out right. Dave went through the obligatory motions—measuring, calculating, setting his saw blade at what he divined as the proper angle. In the end, however, after ravaging several perfectly good lengths of lumber, he resorted to the last best refuge for novice builders—the easy way out: He attached a straightforward, one-story vestibule with a simple-to-frame gabled dormer to the facade of the house.

Inside the house, Dave had smashed the old plaster walls with a sledge hammer. When the dust settled, he put up drywall. "Over two hundred sheets of it," he says, "and I hated every one of them." Just carrying it into the house and up the narrow stairs was tough. The space was tight, so tight in fact that the eventual buyer of the house couldn't get his new bedroom furniture to the second floor and had to send it back. Smearing Sheetrock seams smooth, Dave went through miles of tape and barrels of joint compound, or "mud," as it's called by the building crowd. The job seemed endless. And dull. "Mudwork," Dave says, "was the worst."

Then Dave reconsiders. "No, it was second worst." The prize went to his perpetual struggle with mistakes made by the long-gone builder of the original house. "Whoever built it," Dave asserts, "couldn't have owned a level or a square." No floors in the house were level, no walls plumb, no corners a

In the end, Dave attached a one-story vestibule with a simple gable roof to the facade of the house.

true 90 degrees. "Try putting up Sheetrock on a wall or ceiling that isn't square—that's murder," Dave says. "When I started the work, I was naive. I thought that if you want to install Sheetrock, you just measure the height and width and cut it. It doesn't work that way. You have to measure it several different ways." Indeed, to fit Sheetrock onto his walls, Dave often trimmed the ends at an angle other than 90 degrees, turning what began as a rectangle into something vaguely rhomboidal.

The outside walls presented another kind of problem. Brick facing covered the entire first floor of the house. Once painted white, its surface was now flaky and badly chipped. Rather than scrape and repaint it, Dave decided to restore the brick to its natural red color. He could have used one of several chemical paint-removers that strip old paint efficiently but, at roughly $2 a square foot, expensively, too. Since chemicals also excel at removing skin from the hands that touch them and have been known to scar the substrate, or brick, unless applied properly and hosed off in a timely fashion, Dave chose to blast the paint from the walls with sand.

Sandblasting, while somewhat less pernicious than chemicals, offers few pleasures except that it gets the job done quickly. To pay for speed, however, you must be willing to cover every square millimeter of your body in protective gear: heavy gloves, goggles, tight-fitting hat, and above all, a good respirator that will keep your nose and mouth free of dust, sand, and paint particles, which on old houses like Dave's, are apt to be full of toxic lead. The sand used to peel a wall differs from beach sand. Made of iron-ore slag, it is black, sharp-edged, and abrasive. It is shot under terrific pressure through a nozzle and would have little trouble damaging a person that wandered into its line of fire. Rebounding from the wall, granules sail twenty or thirty feet, coating everything in sight with a dull gray film.

Dressed like a moonwalker as he blasted the wall with sand, Dave came to understand that building doesn't lack its share of nastiness: dirt, boredom, exhaustion, blisters, scrapes, splinters, and for an inordinate number of do-it-yourselfers, lower back pain. None of these annoyances, however, weighed on him like his own inability to work faster. Without George to set the pace, Dave's progress slowed to a crawl.

Builders will swear that a one-man crew is only one-third as productive as a crew of two, an arithmetical anomaly that caught the eye of Dave's sister-in-law Marti Kirschbaum and her husband Ira, who had put $25,000 into Dave's project. Observing Dave's glacial pace, they began to worry about their investment. Dave had led them to believe that he would return their principal within a year, along with earnings of at least 10 percent. "My estimate was a shot in the dark," Dave admits in retrospect, "but for a beginner, it was a reasonable guess." Ira had a particular interest in having Dave keep his word because he had convinced Mike Quinlan, his boss at the

U.S. Bureau of Prisons, to invest $25,000, too. When George's early departure scuttled Dave's plan to complete and sell the house in a year, the specter of catastrophe crossed Ira's mind.

"When I began," Dave says, "I thought a year was a long time." Apparently not long enough, however, because after twelve months the place still looked like a wounded warrior in need of a lengthy convalescence. During the months that followed, Dave repeatedly assured his bankrollers that the house would soon be ready for the realty market. Marti and Ira thought otherwise and urged Dave to pick up his pace. Every day's delay eroded their profit. It meant paying more property taxes, more insurance premiums, and more interest on their home-construction loan. And since mortgage rates were shooting skyward, they feared being stuck with an urban albatross for a long, long time. Their anxiety grew further when Dave dunned them for an additional $10,000 for unanticipated expenses: Dumpster rental, electrical work that far exceeded his estimates, driveway paving, and more building materials—more insulation, more vinyl siding, more lumber to build a small deck and steps outside the kitchen door. And because the D.C. building code forbade amateurs to do their own plumbing, Marti and Ira were forced to pay for a licensed professional.

Engulfed by pressure to hurry up and complete the work, Dave staggered between the house and his job, stealing a few hours' sleep in between. "I wasn't that young then," he says. "If I'd been twenty-one and single it might have been different." He passed like a shadow in and out of his family's life. "I hardly ever saw my wife and kids," he recalls. Beth bore the brunt of Dave's absence. Reduced almost to single-parenthood, she held a full-time job, tended to their home and to their adolescent kids, Mark and Laurie, while also going to class and writing term papers. Had Dave even noticed Beth's struggle, he was in no position to help, for he carried millstones of his own. Looking back, Dave calls that time "one of the most stressful periods of my life."

"Dave and Beth had their problems," says Marti. Journeying back in thought, she vividly recalls that during the D.C.

house project Dave and Beth became like strangers to each other. "It almost ruined their marriage," she adds. A marriage that includes a husband with attention deficit disorder can be a tense and torturous affair in any case, even without a crushing building project on its back.

Whatever the ADD-induced emotional torments Dave suffered while mired in the D.C. project, they haven't prevented him—more than two decades later—from thinking about taking a crack at another D.C. house: "I'm not looking for it, but I wouldn't hesitate if the price were right. I'd go in with my eyes open this time," he says. "I'd know what I was doing."

Apparently, time has blurred Dave's memory of his experience in D.C. Some data about the house he recites as readily as his PIN number—the exterior dimensions, the amount of Sheetrock he used, the height of the front door above the street. But other facts have faded. Offhand, he can't recall the year he bought the property, for example, and how much he paid for it. Nor does he remember his own earnings. But he assumes—since he didn't keep a time sheet—"probably less than the minimum wage." As for disbursements to investors, the figures have flown from his mind. "Less than they expected," he says, "but I don't know how much less." (Marti does, however. She and Ira made about $4,000, a third less than they anticipated on a two-year outlay of $35,000.)

Even before Dave put the house up for sale, he sold it. One Sunday morning, while he was finishing a floor, a neighbor knocked on the door and said he'd like to buy the place for his daughter. In a few minutes he and Dave struck a deal. Dave was ecstatic. The gods had finally smiled on him, releasing him from a project that had held him captive for two years. Having the house virtually sell itself after all he'd been through Dave calls "a true blessing." Transcendent relief greeted him four weeks later when he handed the title to the new owner.

Unburdened at last, Dave began to pour his energy into police work. He studied for a promotion and earned a sergeant's stripes. One night in December, 1987, responding to a "man-with-a-gun" call, he shot a man to death. The man he killed had gone berserk on PCP. As Dave tells it, "The man jumped into the back seat of a car stopped at a red light at the intersection of Minnesota and Ames. As I ran toward the car, I yelled to the driver that the man had a gun. Immediately the driver and front-seat passenger abandoned the vehicle. Approaching the left rear door of the car, I ordered the man to take his hand out of his pocket and to put both hands on the roof of the car. He looked at me with crazy eyes and said, 'Shoot me.' As he said this, he began turning his body toward me, obviously to bring the muzzle of his pistol around to fire at me through the window. I fired my service weapon, but the man kept rotating toward me. It took three more rounds before he stopped."

Immediately Dave was put on administrative leave, a standard police-department procedure following a shooting. Until the incident could be investigated and presented to a grand jury as a possible homicide, Dave drew pay but could not work. The case took five months to resolve. During that time, Dave stayed close to his home in Bowie. Growing restless, he decided to add two rooms to the back of his house. He hadn't built anything serious in nearly a decade, not since his two-year term at hard labor in southeast Washington. If any ill effects lingered from that time, they didn't hold him back. Besides, here in Bowie the working conditions were completely different: no long commute to the site, no deadlines to meet, no investors to satisfy, no more threat of theft and arson. And best of all, he now understood a builder's job. He was past agonizing over what to do and how to do it. In contrast to his D.C. quagmire, this adventure in building would flow like a swift river. Dave's labors produced a palatial twelve-foot-by-thirty-foot, two-room family recreation center that spanned the rear of his house. In the smaller of the rooms, a family spa, Dave installed a six-person Jacuzzi. "Instead of sitting it on the floor like an ordinary bathtub," Dave says, "I sank it halfway so that people would step down into it." By recessing the tub, which, when full of water and hot-tubbers, weighs two and a half tons, Dave eliminated the need to construct a massive supporting platform. Instead, he built a deck with treated plywood, then framed out a round hole for the tub. "Underneath," he explains, "I built an insulated concrete pedestal for it to rest on." Italian terrazzo tile covers the floor of the room, and elegant French doors mounted in a wall of glass open to a brick patio. The remaining walls are lined with redwood. When night falls, indirect light from behind a redwood panel bounces off the ceiling and walls, bringing the room to life, like the prince kissing Sleeping Beauty. "That spa is the best thing I ever built," he says.

Next door, he constructed a TV/media center with skylights and a sixteen-foot-wide glass wall with sliding doors. "I got help putting up the wall," says Dave, but he was left on his own to fashion a mighty eighteen-foot header to support the shed roof above it. He made the header with a pair of two-by-twelves and a one-quarter-inch piece of steel called a flitch plate that he locked between the boards with fifty half-inch bolts. To lift the big beam into place Dave contrived an ingenious derrick made of two-by-fours and a come-along that he attached to a pecan tree in his back yard. Single-handedly, he hoisted the beam with cables and gently slid it onto the frame.

To Dave, that was the easy part. More difficult was hoisting four-by-eight pieces of Sheetrock onto the room's sloped ceiling. For that, he had only the lifting strength of his own arms and back to count on. Dave carried each piece up a ten-foot extension ladder and rested it on his head while struggling to drive in enough nails to hold it aloft. "That was fun," he says, his eyes rolling skyward.

Reinstated by the D.C. Police Department when the addition was almost complete, Dave again took up his duties on the streets of Washington. But an incident during his first night back changed the trajectory of his life once again. Dave was called to back up Jeff Hoop, a fellow officer, on another man-with-a-gun run. He says it turned out to be a "bad call." That is, neither gun nor man was found. But Dave wondered afterward what the grand jury might have concluded had he shot someone on two consecutive radio runs, even though five months apart. The question bothered him, and he began to worry whether he had it in him to shoot again. "What if I hesitated a little too long, perhaps endangering Jeff's life?" The thought alarmed him. Could he act decisively in an emergency? What if his indecision were to cause someone to die needlessly? He brooded about the possibility. It gnawed at him day and night. "I got to the point," he says, "where I had almost no short-term memory. On the job, I grew short-tempered with my officers and with civilians."

Months later, reading a police union circular on the symptoms of post-traumatic stress disorder, Dave felt as though he were reading about himself. "It described me perfectly," he says. "I immediately put my name in the sick book and drove to the union psychologist's office. She referred me to the department's psychiatrist, and I never went back to duty. I was retired from the department on April 14, 1989."

OUT IN DUNKIRK, MARYLAND, Dave has revamped his lifestyle. Instead of walking a beat, he builds. Over time he has compiled a dazzling dossier of completed projects, some at home, others as a self-employed contractor in North Beach, Chaneyville, Bristol, and the other scattered towns of Calvert County. For friends and relations, he's gutted and renovated kitchens, redone roofs, knocked down and erected partitions, installed skylights, and more. He does quality work and is paid well for it. But the money matters less than the craft. He works not to pay bills or fill up his days but to do the work. Not all the work is pure pleasure, but neither is it drudgery. It can't be when it gives his life focus and meaning.

Frankly, this is my own inference about Dave's present work. I couldn't get Dave to discuss the emotional perks of being a builder. He'd probably find that kind of talk fishy, anyway. When two builders meet, they exchange facts and figures, the names of things—two-by-tens, oriented strand board ("OSB," that is), and soffit vents. Beyond that, a pair of veteran do-it-yourselfers might boast a bit and swap anecdotes, mostly about others' damn-fool building mistakes. As for the personal rewards of building, either they don't count for much or they are not what guys like us are meant to talk about.

Dave's reticence leaves me guessing. Why does Dave build? Does he hope to find a more accurate alignment with the physical world? Is he attempting to fulfill his destiny as a human being? Is he trying to maintain the illusion of control of his life? Does building light a fire in his belly? If it does, he won't say so. He doesn't analyze his behavior, not in terms like those. During many hours of conversation, I wanted to find out what it was like for him to rebuild a burnt-out house and what the experience meant to him. As we talked, however, it became clear that Dave is more the story-teller than the inter-preter of experience. He tries to get the details right but leaves me to dope out the text between the lines. He showed me what he's done and told me how he did it. As for catching a glimpse into the soul of a builder—well, I evidently came to the wrong place.

Resident Artist

Browsing in do-it-yourself heaven—otherwise known as the Builders Booksource, a Berkeley shop that sells nothing but books on building, architecture, home care, and crafts—I came across a reference to Leona Walden, a northern California artist and sculptor who built two cabins by herself and afterward designed and supervised the construction of two houses, one her residence for ten years, the other her present home. Such credentials suggested to me that Leona would be a fertile source of insight into the mysteries and visual delights of home building.

Weeks later, when I phoned her from New York, she agreed to an interview but declined to make a specific appointment. "We'll talk sometime," she said. "Call me when you get to California."

On my next trip west I rang her from the San Francisco airport. "I'm here," I said, and tried to set a time—2:30 the following day.

"Oh, whenever," Leona responded casually. "I guess I'll be at home around then."

How mellow, how California! I thought to myself—and she's an artist to boot. Hanging up the phone, I figured the odds at fifty-fifty that I'd be stood up.

THERE COULDN'T BE A more idyllic spot in May than
Albion, on the Mendocino coast. The land, strung between
redwood groves and the ocean, is lush with greenery and flowers.
Summer crowds are weeks away, and it's still possible
to find a quiet beach or stroll the cliffs above the sea without
seeing another soul. Four miles from the coastal highway, the
road narrows, soon loses its paving, and curves into the woods.
A graveled driveway marked "Walden" winds to a graceful
house close to a pond and surrounded by park-like grounds. In
the dooryard groupings of rock are displayed like abstract
sculptures. A hand-lettered sign in the plantings says, "Free
Weeds." Around the property, fire-blackened tree stumps,
wider than my car and as tall as the house itself, stand like sentinels. They are redwood tree stumps, the remains of the old-
growth forest, now lawn ornaments. Flowering vines curl up
their sides. Some serve as planters. Another holds a water tank
aloft. The effect is to deny the traditional role of tree stumps
as blemishes to be removed from the land. Instead, an
unabashedly arty transformation has taken place.

A trellis of heavy interlocking timbers draped with vines
leads to the front door of the house. A Chinese lantern hangs
overhead. From high on a post a clay mask, vaguely demonic,
stares at passersby. Pieces of driftwood lie on a wooden bench
weathered to silver-gray. A Plexiglas roof lets daylight pour
into the portico below and shields callers from the rain.
Attention has been paid to create an interesting transition between the yard and the inside of the house.

Leona answers my knock quickly, as though she'd been
waiting. I feel relieved. She flashes a winning smile. Perhaps
I've misjudged her. Light brown hair going gray frames her intelligent face. She is tall like a model, fine-boned and graceful.
She greets me barefooted and says apologetically, "I ask everyone to take their shoes off when they come in."

This I am not prepared for. I have arrived for the interview
with a tape recorder, extra batteries, a clipboard, lots of questions and also, alas, a sock on my left foot with a hole in its toe
as big as a silver dollar. Nevertheless, I leave my Reeboks in

the foyer, expecting Leona to explain why her guests must shed their footwear at the door. Probably some weird custom, something cabalistic, like letting the life force of the building flow into your body through the soles of your feet. But no, Leona says simply that she can't stand housekeeping and wants to keep her carpet clean. Indeed, her floor is immaculate. And through the whole afternoon she averts her eyes from my big toe sticking out in the air like a peeled potato.

"Won't you sit down," she says, leading me to an overstuffed chair in the living room, and offering tea ("Any flavor you'd like"). Not at all the California dreamer I expected, Leona is a sophisticated and practiced hostess. There is an atmosphere of studied tranquillity inside her home: spacious light-filled rooms, antique furniture, pale green broadloom, an ornate grand piano. Posts and beams—"fir stained to look like redwood," she tells me later—are set off against whitewashed walls and a vaulted ceiling. A fireplace and raised hearth of forest green marble sit in one corner. Expansive picture windows frame views of Leona's gardens and the pond. The place deserves a spread in *House Beautiful*.

The house is a Leona Walden original, designed and built in 1990 only half a mile but a world away from the first house she built some twenty-five years ago at Salmon Creek. "In the early 1970s," Leona begins, "I was living in Mexico with my friend Max Efroym and my daughter Juli, who was three at the time. But it wasn't working out very well. So I said 'Let's go up to the Mendocino coast. It's pretty there.' So we came up here to Albion to join the commune at Salmon Creek Farm."

What Leona calls a commune was little more than two families, ten people in all, settled in tents alongside a creek at the bottom of a small canyon. In time, the group grew to fourteen—seven kids and seven adults. "It was raining when I arrived," Leona recalls, "so I decided quickly to start building a house. The site I picked was the only level piece of land I could find—on an old dead-end logging road near the rim of the canyon. In four months, from July to October, I built a cabin."

Leona pauses for a moment. "No," she says, "that's not quite right. To give credit where it's due, Max helped. He was pretty good at hammering nails, but he didn't have a logical mind and was clueless about design and construction." Leona's cabin, taller than it was wide, measured twelve by sixteen feet and had two stories. "I chose those dimensions," she explains, "because the road was fourteen feet across."

Until then, Leona's building experience had amounted to brick-and-board bookshelves—period. What gave her the confidence to think that she could build a house were what she terms "a logical mind and good eye. I've always been mathematical," she adds, "and I'm also an artist. To build the cabin I simply used both sides of my brain—the right side to visualize it, the left side to figure out how to do it. But the real impetus was that we needed a house to live in and had no money to pay someone to build one for us."

Leona speaks softly about her feat, from time to time barely louder than a whisper. She often starts a sentence, stops, alters her thought, and heads in a different direction. At times she seems wary, a bit uneasy, as though she's revealing classified information. Maybe she regrets consenting to this interview and allowing a total stranger to root around in her life. But as we talk, she begins to relax and warms to telling her story.

"I LEARNED TO FRAME A HOUSE BY IMITATION," she says. "I studied photos in a four-dollar paperback book. It showed how pieces of a house fit together—how to frame a wall with a window and how rafters are attached. It also explained building codes and told me that studs are sixteen inches apart and should be measured o.c., you know, from the center of one board to the center of the next." In short, the book—she can't recall its title—led her step by step from the foundation to the ridge pole. If anything puzzled her, she consulted experienced builders. When three out of four told her the same thing, that's what she did. A consensus affirmed for her, among other things, that a shed roof was the simplest kind to build and that no other material could beat roll-roofing for ease of installation.

To build her cabin Leona relied solely on hand-powered tools. No electricity, no gasoline engines, no battery-operated drills and drivers. "I prefer not to use power tools," she says. "I don't like the noise and the fumes. I'd much rather work with hand tools." Like other traditionalists, Leona asserts that what you make up in speed and ease with power tools, you lose in humanity. "By giving in to a machine you lose your feeling for the work. You become an accessory—a robot as opposed to a craftsman." Had Leona owned a circular saw or electric drill, she couldn't have used it anyway. The residents of Salmon Creek Farm were committed to leading simple, close-to-nature lives. Neither Leona's building site nor any other part of the commune was wired for electricity. (During her time at Salmon Creek, Leona heated and cooked with a wood-burning stove and lit her cabin with candles and kerosene lamps.)

Leona took pleasure from the languid pace that hand-powered tools imposed on her. With no deadline to meet, she tried to enjoy every moment of cabin building. And although she worked conscientiously, she also worked slowly, seeing no need to push herself to the brink of exhaustion day after day. Hand-powered tools encouraged her to work carefully, forcing her to focus. When every cut demands a hefty investment of muscle and willpower, you learn not to err, not to make incorrect cuts or bore holes in the wrong place. The carpenter's cautionary adage "Measure twice and cut once" sounds positively oracular to a builder about to cut a two-by-ten with a handsaw. What's more, using hand tools is meditative. Turning a hunk of lumber into a rafter takes more than brute strength. The physical act of holding a saw on the cut line and maintaining a consistent cutting angle requires intense concentration as well as patience and perseverance.

Through the dog days of summer and early fall, construction progressed at tortoise speed. "The building site was a quarter-mile from the road," Leona says. "Every scrap of the house had to be carried in along a narrow trail through the

woods." A dozen times a day she and Max, like beasts of burden bearing house parts, shuttled between the road and the
work site. Having started construction with a minuscule budget, she made ends meet by scavenging the state of California
for free wood. A Petaluma chicken farmer gave her most of the
framing lumber—"true two-by-four redwood," Leona exclaims, "but Max and I had to tear down his old chicken coops
to get it." The coops must have been well past their prime because "true" two-by-fours—lumber that literally measures
two inches by four inches—haven't been widely used for construction since late in the nineteenth century. Today's nomi-
nal two-by-fours are usually a half inch smaller all around,
having lost their true girth while being planed and dried at
lumber mills. "One of those old-growth redwood studs
weighed as much as three new ones," says Leona.

Using recycled lumber, while saving trees and money,
prolonged Leona's work still further. The ragged ends of each
hand-me-down board had to be sawed off. Rusty nails had to be
extracted. Unlike new lumber, which can be counted on to
have specific dimensions, every old piece needed to be measured and trimmed. Antique wood tends to be brittle. If Leona
hammered nails too close to the edge or the end, the dried out
fibers would split or splinter. Since old boards don't shrink,
twist, or warp, however, the nails she sank into the studs and
joists would never loosen or pop out.

Another windfall enabled Leona to put siding on her cabin
virtually for the cost of the nails. From a mill owner in
Woodside, south of San Francisco, she wheedled a bunch of
lath, one-quarter by four inches. With the lath, she conceived a
type of board-and-batten siding. As she tells it, "I put up pairs
of boards vertically, then covered the seam between them with
a third board."

Following the photos in her four-dollar how-to-build handbook, Leona framed her house balloon-style, a mode of framing
that's going out of fashion. While not yet extinct, it won't be
long before builders stop using balloon framing altogether—and
for good reason: it is harder, slower, and more labor-intensive

than its more popular alternative, platform, or western, framing. The chief difference between the two methods is that balloon framing uses wall studs that extend in one piece from the mudsill to the roof, and floors are hung on the studs. Therefore, a balloon frame on a two-story house like Leona's called for cumbersome and hard-to-find eighteen- or twenty-foot studs. Also, numerous short lengths of lumber to be used as firestops between the studs had to be cut by hand and nailed into place in every bay. Platform framing, in contrast, is simpler and more compact. Being compartmentalized—that is, each floor is separately framed, and each subsequent floor is built atop the one below—it requires less cutting and lightens the loads that a solitary builder must handle.

In general, platform-framed houses wobble less, although some carpenters disagree, arguing that balloon framing is the method of choice on houses to be sided with stucco. The more rigid frame, they say, inhibits the cracking of the walls' brittle skin. Such a frame also tends to stand up better to earth tremors and quakes, not a frivolous concern in Albion, which lies almost atop the San Andreas fault. Since the time Leona framed her cabin, however, all sorts of bracing and anchoring techniques have been devised and inserted into building codes up and down the California coast.

For Leona, the effect of four months of construction work was electric. She says, "It was one of the most exciting things I have ever done, a highlight of my life." Her building site was a stage for miracle-working, each day on the job a day of magic. In contrast to her usual line of work—as she describes it, "scraping by as an illustrator and artist specializing in pen and ink drawings"—building yielded unexpected thrills. "My drawings tend to be very intricate," she explains. "They contain a great many lines. A single illustration often takes me thirty to forty hours. But framing an entire wall on a two-story building took me only eight hours. When we stood the wall up, I was truly amazed." Leona pauses, aglow with the rekindled memory of the moment. "Imagine," she adds, "spending thirty hours on a piece of paper that ends up in a drawer and only eight hours on a wall of a house you can live in. Isn't it a fantastic accomplishment to do that?"

Such enthusiasm is not what Beverly Hills-born women are ordinarily presumed to feel about construction work. But in Leona's case presuppositions are bound to be wrong. While growing up in Beverly Hills and attending its chic high school, she was a maverick and proud of it. "I didn't belong there," she says. "It was too uppity." But just as she snubbed the Rodeo Drive scene, her sybaritic classmates turned up their suntanned noses at her. Leona thinks that few of them could ever become charged up about building a rude country cabin on the rim of a canyon. And Lord only knows what they'd think of Leona's current circle of friends, some of them women who don work boots and do building projects together. At present, Leona's crowd is hacking out a trail along a nearby creek. Next on their list is the construction of an Albion Ridge community bulletin board.

"The other day," Leona says, "a few of us were comparing notes about what we got for Mother's Day. One of them received a three-and-a-quarter-horsepower plunge router, one got a Japanese saw, and another a special hand drill. We all laughed about that but, believe me, they all appreciated such gifts a lot more than flowers or candy." Leona says nothing about her own gift but mentions that next year—her aversion to power tools evidently eroded by time—she hopes to get a twelve-inch compound chopsaw.

When I ask Leona how people react when she speaks knowingly about routers and chopsaws, she replies, "Men have an odd reaction but less now than they used to. Age helps, I think." A recent boyfriend once told her, after she had sung the praises of a big, flat boulder she had found for the front-door step of her house, "You're different from other women, Leona. You never get excited about flowers or jewelry. You get excited about rocks."

I asked whether he was right.

Chuckling at the thought, she replied, "I suppose so."

During Leona's career as an owner-builder, hardly an event shines brighter in her memory than taking up residence with Juli and Max in her new cabin. The first night, when she climbed the ship's ladder to her bed, she couldn't sleep. Under the roof that she herself had nailed and stapled and tarred together she laid back, eyes open, basking in the moonlight that cascaded through the window above her sleeping alcove. Had she been a weeper, this would have been the opportune moment to let the tears flow. How blessed she felt and how lucky to have had the wherewithal to build a good home.

Just how good the structure turned out to be, however, became clear only with the passing seasons. In summer the wide overhang of the roof shaded the south-facing windows. During the winter it let the low-slung sun shine in—a happy accident Leona transplanted to the design of three subsequent homes. Also, the bank of windows that lined the southern wall never failed to please her. She often sat meditatively, rejoicing in the view of the canyon below her.

Regardless of such amenities, the fact remains that her cabin was basically a crude piece of work. It lacked both insulation and utilities. It stood on a modest pier-block foundation and in places fell short of professional construction standards. Sometimes, Leona chided herself for "pretty shoddy building practices," citing a single miscut stud as an example. "The top plate didn't meet the stud squarely. It rested on only one corner." Later, Leona found that her transgression was hardly worth a second thought. "I was visiting a friend who had a professionally built tract house in southern California," she explains. "They were tearing out a wall and I saw a stud supporting nothing but air. It was actually two feet too short. I realized then that I wasn't such a bad builder after all."

Leona's building debut occurred at a time, as she describes it, "when many struggling hippies came up to the Mendocino area. Since we had no money, we helped each other—planting gardens, sharing food, helping with building chores." Consequently, it was also a time when the local building authorities, not altogether thrilled about the rustic homes being hammered together in their jurisdiction, undertook a crusade to clamp down not only on newcomers but on predatory landowners who, out to make a buck, had erected flimsy shacks on their property, called them cabins, and rented them out for a few hundred a month—essentially creating latter-day Hoovervilles in Mendocino County. The building inspectors "red-tagged" many of the new structures, indicating that they were non-code dwellings. But a hardy band of people, including Leona, petitioned for changes in the building code, in particular for a relaxed set of standards for the simple homes that she and others had built. In time, their voices were heard and new rules effected: Any existing structure such as Leona's that was safe electrically (not an issue in her power-free home), that had a properly installed stove, and that posed no threat to the health and safety of its inhabitants, would pass muster. Strict new codes applied only to future construction.

Two years after moving into the cabin, Leona and Max called it quits. "I had to make a choice," she remembers, "either to evict him or to leave. Because I knew that Max would never get his act together, I sold the house to him for $300, the amount it cost me to build, and moved out." Leaving Salmon Creek Farm, she made her way to San Francisco, there to put her creative talents to work as a street artist specializing in jewelry. While not exactly a step up a career ladder, her stint making bracelets and brooches at Fisherman's Wharf and on the sidewalks of Haight-Ashbury gave her a chance to figure out what she really wanted to do with her life. Considering her background, she had numerous options.

"I've had lots and lots of education," says Leona. An academic nomad, she dropped in and out of four different colleges and took seven years before she could lay claim to a B.A. in fine arts. Now, decades later, she's still dangling "just short" of a master's degree. Leona also braved courses in auto mechanics, woodworking, plastics, and metalworking. "I was the only woman in those classes," she says, "and it was hard to get to do my own work. The guys would always want to help me. I had to convince them that I was taking the class because I wanted to learn. I didn't want to watch someone else do it for me."

I didn't want to watch someone else do it for me. Leona's remark encapsulates what has been a basic tenet of her life, a kind of guide to action. Innate self-reliance disposed her to build her first cabin and explains why she returned to Salmon Creek Farm to build another one after a scant two years in San Francisco. In the city she missed the dubious charms of living without power or plumbing. She grew nostalgic for the long uphill treks carrying buckets of water from the creek and yearned once again to hitch her days to the rise and fall of the sun. She wanted to work the soil once more and hear the wind rustle the trees outside her window. But the real attraction of Salmon Creek Farm was the chance it afforded to pick up a hammer and saw again. Having once tasted the delights of designing and constructing a home, she could barely contain her urge to do it again. Therefore, back on the abandoned logging road once more, Leona set out to construct a second cabin, roughly the size of her first and only a stone's throw away.

Cabin number two has more panache than the first and is more consciously the creation of an artist. Long before becoming a builder, Leona had been a sculptor given to abstract acrylic assemblages composed of concave and convex surfaces that formed amorphous shapes and optical illusions—"Very L.A.," as she likes to say. Although her second cabin looks nothing like a museum piece, she dared to build it boldly. One exterior wall, like a bay window, faces in three directions. On her hip roof she constructed a gabled dormer. She installed tempered glass panels all around, so that in the daytime the rooms are perpetually flooded with light. "Floor-to-ceiling windows in the second story opened up the space," she says. "All of a sudden you'd want to sit on the carpeted floor to do yoga or enjoy the views of the canyon." On one end of the cabin Leona built a small deck and an eye-catching entry of vertical boards topped by an rounded Italianate arch. The door itself is hung with large wrought-iron strap hinges shaped like arrows in the colonial style. Both ends of the cabin are sided with diagonal tongue-and-groove redwood boards. "Since the cabin was so tall," she says, "I tried to make it really strong." Indeed, the rakish angle of the siding strengthens the building both structurally and visually.

Leona says she sought no help while erecting her new home except to raise walls and lift rafters. "I even taught myself to use a chain saw." Ignoring its roar and noxious exhaust, she handily cut girders and joists, accelerating construction to twentieth-century speed. It still took her half a year, the details and decorative touches gobbling up more time than she expected. Leona worked no less contentedly on her second home than on the first, but having taken greater pains to create a visual tour-de-force, derived greater satisfaction from its design than from its assembly.

To pay for materials, Leona continued to work as an artist. One of her early projects was *Country Women: Handbook for the New Farmer* by Jean Tetrault and Sherry Thomas. A thick volume of instructions for close-to-the-earth women on how to perform scores of homespun tasks, the book is profusely illustrated with Leona's line drawings of outhouses, chain saws, compost piles, septic systems, and other accoutrements of country life.

Her sharp eye and sure pen eventually led to other commissions. "An innkeeper in Albion asked me to create an advertisement for his inn," she reports. "He loved the ad I made for him and jokingly suggested that I start an ad agency so that his future ads would cost less to produce." Leona took the suggestion seriously. She probed the ins and outs of the business and founded Pacific Ridge Advertising, a one-person agency, now two decades old.

In the 1980s, as computers changed how ads are created, Leona faced a decision: to become digitally savvy or to quit the business. In order to stay current Leona needed technology. But knowing the consequences of going electronic—she already knew how power tools simultaneously speed the work and diminish the builder—she felt ambivalent. In the end, however, she caved in. "I learned to use a computer," she says,

"but lost part of the physical creativity I always found in drawing. A computer takes out much of the joy."

A mouse and modem, however, couldn't change Leona's
preference for working alone. Once, as an experiment, she
hired an assistant. But the burdens of being a boss weighed her
down and after two months she decided to work on her own
again. Not long ago she was invited by a graphic arts concern
in Fort Bragg, thirty miles up the coast, to merge her business
with theirs. "I was flattered but said no," she says. "Why
would I want a partnership? I have a lot of freedom now. I don't
have to work in an office and can travel whenever I want."
Leona, in fact, is just back from a month in Europe.

LOVE, THE POET DANTE TELLS US, can move the sun and
other stars. In 1978 it also moved Leona right out of her new
cabin, in which she had slept but two nights. Long before hammering the last nail, she had met and fallen for Jack Price, a
well-heeled widower with grown children and a rented house
in town. When she finished the cabin, therefore, she sold it and
made haste to Jack's, for all intents and purposes, ending her
career as a do-it-yourself builder.

It may have been a fortuitous move, because Leona was
about to take on a big-time building project too large and too
complicated to handle alone. It was a timber-frame barn meant
as a facility for Jack to stash his earthly goods, including his
collection of antique cars and twenty-two motorcycles, while
he and Leona sailed around the world. To save Jack the cost of
renting storage space, Leona volunteered to design a barn and
serve as general contractor during its construction.

Leona picked a site on the 140-acre tract that Jack owned
in the Albion highlands. As she drew plans, Jack repeatedly
looked over her shoulder and said, "No, it's too small. Make it
bigger." Jack wanted space, but more than that he wanted the
barn to be framed with used bridge timbers that he had once
bought. "He couldn't resist the deal," Leona says, "but he didn't
know what to do with them. They just sat there in a pile. So,
my plans included this bunch of twelve-by-twelve timbers

from a bridge in Oregon that had been torn down." The building Leona designed eventually spiraled into a forty-by-sixty-foot colossus with 4,600 square feet of floor space.

A carpenter using the proper equipment can frame a small post-and-beam house by himself, but on a building the size of Leona's barn, it wouldn't be much fun. Tree-sized pieces, some weighing eight or nine hundred pounds, give even experienced professional crews a run for their money. Timber framing is like that. It's not for the weak, the impatient, or the unskilled. The main timbers, peeled, planed to size, and precisely joined to assure the frame's strength and squareness, must be at least eight inches thick and strong enough to hold up both a large house and everything in it. Besides being muscular, the timbers that remain exposed as part of the interior decor must also look good. For a finished appearance, they need to be planed and oiled, and sometimes stained or varnished. As some have aptly said, a timber frame is like a piece of furniture on steroids.

To design the barn, Leona mined her knowledge of art and architecture and pulled out an eclectic style she calls California Gothic. The building—rustic, earth-toned, and rambling—consists of a three-story rectangle with large sheds attached like massive wings to both sides. From the Gothic tradition Leona drew high-peaked ceilings, clerestory windows, and an exuberance of detail such as leaded-glass windows, an octagonal window on each gable end, and elaborately carved doors and hinges.

The barn is only a ten-minute walk from Leona's present home. En route to see it Leona tells me about her experience as a general contractor. "I had trouble with some of my subs," she says. "It was a huge project, I was unlicensed, and some of the men had real trouble taking directions from a woman." In fact, Leona had to fire Richard, the head carpenter, not for any particular breech of courtesy, but for his generally resentful attitude. He just couldn't accept a woman boss. "My theory of building," Leona says, "is that you should enjoy it." Apparently Richard saw it otherwise.

Leona's barn consists of a three-story rectangle with large sheds at-
tached like massive wings to both sides.

Swishing toward the barn through knee-high grass, Leona
also tells me that partway through the barn's construction,
Tony, the new head carpenter, passed a remark to her and Jack
that set their building plan on a new course. Tony told them,
in effect, "With all due respect, you are out of your mind to use
a gorgeous storage facility for your belongings and live in an
old trailer. The barn should be your home." Leona and Jack
thought about Tony's words, agreed, and canceled their cruise.
Then they converted the barn into a residence, and, after their
marriage, lived there for almost a decade.

When Jack died of cancer in 1989, his children inherited the
building. Suddenly homeless but heir to some of Jack's acreage,
Leona set out to build the house she now calls home. She designed an economical, no-frills structure, easy on the eye and a
balm for the spirit. "It's a very simple house," she says, "one
rectangle with a shed on the side. And half of the rectangle is
two stories high—no odd angles, nothing complicated." Yet,
the house is more dashing than Leona suggests. Maybe it's the
dual pitch of the upper and lower roofs or perhaps the wide-
brimmed eaves and visible rafter ends that dramatize this bit of

rural landscape. Certainly the house derives a degree of visual grace from its decks: a second-story sundeck on one end, a glass-enclosed deck off the living room at the other, and a third that spans the rear of the house.

Leona declares, "In my design for this house, proportion was very important." Inside, she points to the ten-foot-high living room and its vaulted ceiling. "These are very tall walls," she says, "but the space doesn't feel awkward because of its relative width and length." If the room were narrower, one would feel dwarfed, lost in towering emptiness. Instead, Leona has created space that has rapport with its occupants. Like the house and its setting, the room is bold, yet balanced and serene. Leona remarks, "It gives you a sense of well-being, of feeling good to be here."

The house combines extreme good looks with everyday practicality—not a minor achievement for a self-taught architect like Leona. The cabins she built at Salmon Creek Farm had been circumscribed by the terrain, the size of the site, and—at least for the first cabin—Leona's limited technical expertise and a shoestring budget. The barn had been designed as a warehouse. On this house, though, Leona had *carte blanche*. With no constraints (except money) and infinite possibilities, she faced a more daunting challenge by far. Where do you begin when choices are unlimited? As an artist and a sculptor she had designed and fabricated three-dimensional objects before, but none meant to both attract the eye and be put to use in her day-to-day life for years to come.

Spurred by the challenge, Leona used a technique she calls "inside-out" design. That is to say, before drawing a line on paper, she measured her furniture and thought a lot about house details that tended to give her soul a lift. "That was better than designing a house in the abstract and then adapting your life to the plans you drew," she explains. "So, basically, the house was built to fit my furniture and to fit me." Put another way, Leona's bed, dressers, dining room table, breakfront, and every other stick of furniture virtually preordained the dimensions and shape of each room. She doled

out space generously. "You can never have too much room,"
she believes. Also, because Leona is tall, she had tall cabinets
built for her kitchen. The counters are higher than the customary thirty-six inches. "I love them," she says. "I don't have to
bend over to do dishes." Leona is especially pleased with the
design of the bathroom. "It's in the center of the house," she
points out, "and is accessible from both the bedroom and the
living area." Actually, the bathroom is a mini-suite. "My
daughter told me, 'Mom, don't put the toilet in same room as
the shower.' I took her advice. Guests can use the bathroom
while I take a shower. It's very convenient—like having two
bathrooms."

Leona keeps an office upstairs. Accessed via both an inside
and an outside staircase, the second floor also contains a private studio apartment, occupied at present by her grandson,
Ted, the twenty-year-old child of Jack's daughter. Leona is content to live on the ground floor. In fact, she says, "I planned the
house with the idea that I could be an old lady here." Yet
she also thinks about possibly spending her dotage in a community. "Not a group home," she says, "but in a place you can
live separately on some land with a central house and with
communal meals, a communal shop, and communal gardens
and greenhouse." Long ago, at Salmon Creek Farm, Leona
learned that, by joining together people tend to conserve resources, from gasoline to firewood. "Living communally,"
Leona continues, "is living in concert with the Earth, treating
it with the respect it deserves." For the time being, though,
Leona claims the house is perfect for her. She could do no better anywhere.

Such perfection wasn't easily won. Short of driving the
nails herself, Leona could not have been more deeply immersed
in building the house. She got the permits, ordered the materials, engaged subs, checked the work every step of the way,
and stood by as chief problem-solver. She also chose the
builder, and during interviews for the job, laid out her expecta-
tions. "I want to enjoy the process," she told each applicant.

"One contractor informed me that he had lots of building
ideas and was interested in hearing mine," Leona recalls. "But

then he said, 'Lady, if I'm going to build this house, my ideas have to be paramount.'"

Leona glared at the man homicidally and gave him a curt, "Good day."

The builder she picked, Rob Kirby, was a man she could trust. "He was an artist," Leona says, "very visual—like me. In fact, if you took the Sheetrock off these walls you'd see lots of drawings of things we figured out together as we went along."

Rob sometimes scratched his head over Leona's plans. She wanted angled rafter tails with a quasi-Oriental look along the eaves.

"Impossible," Rob told Leona. "The angle of the rafter tails can't be the same as the angle of the main rafters on a dual-pitched roof. It can't be done the way you say."

"I think it can," she responded. "If I make one out of foam board, can you build it out of wood?"

"Of course," Rob replied.

Leona set to work with foam board and an X-Acto knife and thirty minutes later presented Rob with a model of the "clip-on" rafter tail she had envisioned.

Word of Leona's design talents has spread along the Mendocino coast. From time to time, friends about to build or renovate a house seek her advice. She walks their land with them, points out favorable building sites and barrages them with questions: Do they like to cook? Meditate? Play bridge? Do they have big parties? Do they need a studio, a solarium, a sauna? Would they rather view the sun coming up or do they prefer to watch it set? Once she understands the tone and tempo of their lives, she draws a floor plan. "I do it infor- mally," she says, "just a pencil sketch to show their architect. Some have actually built the house exactly as I drew it on a scrap of paper torn from a notebook."

In all, Leona has built or designed six homes and left her imprint on the design of several more. A generation from now, however, no one will know it. She's never left a mes- sage or memento behind, not even her initials inscribed in wet concrete. "That's not important to me," she says. "I don't sign my artwork either and rarely put my agency's name on my publications." Leona would rather let her work speak for itself. "A house is either attractive or it's not, and knowing who designed all or part of it won't change that." Leona has a point. The stamp of a big-name architect can alter the way we perceive a house or building. A work by "anon." stands or falls on its merits.

Explaining further why she shrinks from public recognition, Leona says, "Building just isn't an ego thing for me. I remember that during the construction of the barn, Jack and Tony the carpenter signed the inside walls, but I didn't. That's not my style." She also reveals that for years the Mendocino Arts Center consistently asked to include her home and backyard on its annual Garden Tour. For years she declined. Recently, however, she finally agreed—but with reluctance. It's not that she isn't proud of her work. She's just not sentimental about it. "Basically, I'm a practical person," she declares. "I don't feel a lot of attachment to this house or to any of the other houses I built. If necessity forced me to leave and build another house, I could do it without shedding a tear."

LEONA'S READINESS TO PICK up and move on stands to reason. It's the course you'd expect from a woman who built two houses and who made a point insofar as possible to build them without help. I'm momentarily struck by a trifling coincidence: Leona—surnamed Walden—lives on the shore of a sylvan pond. Like Thoreau, the consummate individualist, she protects her independence passionately. Her vacillation on the telephone, I realize later, had nothing to do with either Californian nonchalance or an artistic temperament as I had briefly supposed. Rather, Leona instinctively steers clear of unnecessary entanglements. She savors freedom and is wary of anyone or anything that may complicate her life, including, I suppose, interviews with oddball authors from New York.

A house, especially one you built yourself, can enslave you emotionally, but Leona won't let herself be bound. As someone infatuated with personal freedom, she keeps cuddly feelings for her house in check. What's more, she cites deeply philosophical reasons for maintaining loose ties. "I'm caretaking it," she says, "and I'm caretaking the land around it. It's all on loan to me." In short, she subscribes to a spiritual belief, widely held in Native American cultures, that we have been granted temporary stewardship of our lands. "I have some Indian blood in me," Leona says, as though to justify her view. "Maybe that's why I feel that I don't own this land. Yes, I own it legally but in the cosmic sense I don't. I just happen to be the lucky person who's borrowing it and paying the bills."

As the interim custodian of her land, Leona feels obliged to protect it. To illustrate her point, she takes a book from her shelf. It is a treatise on hand-made houses entitled *Dwelling* by an author who goes by the name River and who discusses at length the relationship between man and nature. River, a founder of Salmon Creek Farm, urges readers to treat the Earth tenderly. In particular, she espouses the construction of simple, virtually biodegradable, dwellings. "Build no house," writes River, "that will permanently scar the land or interrupt the flow and cycles of natural life."

River's ideas and intense spirituality have rubbed off on Leona, although she is quick to assert, "I'm not particularly spiritual, not when it comes to building." A moment later, though, she backs up: "No, that's not quite true," she says. "On some levels I am. I have one foot on either side of the fence. I've loved building a home and a garden. But to do it, I've had three acres of woodland cleared. The lumber and siding for this house—mostly fir but also a couple of downed logs of old-growth redwood—have come from my own land. As a result, there are three acres of trees that don't exist any more. That bothers me."

Not all home builders share Leona's concern for the environment. As a matter of conscience, bona fide save-the-Earth types won't use ecologically hostile building materials such as Styrofoam, particle board, urethane, pressure-treated lumber, or anything else laced with toxic chemicals. Many other do-it-yourselfers pay lip service to clean air and water, deplore lumbering on federal lands, and snarl a bit about clear-cuts, but you'll find them at the Home Depot on Saturday mornings loading two-by-fours into their SUVs. Leona, on the other hand, is genuinely vexed about razing a thousand trees to build her house. "I feel terribly guilty," she says. "I occupy a big space on the Earth and use up vast amounts of resources. So, I continually ask myself what I can do to make up for it."

Until she returns someday to communal life, Leona eases her conscience by sharing her bounty with others. In particular, she has opened her home to her grandson Ted. She tells me that Ted had been reared by troubled, eccentric parents in hyper-primitive conditions: "not even an outhouse; he had to go dig a hole in the woods." Given the chance to offer him a genteel sanctuary, Leona has embraced it. It makes her feel virtuous and, as she says, "justifies having this nice house."

She's also reached out to the local populace, offering neighbors the use of her pond. "At one time the pond was off limits," she says, "but ever since Jack and I owned it, it has become the old neighborhood swimming hole. I like to think that it doesn't belong to me but to everyone." Hoping that neighbors would continue to flock to the pond even after her house was built, Leona chose a site close to but not directly at the water's edge. "From my windows," she points out, "I see swimmers only when they're out in middle. I don't disturb them and they don't disturb me. We live in harmony with each other. It feels good to be able to share. If I had to keep it all to myself, I'd have a real hard time."

A Work in Progress

A byline blurb for a This Old House *magazine article about cabinet and door hinges noted that the author, George Nash, was building his own shingle-style house in a small mid-coast Maine town. As the owner of a few well-thumbed copies of Nash's books, I knew him to be well-acquainted with the spiritual content of building. His "how-to" manuals make clear that renovating old houses and do-it-yourself home building are in large measure inner pursuits that focus the mind and nourish the soul. In fact, Nash's writing put in my head the notion that, if America's weekend builders ever required the services of a spiritual foreman, he'd be the best man for the job.*

Suspecting that Nash would have a good deal to say about his current building project, I e-mailed him a letter that described my plans for this book. In response, he invited me to visit him and his house.

In Orland, Maine, April is the season for mud, a fact I discover on the bright morning I sink my Hertz rental into the clay strip of ruts and puddles that George calls his driveway. Waiting nearby in his pickup, George sees me stuck, then leaps from the cab and leans his thick, compact body—175 pounds and built like a fire hydrant—into my Mazda's hood. His push gives me just enough purchase to back onto the road

*again but not before my spinning tires muddy the legs of his
jeans but good.*

*"Don't worry, I'm used to it," he says, standing shoetop-
deep in brown soup.*

GEORGE'S BUILDING SITE LIES at the end of a three-
hundred-foot driveway, past broom straw meadows stretched
out on both sides. Where the trees begin I see what amounts to
George's new house.

Actually, there's not much to see. Only a concrete footing
and on this occasion an adolescent boy struggling with a crowbar to dislodge cement-encrusted form boards from the outside
edge of the concrete. The boards, half-buried in dirt, resist the
boy's best efforts. "That's my neighbor's kid," George says.
"It's his first day on the job." Considering the progress he's
making, the kid is in for a long first day.

George points to a large slab of poured concrete that lies
between the footings and the front-door steps of a house
trailer. "That'll be the floor of our entry and mudroom," he explains. Gesturing toward mounds of earth and some giant
boulders, he adds, "There's the main part of the house, and
here, where the trailer is, that's the garage and workshop. It'll
make more sense when I show you the model I built," he says,
scraping mud from his boots on the edge of the slab.

Inside the trailer, George holds up a cardboard rendering of
his house-to-be and says, "I made this because I couldn't visualize the roofline." His fingers run over the model's meander-
ing hip roof, its series of gabled dormers and a shed-like
extension over a wraparound porch. "Fitting all the parts together was tricky," he adds.

To build the roof will be trickier still, for George intends to
flare its bottom edges pagoda-style. "I like little touches like
that," he says. He explains further that the house will consist
of two modules joined by an enclosed breezeway that contains
an entry hall, a mudroom, and a utility area "where you can
take a shower and dump your dirty clothes." Turn left at the
entrance and you'll go toward the main section of the house, a

one-and-a-half-story structure with a country kitchen and the usual array of living spaces, plus guest rooms, a porch, and two areas for work—one a project room for George's wife Jane Waterman, the other a cubicle where George will do his writing. A turn to the right at the front door will take you to the garage, to a storage area, and to George's 320-square-foot workshop.

"This trailer has been home since last fall," George says while serving up mugs of Lemon-Berry Zinger at the kitchen table. "We used to own a house nearby but sold it and rented a cabin down the river a couple of miles from here. We planned to live there while the house was under construction."

From the living room sofa Jane picks up the narrative. "But we couldn't stand living in a rental. It was too confining. We go crazy if we can't putter around, go outside and do little landscaping projects. After two months we moved to the trailer. It would be scruffier, but at least we'd be on our own."

"Scruffier and more primitive," George continues. "For weeks the trailer was parked in a field while I cleared this site. It leaned a foot and a half from one side to the other. We camped inside with no power and no heat except for a little propane heater and a tiny cook stove. We were in our twenties again: no running water and shitting into a bucket on the floor."

Jane, an offstage chorus, comments, "That's what we all did back then. It was normal." But now she grants that, as a pair of grandparent boomers, she and George have probably chosen a "pretty eccentric way to behave."

George agrees. "Financially and structurally we're still in our late twenties. I'm fifty this year. Sometimes I tell myself that I'm too old for this. But I am pumped up to build our house. I've built houses for lots of other people. Finally, I have a chance to build one for us, and I'm going to do it the way I want."

The way George wants, however, isn't the way it's been— so far, at any rate. "I started in mid-October, when Maine weather is usually pretty decent," he explains. "But last fall it was terrible. November was like the dead of winter. It shut me down, leaving me far from where I expected to be. Two days before Christmas it happened to be warm enough to pour the concrete footings. But that night the temperature dropped again, so we poured the slab in nineteen-degree cold. The job lasted until two in the morning."

Wet concrete is extremely sensitive to cold. If the water freezes before the concrete hardens, a wall can crumble like bleu cheese. To shorten the concrete's set-up time, George added calcium chloride to the mix. He also used a type of Portland cement that generates heat while curing. Like other builders in sub-freezing cold, George heated the water and the gravel, then wrapped the poured concrete into a layer of foam board and polyethylene that, like a cozy on a teapot, keeps warmth from escaping.

Had last fall's weather been less unruly, George might have had a foundation wall and a first floor deck in place. "I could have been framing by now," he says, "and I would have had the house closed in during the summer. Jane and I then could have moved in by this Christmas." But El Niño, crossed stars, bad karma—or whatever—savaged George's plans. His voice suddenly turning plaintive, he declares, "I ought to know it's crazy to have an artificial deadline. I've already done that too often. Besides, I hate having schedules forced down my throat."

Brightening again, George adds, "This time I'm going to do it my way. I'm going to build it right." Not *right* in the sense of *correct*, he explains—adhering to standard construction practices—but "right" according to his own taste and temperament. At present, with the house still in gestation, he is charged with possibilities, foreseeing in perfect detail how the design, look, and feel of the house will be an expression of who he is and what he has become in half a century of life. George's musings about home building imply that, for him, the construction of a house springs from an inner necessity to create. "The moral order has been replaced by the technical order, intuitions with institutions, beatitudes by bureaucracy," he writes in one of his books. "We build our cathedrals in our backyard and find transcendence at the hearts of our homes." As he builds his new home George is making a bid for a transcendent adventure. He is bent on tapping into some sort of flow of divine energy, or, as he puts it—since he's not disposed to religiosity—"to feel an inward grace."

George is no stranger to such spiritual high jinks on the work site. He's fond of recalling a distant summer on an island off Nova Scotia where he had under his wing a group of teenagers from a work camp. In one month, they intended to build a log cabin using only hand tools—adzes, hatchets, drawknives. He had just put in a beam to support the loft and started to flatten it with a steel broadax. "I was hewing the top," he says, "when all of a sudden it hit me that for the last twenty minutes I had been doing it effortlessly, perfectly, and without any awareness of myself and my surroundings. It was a *satori* moment. Wham! It just struck me—a perfect fusion of action and mind, with no ego or intellect to get in the way. Of course the minute I realized it, I was back to normal. But it was beautiful while it lasted."

Such episodes don't often happen when you build to put bread on your table, as George did for eighteen years as a professional contractor. Nothing kills an existential epiphany like the pressure of an approaching deadline, a shiftless work crew, or an architect you'd like to strangle because, in George's words, he's "an egotistical little prick who doesn't know anything about building." No, professionals, unlike most amateur builders, focus on getting the job done and going on to the next one. "Especially young ambitious carpenters," says George, remembering a slice of the past when he worked alongside an old Vermonter named Russell Martin who believed that speed was not the end-all of building. "One day I was nailing blocking between some studs. Because the blocks were too long, I slammed them into position, beating the shit out of them with my hammer. The old-timer noticed my intensity and said, 'Hey, take it easy, George. If you're going to do this all your life, you might as well try to have a good time. Take the blocks out and cut 'em shorter. Don't be in such a damn hurry.'" George heard Russell's message, but slightly short on self-restraint, couldn't always heed it. Nonetheless, George was grateful enough to dedicate one of his books on old-house rehabbing to Russell, "who taught me to slow down and enjoy." As George approaches the age of the man he once called an old-timer, he finally understands the wisdom behind Russell's words.

And none too soon, because plans for the house he has started to build outside the trailer have recently been upended by Jane's unexpected decision to switch career paths. Jane is a physician. After years as a hospital staffer, she is about to start a private practice in nearby Bucksport, and George must convert a *fin-de-siècle* Victorian house into a doctor's office for her. "Renovating Jane's office is my priority," he says. "Jane makes a lot more money than I do, so it makes sense to get her off and running." In short, the house—along with its promise of spiritual pleasures and satisfactions—will have to wait.

No wonder that George ignores his neighbor's son struggling to peel the boards off the footings outside. The boy has weeks to finish the job. Eight of them, to be exact, for George expects to be renovating Jane's office for the next two months. "I'll mobilize a large crew of the right people," he says, "and do a complete rip-and-tear job."

"If I know George," says Jane, as she unfurls architectural drawings at the kitchen table, "he'll do most of the work himself."

Her drawings show an office suite and waiting room on the first floor and two rental apartments upstairs. "The job is much more complex than building a house," she says, "because it's a commercial building. The codes are much stricter, and the ADA rules are impossible." (She is alluding to the Americans with Disabilities Act, which requires ramps and other facilities for the handicapped to be installed in public buildings.) Jane resents being forced to locate a storage area on the main floor rather than in the basement solely to accommodate a hypothetical future employee unable to climb stairs. According to ADA guidelines, buildings with basement storerooms require an elevator, an installation that Jane can't afford right now.

Indeed, money is her most pressing concern. "The bank will lend me only 75 percent of what I need because the appraiser can't find a good 'comp,'" a recently sold comparable house used to assign a fair market value to hers. Now she's worried. No financing means no job, or at least, no independent medical practice for a while.

George and Jane feel caught in a Chekhovian drama. The characters, longing to begin what they've termed their "second life," find themselves in gridlock. She yearns to start work as a family doctor but can't. He'd like to build their house but won't—not until she starts to work. Two people in quasi-crisis. "This was going to be the original sane project," says George, shaking his head. "I planned to devote a year to the house. After that, I was going to settle down and write. While Jane practiced medicine, I'd work on my novel."

AS A YOUNG MAN GEORGE was a carpenter, then the co-owner of a home-building business in rural Morrisville, Vermont. "We were a big fish in a small pond," George says with pride. "We had twenty-six employees and sometimes built twenty to thirty houses a year." That line of work was something he had never considered while growing up in Hamden, Connecticut, although he might have guessed that building would somehow become a major theme in his life. "We built our own house in Hamden," George recalls. "My grandfather was a roofer. When I was seven, he'd bring home loads of old boards. I'd pull the nails out and get a big pat on the head. By the time I was ten, I was crawling around on roofs every weekend." As a teen George insulated apartment houses after school. "My father's best friend owned an insulation company," he explains. "I still remember the constant itching. Of all building jobs, I hate insulating the most. The smell alone makes me cringe."

At eighteen, George entered Wesleyan College, where, intending to be a writer, he majored in English. For his senior thesis he wrote something he thought was a novel but which he now calls "an incomprehensible mess." Today he is a professional writer, although he's earned the bulk of his fortune doing other things. While in college George found weekend work in the theater and dance department of Sarah Lawrence College in Bronxville, New York. He built sets, rigged lights, worked on sound—a one-man tech crew. After graduation he drifted west, where his bachelor's degree in English managed to land him a job in an Oakland, California, scrap yard. He operated a grinder. "We shipped ground-up American cars to Japan," he recalls, "and they sent them back as Toyotas." Within a year he returned to Sarah Lawrence for more behind-the-scenes work. A natural techie ("It's in my blood"), he was so skilled that he found himself turning down an invitation to join a prestigious theater group about to embark on a grand European tour.

Instead he followed his girlfriend, Dai Kappel, to Vermont. Dai's brother-in-law ran a real estate and home-building business near Stowe and offered George an apprenticeship in carpentry. On the job he met Russell, the grizzled, common-sense Vermonter, and Albert Bedell, a part-time game warden who taught him a lot about building and even more about life. "They were great," says George.

George's father, however, could find no greatness whatsoever in his son's career choice. He couldn't fathom why anyone with a top-of-the-line education would want to saw wood and bang nails for a living. "To him my job was just another in a long string of disappointments," George recalls. "I was nearly thirty before we could talk to each other civilly." Years later, George wrote in the dedication of *Do-It-Yourself Housebuilding*, his 700-plus-page house-building book: "For Dad. This is the answer to your question, if I wanted to be a carpenter, why did I spend four years in college?"

On weekdays George toiled for Dai's brother-in-law, at other times for Dai, restoring to useful life her derelict old house in which he was a tenant, lover, and resident rehabber. In three years he was finished with both the house and with

Dai. "My fanaticism destroyed our relationship," George confesses. "The work became more important than the reason it was being done. When she raised my rent, I cashed out my equity and left."

With him he took a wealth of information about rehabbing time-worn houses, enough indeed to eventually turn his knowledge into a book, *Old Houses: A Rebuilder's Manual*. In the book George airs his views on matters from sagging floors to solar heating. He shows why resurrecting a cast-off house "is a profoundly spiritual as well as physical undertaking." Much of the practical wisdom in the book he derived from his work on Dai's house. The bulk of it, though, he gathered from men he calls "old country carpenters."

"Their pool of knowledge," George writes in the introduction, "has remained largely inaccessible to the novice builder." He observes that their collective wisdom, part of an oral and manual tradition learned and passed on by generations of carpenters, is being lost in the rush of mass-manufacture and high-tech home building. "Once the cycle started," he notes with regret, "the old ways were tossed aside and simply forgotten, like the rubbish heap at the edge of the sugar woods." In *Old Houses*, he attempts to preserve that slice of a disappearing culture.

Writers understand that the first commandment of their trade is "Know your subject." George took that dictum to heart. He chose not merely to write about country carpenters, he decided to become one. In pursuit of the authentic experience, he put a down payment on sixty-eight acres of Vermont wilderness and set up shop as a part-time carpenter and a part-time homesteader. "My place was nine miles from town at the end of a long dirt road," he recalls. "With a generator and a Skilsaw, I built a sixteen-by-twenty-foot cabin. I worked for nine days, twenty hours a day, until it was done. I was young and crazy at the time." The cabin was meant to be temporary quarters. Some day, using income earned as a carpenter, George planned to construct a more permanent home. The day arrived sooner than he expected because he met and married

Jane, acquiring with a simple, "I do," a wife and three kids. (Later he and Jane would have a fourth.) "Therefore," George says, "I had to build more and build it fast."

The cabin gradually morphed into a sprawling family complex—a main house and several out-buildings. "There was only an abandoned field when I got there," he boasts. "I made something real out of nothing." Describing the house, George turns rapturous, like a poet reciting an elegy. "The house had a curving roof like a Japanese farmhouse. The front flowed into a rounded greenhouse that curled around three sides, and its long covered portico led to the barn. Inside, the house had wonderful little touches such as a staircase that was really a sculpture made of big beautiful slabs of hardwood that had been sitting in a neighbor's barn for a generation. The stringer was a three-inch-thick slab of a pine-tree trunk. For railings I split a cherry tree down the middle. Wood was everywhere—all polished and very sensual."

Although George basks in the memory of his home on the land, he can't recall anything particularly blissful about being a homesteader. "Homesteading is not a way of life," George says. "It's an expensive hobby, that's all. Jane and I couldn't have supported our homesteading habit unless we had worked outside the home." Jane, a trained midwife at the time, delivered half a dozen babies a month, and George hired himself out as a journeyman carpenter.

"Building jobs kept falling into my lap," he says, and before I knew it I had a partner, Trim Conklin. Suddenly, we were running a company—Conklin-Nash Builders." Regardless of what he did all day, however, George couldn't get out of his head that he was a writer first and a builder second. He wrote how-to articles and also gathered material that eventually found its way into his books. "I never intended to be a contractor," he adds.

As an author-builder, George fit neatly into the corps of bright, idealistic college grads of the early '70s for whom the construction site held more appeal than the corporate office or law firm. As George describes it, "Building attracted an influx of overeducated, Ivy League types like me. We rejected the standard way of doing things. My first framing crew consisted of Harvard, Northwestern, Wesleyan, and Yale alumni. They had more advanced degrees than you could shake a stick at." George's associates didn't talk guns or fishing over the quiche and Perrier they brought in lunch buckets, they'd hold physics colloquia. On the job, they listened to music. Not heavy metal or rock. "That's too distracting," says George. "Rather, I brought tapes of Vivaldi and Mozart. When I hear Mozart, I always feel little fingers massaging my brain."

Whether he was influenced by *Eine Kleine Nachtmusik* or inspired by *Figaro* remains unclear, but George claims to have developed into "a helluva good framer." He can visualize the anatomy of a house. "I don't need drawings," he says, "but solve structural problems without puzzling about them. I take it on faith that the solutions will come to me. I can just feel them."

George regards framing the preeminent building craft. "It's poetry," he says. "I love the way rafters look silhouetted against the sky. They are incredibly dramatic. In raising something to the heavens, you see the archetype of defiance. By lifting out of the earth something that by nature wants to go back down again, you make a Promethean statement." Forming a triangle in the air with his fingers, George emphasizes, "Everything in carpentry is built on this shape: opposing forces in equilibrium, a perfect balance. I admire that tension." To celebrate the achievement of such perfection, George follows the centuries-old building tradition of nailing a small evergreen tree or bush to the peak of the frame after the last nail has been driven, a ritual said to pay homage to the forest for its beneficence. "It's a powerful custom," says George. "I'm always moved by it."

Did George's crews revere the work as much as he did? "Some of them talked about it," he remembers, "but even if they said nothing, they felt it. Let me put it this way: They knew the dance." George elaborates with an anecdote about a four-man framing ensemble on a bitter cold day in Vermont:

"The work was flying. Everyone was focused on building the floor platform. Each person knew the others' functions intimately. Hardly a word passed among us. It was as though we'd been choreographed. The faultless cadences of that moment have stayed with me. Anyone who works on a good crew knows what a dance carpentry can be."

For George, timber framing, the oldest of building techniques, is more lyrical still. He calls it "sort of meditative." Cutting tenons and mortises, the "male" and "female" components of a timber-framed joint, is like an ancient ritual. "As the wood chips fly, you feel connected to artisans of ages past. There's no practical reason to do timber framing," he goes on. "You do it to make a spiritual statement. There's something magnificent about using large pieces of trees hewn from the forest instead of skinny little two-by-fours processed in a lumber mill. The beauty of it lies in taking a super-sharp chisel and this really massive timber and making joints so precise you can't slip a piece of paper inside. You start with really rough and heavy timbers and make them come together—like Whump! That's what I call amazingly satisfying work."

Satisfying but slow. That's why, after contracting for three timber-frame houses, George devised what he terms a hybrid system. "People like exposed beams in the ceiling," he explains, "but not tacky, fake beams." His system combines a stick-built frame—that is, "two-by" dimensional lumber—with real six-by-eight or eight-by-eight timbers. The walls carry mortised beams that remain partly in view after the interior is finished. Pieces are connected by simple lap joinery and secured not by customary wooden pins or dowels but by short lengths of half-inch steel reinforcing bars—a compromise George was willing to make for the sake of efficiency. "It looks just like a timber house but is much faster, easier—and, therefore, cheaper—to build," he says.

George also pioneered an economical wall-framing technique. Instead of two-by-sixes—ordinarily specified by residential building codes to provide space inside wall cavities for five and a half inches of insulation—George used two-by-fours that

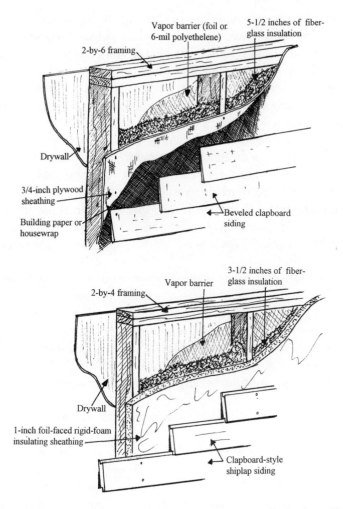

The anatomy of an exterior wall. Top, a conventionally built wall; bottom, George's money- and time-saving innovation.

he sheathed with an inch of rigid foam board. He says, "It was the cheapest wall you could build and still have an R-19 insulation rating." Over the foam George nailed boards of cedar siding. He ordered the boards cut with a square notch, or rabbet, along the top and bottom edges. Milled that way, the boards could be mounted on the house with the square-cut lip of the upper piece overlapping the piece below. Viewed from a distance, the siding looks like traditional New England clapboard. "But," says George proudly, "it goes up a lot faster because it is basically self-leveling once the first course is in." In contrast, each course of standard clapboard siding must individually leveled—a slow, painstaking procedure.

Such innovations kept George and his business partner, Trim Conklin, a step ahead of their competitors. But staying in front stole more of George's time and energy than he could afford. Unable to write or to enjoy a semblance of family life, he felt trapped. When he told Trim he had to reapportion priorities—90 percent for the business, the rest for himself—Trim shot back, "That's not good enough. You've got to give 110 percent."

"If that's the case," George responded, "you can have it; it's all yours." He sold his share of the business to Trim and walked away, leaving behind a company with more than two-dozen workers and over a million dollars in annual receipts.

Sprung from his partnership, he declared himself a "housing consultant," a jack-of-all-building trades. He doled out advice to home builders, supervised contractors' crews, and taught owner-building courses at the New Agey Vermont Institute of Community Involvement. At home he worked on a book, wrote how-to articles, and watched the kids while Jane commuted to classes at the University of Vermont. For a year the family went to Amherst, Massachusetts, where Jane studied biochemistry, and during Jane's residency in an Arizona hospital, the family lived in suburban Phoenix. Since skillful builders are needed everywhere, George readily found work, although for two of the three years in the Southwest he channeled his adrenaline primarily into his magnum opus, *Do-It-Yourself Housebuilding*, published in 1995.

By then George had decided to give up professional building. He had reached the proverbial last straw during a house-framing job for a young woman and her difficult boyfriend. He quarreled with them about money, work schedules, and the quality of his building crew. Then they had words over a design detail. Accusations of dishonesty sent George to the brink of dropping the job altogether. "Finally," George says, "when the boyfriend called me a goddamn shyster, I looked at him and said, 'I'm outta here. I haven't worked eighteen years to take this kind of shit from you or anybody else. If you don't like it, frame your own damn house, I'm done!' I was so pissed that I picked up a 200-pound radial-arm saw and threw it into the back of my truck." Within hours he had struck the set, carting away tools, scaffolding, lumber, and himself—never again to sign another building contract.

In George's view adversarial relationships spoiled what could have been a congenial career. "The work is inherently enjoyable," he says, "but no matter how good your reputation, you have to prove your competence and honesty to every new client. Contracting would be better if clients just let you do your job. Hell, they hired you, they should trust your judgment."

By contrast, do-it-yourselfers dwell in builder heaven. George writes in *Do-It-Yourself Housebuilding*, "Short of having a baby . . . there's little else most of us can do in our lives that involves a greater commitment, requires more energy and expense, or is potentially more rewarding than building one's own house. This is one reason why even people who can afford to do otherwise still choose to build their homes."

But, according to George, the most compelling reason to be an owner-builder is for the joy of it. "Homebuilding," he writes, "represents a convergence of cultural values and self-expression. By giving public shape to private dreams, it's a creative, challenging, and socially valued form of applied art." In George's opinion almost anyone can build a house. "It's not that hard," he says. "It requires some aptitude and skill, but the mechanics are pretty straightforward. While not everything meets the eye, it's not a great mystery either."

Truly, there's nothing mysterious about George's seventy-step home-building process—laid out in the first chapter of his book. George says he wrote the book "by osmosis," letting the knowledge he assimilated as a builder and renovator flow onto the page. A complete guide, weighing more than three pounds in paperback, the book takes readers from choosing a building site to throwing a housewarming bash. George will often refer to his own instructions when he gets around to building his house. He doesn't trust himself to remember everything in the book's 704 pages.

"I enjoy writing more than building," he says, "although it's much harder. When I sit down to write, it may take hours to get the first sentence down. But after that I'm gone and I won't stop 'til two in the morning." In writing mode he doesn't talk or hear what people say to him, "a situation that tends to strain a marriage," he observes. To me, George the writer sounds strangely like George the builder. "That's true," he says, "I tend to be pretty obsessive." He cites a case in point—his latest book, *Fences*. With the deadline coming fast and but a third of the manuscript done—"Jane's illness had set me back," he says—the publishers, Taunton Press, summoned him to their Newtown, Connecticut, headquarters. "They locked me in a room with a computer, brought me food and told me where the bathroom was. For two weeks I wrote every day until I got too groggy to continue. I loved every minute of it," George says.

While researching the role of fences in America, George read colonial treatises on agriculture. His reading ignited an interest in Squanto, the Indian famous for befriending the Pilgrims and later becoming an English gentleman, a warrior, a prisoner of the Spanish, and a cultural oddity. Now George aches to turn Squanto's story into a historical novel. "I have the plot all blocked out," he says. "I even know the first line." But he recognizes that fiction writing must wait. Instead, he'll record in words and photos the construction of his new house. From the effort, he'll extract several publishable articles and perhaps another how-to book.

Whether the house, now barely risen above the excavation floor, may one day fulfill George and Jane's vision of what a home should be remains to be seen. Jane says that she once longed to live in a rejuvenated handyman's special, a desire fueled perhaps by some of George's more evocative prose. In *Renovating Old Houses* he writes, "Like woodsmoke from the cooking fire that has been absorbed into the plaster, the rooms and walls of old houses are suffused with the spirits of former inhabitants. All old houses are full of ghosts." George goes on, "For me, it is this spiritual dimension, above all, that makes the renovation of old houses so deeply satisfying."

Since he wrote those words smoked plaster and ghosts seem to have lost their allure. Immune to his own rhetoric, he chose to build a brand new "old house." He'll run utility lines underground, put in remotely activated radiant floor heat, build his own tiled hot tub, fill gaps and crannies with rigid foam board, and use every other bit of cutting-edge home-building technology he can think of, but in the end he expects the new house to look as though it's been standing on its site for generations.

It will be a classic nineteenth-century shingle-style house. "But with no wood shingles," he points out. "Clapboard is cheaper, faster to install, and more typical of the Maine coast. Around here, there's a fittingness to it." Like most owner-builders, George takes seriously the notion that a house ought to fit into its setting. He says, "A building affects the landscape for a long time. That's why so much modern architecture pisses me off. It makes beautiful landscape ugly. Shopping centers, for example. There's no inherent reason they have to be so butt-ugly." Warming to the topic, he stabs the air with his hands. Eyes flashing behind his round-rimmed glasses, he asks rhetorically, "Don't people realize that ugliness affects them, that unattractive surroundings diminish their lives? Don't they realize there's got to be congruence between your inner life, your house, and your environment?"

George tells me that, if nothing else, his house will be damned sure to harmonize with its surroundings. While planning the house he rummaged through every corner of his heavily wooded lot studying the prevailing colors like a painter planning his palette. For the siding of the house he's chosen a stain of pale green-gray, the same as lichen. For the trim, he'll use a reddish-brown, like the trunks of cedar trees. No garish green lawn will clash with the subtle hues of the house and setting. Rather the yard will be pine needles. "It just rains that stuff around here," he says. The grounds will be landscaped with a rock garden and will have ornamental conifers along walking trails that wind through twelve acres of woodland that reach almost to a tidal inlet of the nearby Penobscot River. "The woods will be filled with lots of little surprises and magical spots," George says. "That's what woods are, well, kind of trippy. You know—the old wood-sprite notion. You'll wander down the trail and think you see something. When you turn around there's a face carved into a tree trunk, a little statue standing in a Zen garden off to the side, or a sculpture lodged in the crook of a tree. I've got a trailer full of funky found objects to place all around."

The house itself won't match the whimsicality of the grounds, but its design will nonetheless reflect George's attachment to the house he built a quarter of a century ago in a Vermont meadow. Mimicking the homestead, the structure-in-the-making will curve up the eaves. It won't be a clone of the old house but will be garnished with equivalent splendors. "God is in the details," asserted the architect Mies van der Rohe. If that's true, the house will be a shrine to things that its owner holds dear—the trees, the nearby river, the spirit of nature, and, to be sure, the house in the country that somehow still stirs George's blood.

Drawing plans was also an exercise in aesthetics for Jane and George. They compiled a dossier of architectural features that caught their eye and moved their spirit. On houses they passed or saw in pictures they noted appealing details, from window treatments to rooflines. Taken altogether, the features they picked formed what George labels a "*gestalt* of their ideal home." In his house-building book George explains his rationale for this design process: "By observation and reflection, you'll make the connection between the general form of your house and your inner sense and image of domestic comfort."

Two layers of 1/4-inch plywood

Rafters

Joists

Cleat

To form a roof with flared eaves, George will use flexible plywood and a cleat to hold the curve.

He argues that such preliminary work is particularly crucial when two people plan their home: "Since 80 percent of homes are built by couples, taking two different, deeply held ideal images and finding a harmonious convergence is likely to be a difficult but necessary prerequisite to the successful outcome of a building project (as well as, perhaps, the survival of the marriage)."

Consequently, George and Jane designed their house together. "Jane has had terrific input," he says, raising his voice enough for Jane to hear the compliment somewhere in a back room of the trailer.

Jane emerges, nodding agreement. "This is going to be *our* house," she says. "When we met, we lived in *his* house, not *our* house, and, frankly, that was always an issue that neither of us liked. This house will be different. Our design will fit us both, so we'll both feel comfortable."

They'll derive some comfort from the auld-lang-syne appearance of the place. Exposed timbers will crisscross the ceiling. Roughly textured plaster walls will be set off by wainscoting and lots of painted wood surfaces. "Old windows, too," says Jane, "but we haven't found any so far." George intends to fill the kitchen with homemade cabinets that look nothing short of homemade. "To create a nice feeling," he says, "cabinetry doesn't require a high level of perfection. On some of the neatest cabinets I've seen, the joints might have been weird, but the overall feeling was just perfect—idiosyncratic, if you will. They had a kind of beauty you can't get with perfection. By putting yourself into stuff, you get more elegance than with something fancy and expensive. Anyway, Jane doesn't want everything to look antiseptic. We like the lived-in look."

George and Jane will also forego top-flight fixtures and appliances. "We don't want any of that high-end fancy shit," he says. "How do you justify spending four hundred dollars on a set of faucets when the world has gone to hell?"

Jane says, "I'd rather spend the money going out to dinner."

For still more *Gemütlichkeit*, they'll recreate a feature of their homestead in Vermont, where George had built an outdoor meditation space with crushed white stone and a garden sculpture. At first, his living room enclosed the space on three sides. But when Jane arrived with her children, George enlarged their cramped quarters by rearranging the walls. He brought the meditation area inside and replaced the gravel with a raised platform that Jane furnished with futons and cushions. Immediately, the space became the centerpiece of the house. "The entire family grew up there," Jane says. "It became the focal point. Since we had no TV, that's where we and the kids would curl up to read stories together." In their new house, George will build another futon-filled platform where he and Jane expect to curl up with their present and future brood of grandchildren.

"When it comes to home design, even the most harmonious couple won't agree on everything," George says. He argues that discord is a certainty because males and females view space differently. "Differences may be reinforced by culture," he notes, "but there's something genetic, too. Men perceive space as shape, light, form, volume, ego, power—penis kind of stuff. For women space is a shell, a nest, a place to inhabit and use. Women see curtains and furniture and wonder where you put down the groceries after you open the door." In other words, when space is at issue, there's still a big divide. George believes such conflicts are power struggles inherent in any relationship focused on a house. "Outside of an affair, there's nothing that will crystallize priorities more starkly," he says.

Evidently he speaks from experience. Not with an affair but with designing houses, especially kitchens. "Jane and I had some screaming fits over ours," he says.

"Right," Jane interjects, "some classic ones. George wanted to put an island in our kitchen, and I hate such kitchens because you can't hang out in them. He argued *work triangle*—the kind of malarkey in kitchen design books about how the stove, sink, and refrigerator ought to be close to each other, all probably written by men who never cooked a meal in their lives. But I say you don't just work in the kitchen, you live in it, so I wanted a big hanging-out space, a big round table in the middle, not a measly island to work on."

Trying to rationalize Jane's rejection of common-sense kitchen design, George says, "Jane grew up on a dairy farm in New Hampshire. She wanted a carbon copy of the kitchen she had there."

Jane concurs. "My old kitchen was huge," she says. "It had a washer, dryer, freezer, and even a couch to sit on."

To settle their differences, George and Jane turned to an arbiter, namely to *A Pattern Language*, Christopher Alexander's definitive home-design book. Alexander specifies that farmhouse kitchens work best and advises, "Make the kitchen bigger than usual, big enough to include the 'family room' space.

. . . Make it large enough to hold a good big table and chairs, some soft and some hard, with counters and stove and sink around the edge of the room; and make it a bright and comfortable room." In such a place meals become special events.

So Jane got her way, although she quickly points out, "It was infuriating that I had to convince George by consulting a complete stranger about the way that *my* kitchen ought to be."

On structural matters Jane deferred to George—no consultants, no discussions, no democratic participation. If two-by-six balloon framing, sixteen-inches on-center made George happy, well, amen to that. Two-inch foam insulation on the exterior suited her fine, and she thought that George's choice of a four-by-twelve rim beam would be just darling.

She also supported George's plan to build a full basement. Nature, however, had other ideas. The excavator found mammoth subterranean boulders too large for his machine to lift. Because blasting them with dynamite would add $9,500 to the building budget, George chose a slab-on-grade foundation instead. But the terrain, which included a four-foot, back-to-front drop, made a slab untenable. Therefore, George settled for a four-foot-high crawl space. "At least I'll have plenty of room to run pipes for radiant heat," he says.

As for his choice of materials, he points outside to a stack of cedar logs higher than the trailer. "I've been cutting trees since last winter," he tells me, "and will make ceiling joists out of the big ones with my neighbor's portable band saw mill." For additional lumber, and for plywood and trim George will haggle with local merchants. "I'm ready to spend thousands," he says, "but they'll have to beat Home Depot's prices if they want my business. That's economic reality." Wood for finishing the interior George expects to order from Bear Creek Lumber in California. "They make a Douglas fir, edge-and-center-bead, tongue-and-groove wainscot that's better and cheaper than anything I can get in Maine," he says. "Besides, I like the folks at Bear Creek. They're a bunch of old hippies turned craftsmen, and they take their wood seriously."

THE LAST TIME GEORGE BUILT a house for himself—in
Vermont over two decades ago—he lacked both time and fore-
sight. "I half-assed it," he admits. As a result, he often found
himself "retrofitting"—that is, redoing work he ought to have
done better the first time. Having learned a thing or two about
quality construction since then, he intends to proceed deftly
and slowly on this job. "I want this house to last at least a
couple of hundred years," he says. "This is the house of my
life. Let it be a statement to the world that says George Nash
was here. At fifty, frankly, I'm running short of time."

George's words sound to me like a too-early valedictory.
Someone with his vitality can't be serious about laying down
his hammer very soon. If anything, the house in progress represents the capstone of a building life, not a conclusion. The
scores of houses that he's built for others were merely prologue
to building his own. When you come right down to it, his past
building projects were shaped largely by business concerns and
customers' wishes. But not this one, which comes from deep
within himself. George used to think that success in building
depended on how accurately he could interpret his clients'
dreams. Now he's taking a crack at figuring out his own. But
until the house is complete and he's tried it on for size, he's not
likely to know whether he's been successful.

Driving away from George's trailer, I'm struck by something incongruous in the image of George finishing his house
and settling placidly into the static, bourgeois existence of a
novelist on the coast of Maine. He seems too restless, his
hands and feet in perpetual in motion. Throughout our time
together, he welcomed chances to get up, make tea, go into another room to find a book to show me. For most of his years he
has thrived on change. By my count, he has lived in seven different states and held at least a dozen jobs—from homesteader
to Christmas-tree salesman. As often as he's run businesses,
he's run from them. He moves fast and makes things happen.
His life, it seems, has been devoted to stalking something just
beyond his grasp. Not wealth. "Jane carries the economic ball,
in any case," he says. Nor love, not with a wife of twenty years

who is willing—for her man—to put up in a trailer month after month at the edge of a muddy construction site. And not with four kids and four grandchildren who often visit from distant places. Nor does he seek fame or the big win. Rather, his pursuits suggest that he's on the trail of something larger, perhaps some intimation of hope or faith that life has more to it than the pitch and yaw of daily existence. He fantasizes about withdrawing from the world like a monk: "If I had my druthers," he says, "I'd be living in the middle of nowhere on the side of a mountain thirty miles from town." But he's not about to head for the hills. He knows the score. "Realistically," he says, "there are no places like that where Jane could make a living."

Epilogue:
Four Walls, One Spirit

Owner-builders, clad in blue jeans and boots, look no different from other working men or women. Nevertheless, they belong in a class by themselves. It's not their omnivorous enthusiasm for the rigors of home construction that sets them apart. Nor does their uniqueness derive from what they get for their toil. Rather, owner-builders can be distinguished from other working stiffs by what their choice of part-time occupation does to them, for there is no other individual enterprise that so thoroughly intertwines the creation of a physical object as large, complex, and useful as a house (or a piece of one) with such a dizzying array of heady and eye-opening consequences.

I can't prove this assertion with facts and figures, nor argue for the uniqueness of owner-builders merely by pointing to the stories in this book. My sample is too small, and its bias— mostly middle-aged, middle-class, and white—too narrow. But I'm convinced that the collective experience of my respondents echoes the experiences of owner-builders everywhere.

While accounts of home-building projects may differ in their details, their main motifs and themes are apt to be startlingly alike. Consider the additional evidence from do-it-yourselfers whose tales of building I came to know but didn't record in these pages: Joice Wright is restoring an 1890s townhouse in Bedford-Stuyvesant. She is undoubtedly fueled by the same tenacity that drives Allan Shope, the architect from Greenwich, Connecticut. Then take Elis Stenman, the builder of an experimental Paper House of Pigeon Cove, Massachusetts. The efforts he expended in fabricating walls out of 215 thicknesses of varnished newspaper nailed to wood lath seem no less heroic than the struggles of Dave Daniel, the restorer of a burned-out house near the U.S. Capitol. And I am certain that Debbie and Brian Sobczak, a low-income couple constructing their own house in Paso Robles, California, with the financial and technical assistance of the People's Self-Help Housing Corporation, long to move into their new quarters as avidly as George Nash, the writer in mid-coast Maine, yearns to take up residence in his. A quest is a quest, after all, and like-minded people in pursuit of their private Holy Grails are apt to be moved by the same spirit.

Whoever and wherever they are, owner-builders clearly share an uncanny knack for picturing things that are not there. They see empty space and fill it with walls and a roof. They walk through nonexistent doorways into phantom rooms. They flick light switches still to be wired and hear water rushing through pipes yet to be installed. In their mind's eye they envision themselves mixing concrete and sawing wood. Trusting their imagination, they refuse to be frozen by timidity, inertia, misinformation, fear of failure, or any of a million other excuses not to start hammering boards together. What's more, they renounce rest and relaxation in favor of a lengthy, fatiguing, and costly home-building project with no assurance that they'll succeed at what they set out to do.

Considering how hard it is to construct all or even part of a house, men and women slip into owner-buildership rather easily—simply by rejecting conventional means to meet their housing needs. They don't shop around for the ideal home in perfect condition or have a dream house built on a site of their choice. Nor do they hire remodelers to expand or improve their homes. Instead, they take cues from an earlier time, when building your own home was at least as common as hiring a carpenter to build one for you. In fact, there is a long tradition of owner-building in America. Until the mid-nineteenth century virtually all single-family homes—except those of the rich—were wholly or partly owner-built. Members of an eighteenth-century family might well have joined in the construction of two, three, or more houses in their lifetime. As their house deteriorated, they built another, or at least, continued to tack new rooms onto an existing structure. In some places—out on the frontier, for instance—a family's very survival depended on their ability to build and maintain their own house. Modern-day owner-builders—the U.S. Census Bureau estimates that 175,000 single-family houses are built by their owners each year—are nudged into construction by some of the same impulses that steered settlers west over a century ago. Driven by a can-do spirit, a lust for adventure, a creative urge, or any number of other social and economic forces, they are to some degree the spiritual heirs of those frontier families.

Owner-builders often set out on life-altering building adventures with a lot of faith in themselves but little know-how. Jennifer Lee's knowledge hovered near zero when she broke ground for her house in the Berkshires; Leona Walden's expertise at Salmon Creek Farm in California was hardly more substantial. West Coast wildlife photographer Bill Pond—a builder who declined to have his story told—didn't know a rim joist from a rafter when he began his building career by making a bid on a cast-off WWII barracks that the U.S. Army at Fort Ord was auctioning off to anyone willing to haul it away. For $51 he and a friend bought a two-story, sixty-by-ninety foot building. Dismantling it piece by piece, Bill learned how it had been put together, then used his newly acquired knowledge and the salvaged lumber, most of it old-growth redwood, to build a new family home in northern California. Some builders learn their craft from fathers, friends, spouses, or big brothers. Or they teach themselves by studying the vast body of how-to lit. Many pick up additional tips by quizzing clerks in lumber yards and stalking building sites. Courses offered by roughly forty home-building schools around the country—even one-shot seminars sponsored free by the local Home Depot—help bring many owner-builders up to speed. But no method is more pervasive and ultimately more effective than on-the-job trial and error. The lessons learned from making and correcting mistakes leave lasting impressions.

None of the do-it-yourselfers I interviewed could tell me precisely how much money they saved by doing their own construction. Some set down expenses in a ledger or notebook, expecting one day to use the data to calculate capital gains. My more fiscally casual respondents stuffed receipts into a shoebox or desk drawer and alluded to rough figures they called "sweat equity," the value they added to their home or property with the sweat off their brows. Since no one punched a time clock, their hourly compensation is unknown. But reckoning the days spent on the work site, along with the time they devoted to paperwork, to ordering materials, and just mulling over the job, they probably earned less than minimum wage. More certain is that no one made a financial killing. Anyone who goes into owner-building to get rich is asking for disappointment.

My respondents, in any case, had more to say about other, less tangible, rewards of building—the wonder of it, the endorphin rush, the intimations of immortality, breaking the borders of the worlds they ordinarily inhabited. Generally pragmatic at the start, some were amazed to find their emotions no less involved in the work than their muscles. One builder described the year he framed his house as "a perpetual high—almost." When he blundered badly, his spirits crashed, but the next morning he charged out to the site raring to right yesterday's wrongs. Overall, the experience nourished them more than they expected it to. They felt elated, more at ease, more confident. Not only had they a structure to show for their pains but they acquired a more vivid sense of themselves. In *Walden*, Thoreau called building one's own house a "simple and natural" occupation, no different from a bird's building a nest. "Who knows," he asked, "but if men constructed their own dwellings with their own hands . . . the poetic faculty would be universally developed, as birds universally sing when

they are so engaged?" Well, as far as I know no one I interviewed either burst into song while hauling concrete blocks or
composed an ode to a vent pipe, but by and large they relished
the work beyond reason.

Why owner-builders should find grueling work blissful
may lie partly in the nature of contemporary life. As it happens, we live in the age of specialization. Workers rarely make
things any more but only parts of things. While the narrowing
of attention on a single task may not always be bad, there is
something demeaning in work that divides workers into sub-
specialties. Eric Gill writes in *A Holy Tradition of Working,*
"Skill in making . . . degenerates into mere dexterity, i.e., skill
in doing. When the workman . . . has no longer any responsi-
bility for the thing made and has therefore lost the knowledge
of what it is that he is making, . . . what is being made is of no
concern of his." In effect, our workforce consists of robots—
both the mechanical and the human variety.

Owner-builders, on the other hand, sink themselves passionately into their work, performing the functions of almost two dozen separate home-building specialists: general
contractor, architect, engineer, surveyor, excavator, teamster,
mason, framer, roofer, window installer, stairmaker, electrician,
plumber, HVAC (Heating, Ventilation, and Air-Conditioning)
expert, Sheetrocker, floorer, painter, sider, landscaper, cabinetmaker, decorator, and the guy who hangs the gutters.

While it may take monumental chutzpah for one person to
assume all those roles, the truth is that a good deal of anxiety
accompanies owner-builders' bravado. Pete Williams, for one,
suffered terribly before his excavation was dug. Jennifer Lee
was forced by uncertainty to depend on the kindness of
strangers to see her through the pouring of her concrete piers.
Allan Shope was up pacing at 2 A.M. on the day of his house-
raising. But Pete and Jennifer and Allan, as well as the
others, toughed it out. On-the-job learning took care of shaky
skills, and dispatching problem after problem on the work site
gradually put an end to early misgivings. When uncertainty
lingered, however, my respondents sent for help, mostly from

electricians and plumbers. Rather than botch a job or endanger themselves, they let good sense triumph over stubbornness. (In some locales, they had no choice; building codes required the use of licensed subcontractors.) Richie Mueller hired experienced woodsmen to fell a dozen giant pines that hung over his Pennsylvania home. At the last minute Fenwick Smith decided not to dig his own well, and Leona Walden handed timber-framing chores to a contractor with the proper equipment and credentials.

While prudence may have dictated doling tasks to others, countless opportunities to stumble remained. Mistakes, as Pete Williams often observed, come with the territory. And in spite of erecting walls that weren't quite plumb, shaping corners that weren't quite square, and in one case, laying a brick patio that its builder termed "a lemon," none of my respondents erred so egregiously that they saw fit to hang up their nailing aprons for good. All, in fact, emerged from their building adventures stronger and wiser—a few a lot older, too.

Apparently, long sojourns in building country are the norm—although the notion of doing your own building undermines the very idea of normality—averaging two to three years per project. However long the journey, though, the after-effects seem to last a lifetime. Building often opens eyes and changes lives. For schoolteacher Patricia Liddle, building a house meant a new career. Once she completed her house in Chatham, New York, she quit the classroom and started an all-women contracting business. Jennifer Lee became an instant landlord by renting out the house she built. More than twenty women builders whose ventures in construction are chronicled in a book by Janice Goldfrank (*Making Ourselves at Home*) took charge of their own destinies for the first time in their lives. According to Goldfrank, "Building seems to have many layers of meaning for women—issues of control, self-esteem, identity, ambition, and their place in society." (Because women builders bear the added burden of proving themselves in a predominantly male occupation, their rewards, being harder won, may be all the more delicious.)

Because her slant is feminist, however, Goldfrank ignores a vital point: Building freshens men's lives, too. While restoring a downtrodden house, Richie Mueller finally came to terms with the memory of an overbearing father who disdained manual labor. Fenwick Smith turned to commercial real-estate rehabbing when his owner-built country home neared completion. Bob Rasero scrapped his deadly accounting job in New York after fixing up and selling two old houses in the suburbs. The prospect of renovating houses for a living lured him to the coast of Maine, where he built his own 4,500-square foot home, became a carpenter, and founded a rock music group he named The Renovators. Allan Shope changed the character of his life by trading more than a year of weekend recreation for the more uncertain pleasures of home construction.

The effect of rehabbing a run-down country home on Norman Rinder was even more potent. Norman, a New York teacher, described his building frenzy this way: "It was a weird time. I must have been insufferable, talking and thinking of nothing but my house in Vermont." Norman's wife Roseanne agreed. "The house swallowed him up," she commented. "It snatched his free will and judgment."

An affliction such as Norman's is hardly uncommon among owner-builders. Sooner or later some sort of building fever seems to strike even the most level-headed among them. But Norman had the fever bad. Alone in the old house with his tools, he sometimes went at it eighteen hours straight. Starting at dawn, he looked up and saw that it was noon. When he looked up again, the sun had dropped from the sky. For Norman, being engrossed in something outside himself was wild ecstasy, like falling in love for the first time. "How Roseanne endured it I don't know," he observed.

But Roseanne knows. She refused to be sucked into Norman's obsession. With her own career, two kids to raise, and a life to live away from sawdust and the banging of hammers, she agreed to accompany Norman to the country only once a month. He, on the other hand, ached for more—holidays, vacations, weekends—with or without her. Roseanne did not object, for she had rarely seen her husband happier than when he held a hammer in his hand. Norman told me that he'd never felt more vital, more energetic, and more productive than he did while slaving away at his home in the country.

Of course, not every borderline obsessive with a tool belt is lucky enough to have a Roseanne in his life to lend moral support. Where Norman found wild ecstasy, other owner-builders found nothing but stress. Juggling a career with a major building project that in itself demands full-time attention can create unendurable anxiety. Two owner-builders I had hoped to interview begged off for that very reason. One said that he'd fallen into a deep funk while tethered to a forty-hour week as a mechanic and building his family home the rest of the time. "I almost cracked," he told me. The other fellow said the experience of building his own house was too painful to recount. It had torn his marriage apart, a misfortune that, he told me frankly, was none of my damn business.

Couples agree that a major construction project has a natural aptitude for testing the mettle of a marriage. It's more than clashes over window placement or the size of the linen closet that strains relationships. Rather, it's enduring the brutal effects of the law of unintended consequences. At the outset Mr. and Mrs. Owner-Builder often fail to grasp what lies in store. Gung-ho to make their building plans a reality, they expect to rise to the challenge of balancing jobs and family life with the demands of construction. But when the physical work begins in earnest, the building half of the team—usually, but not always, the male—appears to reside in another dimension. Even at home he is gone, distracted by thoughts of footings and knee-walls and anchor bolts. Wherever he goes, the work goes too. He carries his project around in his head, thinking of soffit vents and Sheetrock screws. Building thoughts keep him up at night, his mind restless with tomorrow's plans. When he finally gets to sleep, images of mortar or roofing shingles—or whatever work had occupied him that day—dance in his dreams. She notices that he's neglecting his chores, the kids, and her. Energy he once reserved for the family he now expends on laying cinder blocks and sawing wood.

In some scenarios Mrs. O-B gets on Mr. O-B's case. He grows resentful and points out that he's out there on the building site breaking his back, and just when he needs her support the most, she has withdrawn it.

"Withdrawn support? Are you kidding?" she asks. "How can you be so blind and insensitive? Can't you see that I've been keeping the household together? Where's the appreciation that I deserve?"

In effect, each partner has become victimized by circumstances that neither of them wants, and both recognize that they're suddenly living a *mènage à trois*—he, she, and that infernal building project.

Despite such tribulations, though, owner-builders often go on to build again—one, two, or more houses—because on balance, the rewards far outweigh the frustrations. Jennifer Lee barely finished her first house when she began a second. Allan Shope is on his third house as this book goes to press. Once he started building, Dave Daniel never stopped. On subsequent projects, owner-builders work faster, worry less, and as veterans, luxuriate in their hard-won expertise. But first projects, however vexing, seem usually to leave the sweetest aftertaste.

You might expect that home building would attract people with a practical, down-to-earth temperament. Yet, some of my respondents alluded—obliquely or directly—to the spirituality of building, to the presence of inexplicable forces that served as a source of strength and a guide to their actions. They found themselves caught up in the work they were doing, as though gripped by powers outside themselves. As they worked, they often discovered wondrous internal resources that helped them to overcome obstacles and push themselves mercilessly. Their state of mind and heart, it seems, contributed an intangible dimension as crucial to the overall success of their projects as lumber and nails.

Those with a bent to dig for meanings beneath the surface of things spoke of the spirituality of wood, and the symbolism of their building. One mentioned "the Tao of his tools." That they undertook projects more daunting than anything they'd done before also suggests a faith in transcendence, a trust in their capacity to rise above their ignorance of the work and to escape their customary modes of behavior. Some used building as a means of personal expression. "It was probably the most creative time in my life," said graphic artist Richie Mueller about restoring his squalid lakeside house in Pennsylvania.

In *House as a Mirror of Self,* Clare Cooper Marcus writes about "Bill," a lifelong do-it-yourselfer and the subject of a psychological research study. According to Marcus, Bill used his home as an arena for self-expression—as others might use clothes or cooking or gardening. When Marcus suggested that building and remodeling was his *hobby,* Bill bristled. To him a *hobby* suggested something you do to kill time. "The house is me," Bill objected. "Because I built it and because it's everything that I wanted it to be, I think of it really as an extension of our family. It is not an object you buy in a showroom, like a car or piece of furniture. It's us. Its imperfections are as revealing to me as its satisfactions, like a friend or member of the family whose imperfections we can see. If we find something isn't working, we change it. I don't think we change our habits to suit our house, which is what most people must do. We change the house to suit us, so it's constantly evolving. We live it, we don't live in it."

WHEN A HOUSE BECOMES virtually indistinguishable from life—as it did for Bill—and when building becomes a fundamental part of one's existence—as it did for me more than twenty years ago—no project can be taken lightly. One of the most mysterious effects of building is that it tends to draw the builder emotionally up and out of himself. That, at least, is what startled me most when I undertook my first big project, a three-room addition to my suburban home. The discoveries I made on the job fascinated me back then and continue to provoke me to this day.

With no more than a handful of home-improvement projects under my belt, I had drawn a set of elevations and cross-sections with enough grace to convince the town's building inspector that I could probably find my way around a construction site. Privately I wasn't so sure. The Saturday in March on which the work officially began couldn't decide whether to be a winter or a spring day. The sun shone brightly, then stole behind the clouds, forcing me to reach for my jacket again. Ice nestled in the corners of the pond while birds made the morning loud with song. Like the day, I, too, was a waffler—confident that I could build three new rooms but just as certain that I was making a big mistake.

As I steered my wheelbarrow to the south side of my house and marked the corners of the future addition with stakes, I felt a sudden queasiness. Anticipation or terror? I couldn't tell. The string I tied to the stakes outlined a twenty-by-thirty-foot parcel that contained a bower of rose bushes as well as Susan's tomato and zucchini patch. It also lopped the first base side off the family's Wiffle ball field. Near the outer edge of the site was the dirt mound where I once taught my son David to pitch a Spauldeen into a strike zone chalked on the brick chimney. Where the excavation would soon be dug was also the spot where I had once set up a pup tent and taken my daughter Ellie, then four, on her first overnight camp-out. This small rectangle by the side of my house was not just another piece of real estate but a piece of family history that was about to be irrevocably transformed, first into a construction zone and then into half a house. No wonder I felt queasy.

My intention on that day was to dig up the mat of tangled weeds and crab grass we whimsically called our lawn and transplant it on the north side of the house, where grass hadn't grown in years and never would. Absurd or not, I welcomed the task. It ushered me into my project by degrees, like a bather inching into cold water. It may have been fear that restrained me from ravaging my backyard, or just as likely nostalgia for this particular swatch of ground. Whatever the reason, my hesitancy surprised me.

I was in for another surprise when I stabbed the ground with my shovel. The tip sliced through the soil about three inches and then stopped dead. The way was blocked by hard frost that couldn't be dislodged, even by a pickax. Only the sun could make it yield, but that would take days. Could this be an omen? A warning? Was there something symbolic in the refusal of the earth to submit to the blade of my shovel?

Apparently my attempt to disturb the backyard had stirred up the English teacher in me. I was searching for meaning below the surface of things, doing exactly what I nagged my students to do when they read a poem or a novel. Life and literature are interwoven, I often told them. Each imitates the other. And in both, the physical world can express a metaphysical one.

I didn't find anything metaphysical about the moment two months later, however, when an excavator drove his rumbling yellow front loader across the dooryard and began to move tons of earth around. Until that machine sank its teeth into the lawn, the addition existed only in abstract and on a handful of tidy drawings. Now, minute by minute its identity was being transformed into a pit being dug just inches outside the dining room windows. After five hours of rattling and roaring, the machine stopped and withdrew. It left behind not the neat, square-edged rectangle I had envisioned, but a rugged crater of rocks and mounds of earth and a fifteen-foot-high dirt mountain that immediately became a neighborhood playground.

I snapped at the children, "Get out of here, you'll get hurt!" The morning's dig had dissolved my calm. What had shaken me most was neither the din nor the frightful power of the machine, but rather my sudden recognition that this gaping, messy hole in the ground meant that retreat was out of the question. Any trace of self-doubt that I could add three rooms to my house had become irrelevant. Like a skydiver after leaping from a plane or a raftsman on a swift river, I could no longer turn back.

The next step was to "build footings—that, according to Donald R. Brann, the author of a two-dollar, 96-page paperback called *How to Build an Addition*, promised to "take the mystery out of building." Mystery, shmystery, I wish Brann had told me how to take the anxiety out instead, because on the Saturday I poured footings—the sixteen-inch wide, eight-inch deep concrete pedestal on which the foundation wall would be built—the stress almost crushed me. I had hired two high school boys to help, then rented a mixer and ordered the ingredients of concrete—cement (one part), sand (three parts), gravel (five parts)—to be delivered on Friday afternoon. At dusk the sandman called; his truck had fallen in a hole. "Get another, damn it," I yelled into the phone. He must have detected a hint of urgency in my voice, because just before midnight he dumped a load of sand on the driveway. All the next day the boys and I mixed concrete, shoveled it into wheelbarrows, and pounded it into the forms I had built. By Saturday night, wasted with work and worried sick that I hadn't done the job correctly, I'd lost ten pounds. Brann advised, "Allow footings to set three days before laying the foundation wall." I would gladly have waited three weeks.

It took a month and a half of weekends and after-school time for me to lay an eighty-foot-long foundation wall consisting of 420 concrete blocks, a rate I calculated to be about 3.5 blocks an hour. At that pace, an average shopping mall would take fifty years to build. Clearly, speed was not my forte. Instead, I strove to be precise, being sure that the blocks were properly seated in straight rows with just the correct amount of mortar between them. Brann, bless his clever heart, taught me to check my work repeatedly with the cheapest and most ingenious device imaginable, a length of household string stretched between the wall's corners. Unaligned blocks stood out instantly next to the tautly pulled string.

Long before the wall was complete, I began to suspect that building consisted of more than materials and methods. The more fully I poured myself into the work, the more discoveries I made there, not only about how building is done but about what it was doing to me. I felt like a re-made man, and in my new incarnation took it for granted that I had been born with

an extra chromosome for building. The work made ungodly demands on my time and imposed inhuman stresses on my body.
But in return, it nurtured my spirit. Until a quiet evening
when I sat by the foundation wall and meditated on builders
past and future, I'd never so much as given a thought to the
niche I occupied as a man in the eternal flow of time.

One discovery followed the next. It occurred to me, for example, that I might have been driven to build by some primal
urge for shelter. Children play in cardboard boxes to shut out
the world. Most people long for a roof after a day or two without one. Covering the frame of a building in plywood creates
what has been called a womb with a view, a primal image
of the first order and an epithet more serious than it sounds,
for nothing alters the character of a framed structure more
tellingly than its first layer of plywood. The first time I entered
my plywood-clad addition, I stood clamped to the threshold,
transfixed by the loss of space, light, and fresh air. Why did I
stop dead in my tracks? Maybe my eyes had to adjust. Maybe I
wanted to savor the moment. Or just maybe I felt a sudden res-
onance with the first anthropoid who decided to get out of the
rain by stepping into a cave.

Noting the connection between my eye-opening reverie by
the foundation wall and my first step into the gloom of the addition, I realized that for me the act of building cleared paths to
planes of existence that I'd read about but until then had nothing to do with me. What I did with my hands influenced what
happened in my head. Physical work, which is something regular guys are supposed to complain about, took on a new cast.
It proved to be powerfully satisfying—more than I could have
imagined. Hammering, for instance. The sensation of sinking a
nail into wood had become no less familiar to me than, say,
putting on my shoes in the morning. But unlike tying laces,
driving a nail demanded my undivided attention. If I failed to
concentrate, the nail would bend. If I didn't visualize my hammer striking the nailhead, I'd surely blow the shot. Because the
act of driving a nail called for rhythm, timing, and coordina-

tion, it took on Zen-like dynamics. At first, the nail was just an object apart from me. But seconds later, having focused my energy and will into forcing it through solid wood, I briefly entered the nail and left a bit of myself behind as I pulled the next nail from my pouch.

Ordinarily, I have the capacity of a gnat for such spiritual conceits. As basically a no-nonsense fellow, I've made a point of never letting an apostle of spirituality get between me and the nearest door. Building my addition made me no less intolerant of spirit-babble but far more sensitive to the feelings behind it. How else could I account for the inexpressible joy of turning my visions into reality day after day? In the morning I'd look at an empty space and imagine a wall. That evening the wall stood in place just as I'd pictured it. But I could hardly remember putting it there. Because I felt wrung out, I knew that I'd gone through lots of grunting and sweating, but the actual process was a blur. I had gotten lost in the work, so to speak, and didn't find myself until it was over. I'd been wound like a spring early in the day and then let go. In that respect, I felt like a tool in the hands of a powerful force that lifted me out of myself, freed me from my ego, and pushed me to work until I wore myself out.

I couldn't have been more surprised, while sawing myself silly or sitting quietly by the foundation wall after a day of toil, to discover, say, what I took to be a sense of my unity with nature or an awareness of my place in the universe. Such insights, however amorphous and fleeting, were awakening me to possibilities too compelling to dismiss but also too illusory for me to clearly understand. While I didn't find God out on the work site, occasionally I felt the presence of a pretty decent imitation. I'm far more comfortable with the concept of a two-by-four or a pump jack than with the idea of otherworldly powers playing games with my mind. But something touched a synchronous chord in me. In fact, I was rather charmed by the notion that routine building tasks aroused something mystical in the mundane.

As I was later to discover, other do-it-yourselfers collected epiphanies, too. While hewing a large wooden beam, George Nash experienced what he calls a *"sartori* moment"—intuitive, illuminating state of consciousness that is the spiritual goal of Zen Buddhism. By punching a crater in his bathroom floor, Pete Williams was hit with the thought that he had suddenly graduated from a tinkerer to a true builder. At one time I would have thought that George and Pete were mildly delusional, but having in effect walked a mile in their boots, I took them at their word. By the time Allan Shope said to me that a well-designed house was "capable of touching our souls," it was already old news to me. I also understood perfectly why Leona Walden's first wall-raising was such a sweetheart of a moment and why Fenwick Smith felt a "thrilling and joyous sense of shelter" as he watched the rain splash harmlessly against the roof windows he had just installed.

MAKE NO MISTAKE, owner-building is more than crushingly hard work alleviated occasionally by periods of self-satisfaction and enlightenment. On the job, owner-builders also have fun. They laugh, joke, sing, bond with others, fall in love, get suntans, and learn a lot. Their aesthetic sensibilities and appreciation for craftsmanship grow, and they tend to develop respect and admiration for professionals in the building trades—from bricklayers to architects. The physical work itself puts them in touch with their own bodies. It makes them fit and, as a bonus, helps them lose weight without dieting. Building wins the admiration of families, neighbors, and friends, some of whom pitch in and some of whom look on in disbelief. At the very least, building raises self-esteem and incidentally, for a very long time, solves the problem of what to do on weekends.

Regardless of its everyday consequences, however, something reverential seems to happen when you raise walls or see your rafters poised against the sky. Just as a magnificent tree inspires awe and wonder, a house you've built on your own radiates meaning beyond itself. You can't cast an indifferent eye on a structure that has taken months or years of your life to build and consumed a prodigious amount of your physical and psychic energy. Having hammered a house together, you are a different person than you were before. You have, at least for a time, transcended conventionality and—if you allowed it to happen—reached levels of consciousness you didn't know existed. No doubt it takes a vivid imagination to feel transcendent after a wayward two-by-ten bloodies your shin or while you rush to tarp the roof before a thunderhead lets go, but taken all together, the experiences of making your own dwelling, both literally and metaphysically, provide a kind of lift—as though you've been granted a gift of insight or truth. Perhaps most important, building your own house opens you to a sense of presence in the physical world.

Nothing speaks more convincingly about the evocative power of building than the traditional "topping-out" ceremony held after the roof has been framed. Although the custom of attaching a young evergreen tree to the ridge pole seems to be fading, it is still a compelling enough ritual to send even crusty old builders in search of a sapling once they've hoisted the last beam into place. Why they do it is a matter of *maybes*. Maybe it betokens good luck like a horseshoe over the barn door. Maybe it marks a milestone, for after the ridge and rafters go up, a builder can see the shape of the whole house for the first time.

For some builders, the ritual of nailing a tree to the roof may be a way to thank the forest for the lumber it provided, although it strikes me that cutting down a perfectly good tree is a curious way to show your appreciation. Whatever the answer, many sober-minded, otherwise sensible owner-builders observe the custom without having the foggiest idea why.

Aside from such minor eccentricities, owner-builders by and large are neither philosophers nor fools. Instead, they are ordinary people moved by out-of-the-ordinary visions of life's possibilities. Building, after all, is about vision and longing, about a fundamental quest for happiness and a satisfying life. By setting out on challenging and inspiring personal adventures, they try to make damn sure that the sum of their days will add up not to a shapeless gray blur but rather to something that resembles a work of art.

Glossary

After living all his years in rented apartments, Norman Rinder, at age twenty-nine, bought his first house. On the same day he also bought his first hammer and a copy of the *New York Times Manual of Home Repair*, which told him that to survive as a homeowner he would need—in addition to a hammer—a handsaw, screwdrivers, a utility knife, chisels, a set of wrenches, a measuring tape, an electric drill, and boxes of bolts, screws, nuts, and nails.

The acquisition of a basic tool collection, however, made Norman no less of a neophyte: One Saturday morning he drove to the lumber yard in his VW Bug to buy materials to build some bookshelves. The yard was crowded with customers, men in denim and dusty shoes. For a quarter of an hour he watched as each spoke briefly to the boss, a man built like a bus, who wrote their orders on a pad and hoisted boards and plywood sheets into pickup trucks and vans. Finally, the yard-man, his chest heaving, turned to Norman.

"What can I get you?" he asked.

"I want some wood—you know, for a bookcase," Norman replied.

"All right, what do you need?" The man held a pencil poised to write the order.

"Well, I want to add some shelves. You know, for books?" Norman hoped that the giant would know what he meant.

"Yeah, OK. Number two pine. Is that what you want?" He started to write. "How much do you need?"

"Well, I'm not quite sure. You see, I have this wall. . . . Actually, I was hoping to get some advice."

The yardman glared. "Look, mister," he said, "we sell lumber, not advice. I'll give you anything you want, but you got to tell me." He stuffed the pencil into his jeans and turned toward the next customer.

"OK, forget it," Norman called to the man's broad back.

The carpenter's bill came to $475. This is ridiculous, thought Norman, growing angry—more at himself than at the carpenter or the scowler in the lumber yard. He had seen the shelves clearly in his mind's eye but didn't have the words to describe them.

On his next birthday he received from his wife a book that changed him forever—Bob Vila's *This Old House*. In the book's pages the secrets of wall construction were laid bare. Drawings showed the anatomy of a wall with all its parts clearly labeled: studs, top plate, toe plate, cripple studs, and lintel. Norman, who could count on one hand the times he had successfully driven a nail, was amazed to learn that by toenailing, one could join two perpendicular pieces of lumber. He read hungrily about Sheetrock and the marvels of joint compound, or "mud," as it was known in the trade. Then and there he determined to build a Vila-style wall in the basement of his house, whether his basement needed one or not. The next weekend, Norman strode up to the counter in the building-supplies store and ordered a five-gallon can of "mud." No one snickered. He felt as though he'd joined the cognoscenti.

To go with his sixty-five pounds of joint compound, he bought some two-by-fours and a dozen "pre-cut" studs— lengths of lumber 7 feet, 8 5/8 inches long, shorn from eight feet as a convenience to carpenters. Because a standard eight-foot wall is framed with one horizontal piece at the bottom and two at the top, its vertical members need to be shorter than eight feet. Trimming off three and three-eighths inches (hence, the name *pre-cuts*) saves the builder a time-consuming step.

In time, Norman evolved into a handyman extraordinaire. But first he learned the lingo. He gorged on home-building books, studied the tools and hardware, and hung out in lumber yards where people spoke knowingly about such esoterica as mudsills, valley boards, trusses, hip roofs, and cripple studs. *Know the builder's words and you'll know his work* became his dictum. Every piece of a house has its proper name. He learned not to say *stud* when he meant *joist*, and not to say *beam* when he meant *rafter*. *Concrete* is not *cement*, nor are *footings* meant to be called a *foundation*. The words were slippery at first, but after hours of studying how to construct batter boards, set bottom plates, use j-bolts, and install joist hangers, the names began to stick. When he saw how each part served to hold a structure together, it occurred to him that building a deck, a tool shed or a simple partition in his basement was like solving a 3-D puzzle for which he had to cut the pieces and fit them into place, snug and level and plumb.

Builders will tell you that their words are a kind of currency, a medium by which to exchange information. Word-poor builders often find themselves lacking the power to communicate. Big with ideas which they can't utter, and unable to impress upon others the image existing in their minds, they lose time, squander efforts, and occasionally give up entirely.

Knowing terminology won't necessarily transform a bungler into an expert, but the naming of parts will certainly help an aspiring builder sort out the steps of any construction project. Moreover, by getting and spending the words in this glossary—most of them drawn from the pages of this book—an owner-builder will impress his non-building friends, create the illusion of expertise, and, not the least of it, avoid making an ass of himself at the lumber yard.

anchor bolt A foot-long steel bolt that is used to anchor the frame of a house to the foundation. The threaded end of the bolt protrudes from the top of the concrete foundation about four inches, and the sill is attached with a washer and nut. A j-bolt, so called for the bend at its lower end, is often used in lieu of a straight anchor bolt.

backfill   To refill a trench or space around the outside of the foundation. It's risky to backfill before the ground-floor joists are nailed in place because the weight of the fill may buckle the unsupported foundation wall.

backhoe   A heavy piece of earth-moving equipment with which to dig trenches and excavations. A backhoe and its operator can turn a perfectly good backyard into a moonscape in a couple of hours.

balusters   The uprights that support of a railing on a staircase or deck. By code, balusters must be spaced closely enough to keep a small child's head from passing between them.

balustrade   The railing at the edge of a staircase, consisting of balusters, a handrail, and newel posts. For safety, a balustrade ought to be sturdy enough to bear the impact of a professional wrestler falling on it. See *staircase*.

batter boards   Fence-like structures consisting of posts and a rail to which strings are attached for laying out exact location of future footings or a foundation wall. Batter boards are the first tangible evidence that a building will someday occupy an empty site.

bearing wall   A wall that carries the weight of joists, roof, or another wall above it. A bearing wall may be removed during remodeling, but only if a strong beam is put in its place.

bevel   The angle that one surface makes with another when they are not at a right angle. A *bevel square* is a simple in-

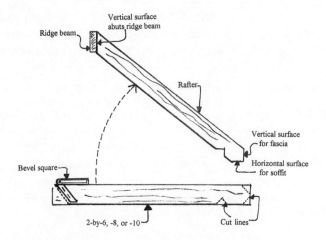

Ridge beam

Vertical surface
abuts ridge beam

Rafter

Vertical surface
for fascia

Horizontal surface
for soffit

Bevel square

2-by-6, -8, or -10

Cut lines

strument consisting of two rules, or arms, joined at a pivot
and opening to any angle. It is often used to draw the cut
lines on a rafter.

blocking   Solid pieces of lumber nailed between joists to add
strength and rigidity to the floor and ultimately to keep
the dishes in the china cabinet from rattling when you
walk across the room. See *frame*.

bottom plate   The bottom piece of a framed wall. Also called
the *toe plate*. See *stud wall*.

brace and bit   The traditional—and now antiquated—hand
tool used to drill holes. With the advent of the electric
drill, the brace and bit has all but vanished from carpenters' toolboxes.

bridging   Pieces of wood used to stiffen joists and keep floors
from wobbling and vibrating. Unlike solid blocking, which
serves the same purpose, bridging is mounted diagonally
between joists, leaving space for stringing wires and installing water pipes. See *frame*.

built-up beam A structural beam made up of several pieces of lumber glued together for added strength and stiffness. Because a built-up beam is far stronger than ordinary lumber with the same dimensions, it can span greater distances and carry heavier loads. Also called a *glulam*.

carpenter's square A steel tool that consists of two arms (the body and the tongue) set at right angles to each other. Both arms are amply engraved with numbers, scales, and tables that can help well-informed builders to figure the lengths of common, hip, valley, and jack rafters for any pitch of roof. Neophytes, however, are often baffled by the hieroglyphics and by such instructions as these (from the manual that comes with the carpenter's square from Stanley Tools): "To find the length of a jack rafter, multiply the value given in the tables by the number indicating the position of the jack. From the obtained length subtract half the diagonal (45°) thickness of the hip or valley rafter." Also called a *framing square*.

casing The decorative molding, or frame, that surrounds a window or door.

cat's paw A handy tool made of forged steel shaped to extricate unwanted nails from wood. Few nails can withstand a tug from the claw of a cat's paw.

chopsaw *or* miter saw A piece of equipment for cutting miters at virtually any angle from 0 to 90 degrees. The head of a compound miter saw can be tilted so that the blade cuts obliquely through the wood, enabling a builder to cut complex angles for valley rafters and such.

circular saw The most common type of portable power saw found around a job site. Once you've used one, you'll put your handsaw into permanent storage. Also called a *framer's saw* or *Skilsaw* (a brand name now used generically).

cleat A strip of wood used to reinforce any piece of the frame that has been drilled full of holes or notched for pipes, wiring, or ducts.

collar ties   Horizontal members of a roof frame. Attached to opposing rafters, collar ties help prevent the roof from sagging under its own weight. See *frame*.

come-along   A device consisting of levers, gears, springs, and cables that all together can exert more pulling force than you'd ever expect. While come-alongs may not move mountains, they've been known to give a truck full of sand a pretty good tug and to straighten a tilted house.

concrete blocks   Literally, the building blocks of a wall. Concrete blocks differ from cinder blocks, which are made with cinders instead of crushed gravel and, therefore, weigh less. Both kinds of blocks, however, are equally hard and immutable.

concrete mix   A mix of gravel (five parts), sand (three parts), Portland cement (one part), and water. In home-building, concrete is used not just for footings and foundations, but also for driveways, patios, steps, and even for countertops.

coping saw   A handsaw with a very thin blade held in a U-shaped frame and used to cut intricate patterns and shapes

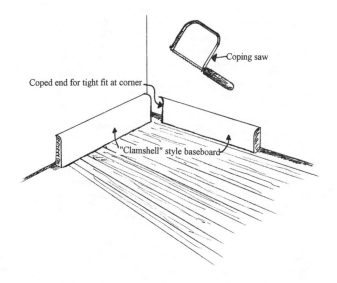

Coping saw

Coped end for tight fit at corner

"Clamshell" style baseboard

in wood. Where two pieces of molding form an inside corner, the end of one piece is often "coped" in the shape of the opposing piece to create a tight fit.

cordless, keyless half-inch drill   A drill that runs on batteries and requires no special key to turn the "chuck" that holds the bit tightly in place. A half-inch drill will accommodate bits with a shank up to a half-inch in diameter.

corner   The juncture of two walls. A corner offers a builder several framing options, each with a different configuration of studs but all equally adept at providing a meeting place for a pair of walls.

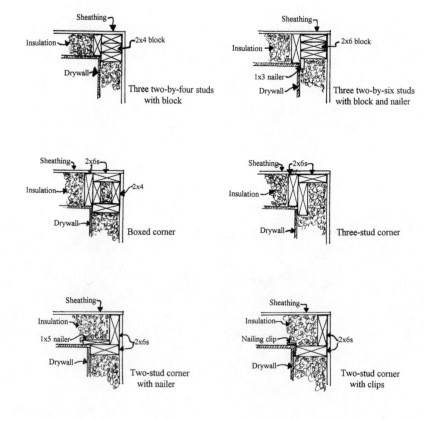

Three two-by-four studs with block

Three two-by-six studs with block and nailer

Boxed corner

Three-stud corner

Two-stud corner with nailer

Two-stud corner with clips

crawl space   The area underneath the first story of any house without a full basement. A crawl space can be a few inches to several feet high. A crawl space is a great place to crouch or stand in a hunched-over position. The term *crawl space* also applies to low-slung attics.

cross-section   A drawing that shows both the profile and the inside of a house as though the house had been sliced open like a loaf of bread. A cross-section shows builders where interior features are located.

dimensional lumber   Lumber cut to standard dimensions; i.e., two-by-fours, two-by-sixes, four-by-fours, four-by-sixes, etc. Lumber cut to nonstandard sizes must be specially milled, and therefore costs more than stock pulled from lumber yard shelves.

dormer   A miniature house atop a pitched roof. Nothing beats a dormer for bringing light and air into an attic room with a sloped ceiling. Dormers also dramatically change the overall appearance of a house. Shed dormers, although not as elegant as other kinds, provide more usable space and are easier to build. See *roof*.

drip edge   A strip of metal meant to carry water away from the rim of a roof. Without this protection, the exposed edge of the roof deck is apt to get wet, stay wet, and eventually, disintegrate.

drywall   A ubiquitous material mounted on walls and ceilings and consisting of plaster and fiberglass sandwiched between layers of tough paper. Also called *wallboard*, *plasterboard*, and *Sheetrock* (a trade name often used generically).

eave   The lower edge of a roof that extends horizontally beyond the face of a wall. Also called the *overhang*.

elevation   A two-dimensional drawing that shows the profile of a building, including the placement of prominent features, such as windows and doors.

fascia   A horizontal band of trim that conceals the joint between the top of a wall and the eaves. Fascia boards are also attached to rafter tails and serve as a backing for rain gutters. See *frame.*

finial   A spindle-like object often used to dress up the tip of a pyramidal roof, a gable, a spire, a dome, or the top of a post.

firestop   A length of lumber mounted horizontally between two studs. Firestops stabilize a wall but are also meant to contain flames that might otherwise swoop up inside a wall cavity, as though through a chimney. See *stud wall.*

flashing   Strips of aluminum or copper meant to prevent roof leaks. Flashing is installed in valleys, around skylights, and where roofs meet walls, as on a dormer or chimney.

flux   A greasy gel smeared on the joints of copper pipes prior to soldering. Flux prevents oxidation on the heated surfaces of the joint and promotes the flow of melted solder into the space between the pipe and its fitting. See *sweating pipes.*

foam insulation   Rigid boards of foam material, ranging in thickness from a fraction of an inch to three inches. Foam is often used in lieu of fiberglass insulation. Some builders refuse to insulate with foam because it contains chlorofluorocarbons (CFCs), which harm the ozone layer. (But even fiberglass insulation has its risks. Manufacturers label it "possibly carcinogenic.")

footings   The wide, shallow concrete or stone pedestal on which a foundation is erected. Footings provide a stable base for walls, posts, piers, and columns. Footings built on different levels, following the topography of the site, are known as *stepped footings.*

foundation   The thick stone or concrete structure on which a house is built. A foundation can be made of stone, concrete blocks, or poured concrete in the form of walls, piers, posts, or columns. Long ago, most houses were built on piles of stone called *rubble*, often without mortar to hold the stones in place and seal the spaces between them. Few such houses remain standing today. Understandably.

forms   Wooden structures used as molds for poured concrete. Forms must be sturdy. Until the concrete hardens, they are like dikes holding back a flood of semi-liquid stone.

frame   The basic structural component of a building; its skeleton. A frame consists of numerous members, each with a name and a function.

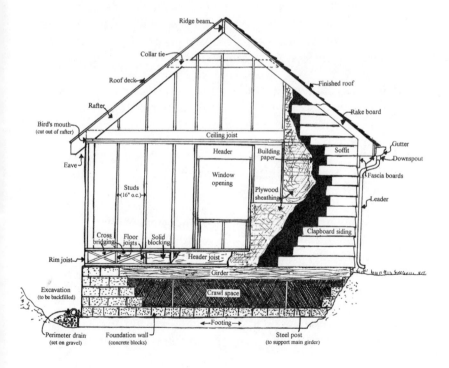

front loader A piece of heavy earth-moving machinery that digs up huge amounts of dirt and rocks with a wide scoop attached to its front end.

girder The most substantial supporting member of a house frame. A girder carries considerable weight and may itself be supported by the foundation and piers or posts. In most homes the main girder is made of wood, but a steel I-beam can carry the same load with eight inches less depth than a built-up wooden beam. That is, ten inches of steel bear roughly the equivalent of eighteen inches of wood. See *frame*.

header A horizontal beam that spans the top of a window or door. Because a header often supports parts of a floor, a wall, or the roof, it must be strong. A piece of plywood sandwiched between two lengths of lumber gives a header its muscle. Sometimes a steel plate, known as a *flitch*, is substituted for the plywood. Now and then, built-up beams or glulams (several strips of plywood glued together) serve as headers. Also called a *lintel*.

jamb The upright surface forming the side of a window or door opening. Typically, a jamb is four to four and a half inches wide. Two-by-six framing, however, necessitates jambs that are two inches wider.

j-bolt A threaded bolt used to attach the sill to the foundation. See *anchor bolt*.

joint compound A pudding-like substance that hardens when dry and is used both to fill in the seams between sheets of drywall and to hide dents, gullies, and assorted dingles on a finished wall. Sometimes called *spackle* or, by those in the know, *mud*.

jointer A woodworker's tool used to plane a true edge onto a piece of sawn wood. Two pieces of wood with perfectly smooth, straight edges can be joined almost seamlessly. Hence the name of the tool.

joists The horizontal beams that support a floor. When the joists are underfoot, they're called *floor joists,* when overhead, *ceiling joists.* See *frame.*

joist hanger A steel device used to secure one or more joists to a header.

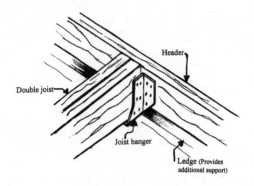

junction box A steel or plastic box inside which electrical cables are spliced.

kneewall An abbreviated wall used to elevate a pitched roof. A kneewall, anywhere from a few inches to several feet high, can help turn an attic into usable living space.

lath Thin strips of wood mounted on walls to hold plaster. Wood lath is rarely used any more, except in restorations. Metal lath, a flexible steel mesh, is the material of choice among today's lathers—if there are any about. Drywall has made lathers as rare as coopers and wheelwrights.

lathe A woodworking machine used to make round posts, table legs, baseball bats—or any other any wooden object that is tubular, conical, cylindrical, ovoid, columnar, or gibbous. As the wood rotates about a horizontal axis, a sharp blade shapes the wood.

masonry hammer   A hammer designed for whacking bricks, concrete blocks, and other stone-like materials. Its head is meatier than that of a carpenter's hammer, and its handle longer.

miter box   A device in the form of a wooden or metal trough that guides a handsaw at the proper angle for a cutting a miter joint. Vertical slots in the sides of the box guide the saw for cuts of $22^1/_2$, 45, and 90 degrees. A swivel in some miter boxes permits the saw to be positioned at any angle.

miter saw   See *chopsaw.*

mortise and tenon   A type of joint found in post-and-beam construction. Mortises and tenons go together, both verbally and physically. The tenon, a protuberance at the end of a beam, fits inside the mortise, a receiving cavity, groove, or slot. Wooden pegs hold the tenon securely in the mortise.

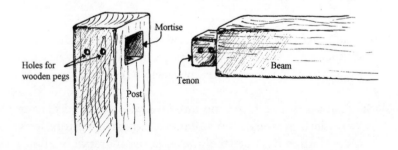

mudsill   The only framing member that sits directly on the foundation. Mounting the mudsill—the initial piece of the frame—marks a milestone in the construction of a house: no more mucking about with concrete. Also called the *sill, main sill,* or *sill beam.* See also *anchor bolt* and *stud wall.*

nail gun A gas- or air-driven fastening tool that sinks nails with astonishing power and speed. A typical nail gun can shoot a three-and-a-half-inch nail into tough southern yellow pine or dense Douglas fir in less than a tenth of a second. Some say that a nail gun is so lethal you ought to have a license to carry it.

nailer A piece of wood that provides a surface to which wallboard or another piece of wood can be attached. See *sleeper*.

newel post A post on a stairway that holds the railing. See *staircase*.

nippers A tool resembling pincers used to trim or shape ceramic tile by nipping off small fragments at a time. Care must be taken while nipping. If a bite is too large, the whole tile may suddenly crack or shatter.

on-center A phrase that describes a system of measurement. In builders' lingo, "on-center," or "o.c.," indicates that the interval between parallel framing members measured from the center of one piece to the center of the next. Framing members—studs, joists, rafters—are typically "sixteen inches o.c."

particle board A synthetic material made of wood chips, chemicals, and glue and used most often as an underlayment for plastic laminate (e.g., Formica) countertops and as subfloors. Gases given off by urea-formaldehyde adhesives used in manufacturing particle board are said to cause health problems for chemically sensitive people.

partition A wall that serves as a separation between spaces inside a building. Unlike a bearing wall, a partition holds up nothing but itself.

pier A pillar, post, or other vertical support, usually made of stone, concrete block, or poured concrete.

pitch   The steepness of a roof. Pitch is described not by degrees but by the ratio between the *rise* (vertical distance) and the *run* (horizontal distance). Thus, a roof that rises ten feet over a span of thirty feet has a "one-in-three" pitch. To keep your balance on a steep roof, say, with a pitch of one-in-one, requires the dexterity of a tightrope walker. Also called *slope*.

planer   A tool that smoothes the surface of lumpy, bruised, or beat-up boards.

plumb bob   A tool consisting of a string and a pointed weight tied to one end and used to determine verticality. Physical laws force the string to hang straight down unless a stiff breeze blows the string out of plumb.

plywood   Thin layers of wood glued together with grains of adjacent layers perpendicular to each other. Plywood usually comes in four-by-eight-foot sheets and in thicknesses from a quarter of an inch to over an inch. The surface of plywood used for sheathing ("construction grade") is rough and knotty. But better grades of plywood have smooth surfaces and solid cores. In fact, cabinet-grade plywood comes with a silky veneer of pine, oak, birch, cherry, or other fine wood, and can be used to make handsome furniture.

post and beam   See *timber framing*.

pressure-treated   A description of lumber that has been treated with preservatives applied under pressure. Because water will decompose most common woods (other than cedar and redwood) pressure-treated lumber is used for decks, mudsills, fences, and other structures exposed to damp ground or to the weather. Handling newly treated lumber is akin to an upper-body workout. The stuff is abominably heavy.

punch list   A "to-do" list of items remaining to be completed on a building project.

radiant floor heat   A system of heating in which a grid of pipes carrying hot water is installed beneath a wood or concrete floor. The initial cost of radiant heat is high, but over time it can lower heating bills. Better still, radiant heat keeps a space toasty on the coldest days and makes cold feet a thing of the past.

radial-arm saw   A shop tool particularly suited to cutting large, heavy boards. Instead of pushing the board to the blade, the operator simply lowers the blade—suspended from a movable arm—onto the lumber.

rafters   The sloping roof beams to which the roof deck is attached. See *bevel* and *frame.*

rafter tail   The bottom end of a rafter that extends beyond the wall of the house. When the eave is left open, the exposed rafter tail serves as a decorative architectural feature, notably in Craftsman, Oriental, and Gothic Revival styles.

reciprocating saw   A hand-held power tool, often called a *Sawzall* (after the popular model made by Milwaukee Tool Company). Because blades protrude from the tip of the tool and are generally long and slender, a reciprocating saw can make cuts in tight places, unreachable with other saws.

ridge, ridge pole, ridge beam   The uppermost piece of the roof frame. Builders often celebrate the completion of framing a house by attaching a small evergreen tree to the ridge. See *frame.*

rake   The edge of a pitched roof, often trimmed with a rake board. See *frame.*

re-bar   A steel rod used to reinforce concrete. Re-bars are inserted into the forms before the concrete is poured.

riser   The vertical surface between treads on a set of stairs. The height of the riser and the width of the tread are governed by strict safety codes. See *staircase.*

roof   The outside cover of a house or building. The slope, shape, size, color, and texture of a roof, along with any add-ons such as dormers, influence the external appearance and character of the entire structure. The roofs of most houses are variations on those illustrated below.

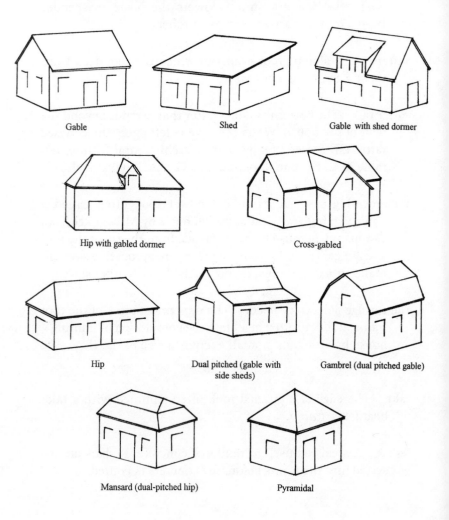

Gable   Shed   Gable with shed dormer

Hip with gabled dormer   Cross-gabled

Hip   Dual pitched (gable with   Gambrel (dual pitched gable)
                    side sheds)

Mansard (dual-pitched hip)   Pyramidal

roofing cement   A gummy, tar-like substance with multiple functions, mostly to seal seams, plug holes, and keep leaks at bay. Roofing cement comes in cans and tubes and tends to soil hands, stain clothing, and get onto everything else in sight.

router   A versatile shop tool used to shape wood. Routers enable a woodworker to fashion decorative moldings and casings, to make dovetail joints, to raise door panels, and engrave letters on wooden signs. A variety of router bits can dress up the edge of a board with rounded corners, flutes, channels, curves, grooves, and fillets.

screed   An overgrown squeegee made of wood used to smooth the surface of newly poured concrete.

shakes   Pieces of cedar used for roofing and siding. Shakes, which are hewn (not sawn) from cedar logs are rougher, thicker, and more durable than shingles. They give a house a rustic look.

sheathing   Usually plywood—but also diagonally mounted solid wood boards or waferboard—used to enclose the frame of a house. If the frame is the muscle and bone of a house, sheathing is its skin. It stiffens the frame and keeps a house on-kilter. Sometimes called *plyscord*.

Sheetrock   See *drywall.*

shingles   The most common roofing and siding material. Made of asphalt, each three-tab roofing shingle covers about one and a half square feet. Cedar shingles, used to cover both roofs and walls, are expensive and slow to install, but make up for these shortcomings in durability and good looks. Siding can be painted, stained, or left to weather on its own. Over time cedar shingles take on an attractive silvery-gray patina.

siding   The outside protective surface of a house. Siding comes in many forms, each with its virtues and shortcomings. The perfect siding—one that looks and feels like wood, that requires no maintenance and will last forever—has yet to be invented.

sill beam   See *mudsill.*

Skilsaw   See *circular saw.*

slab   The simplest concrete foundation for a building, consisting of a bed of gravel and four inches of concrete. The slab is often thickened underneath heavy loads such as the chimney and supporting pillars. Of all foundations, the slab is the fastest and cheapest for a do-it-yourselfer to build.

sleeper   A length of lumber used to provide a nailing surface for another piece of lumber or plywood. Sleepers are used, for example, when installing a wooden floor over a concrete slab. Also see *nailer.*

soffit   The horizontally mounted trim piece that encloses the eaves. See *frame.* A vent that promotes air circulation is often installed in the soffit to prevent condensation from forming on the underside of the roof deck. The boxed-in space between kitchen cabinets and the ceiling is also called the *soffit.*

solder   An amalgam of tin and lead used to sweat water pipes. Melted solder flows into the space between a pipe and its fitting. When the solder hardens it creates a watertight seal. See *sweating pipes.*

Sonotube   A cylinder used to form concrete foundation columns. Sonotubes, which are made of thick cardboard, need not be removed after the concrete hardens. Buried in backfill, they will disintegrate over time.

spirit level   A device for finding a horizontal or vertical plane by means of a bubble in a vial of alcohol or other liquid. Movement of the bubble to the center of the vial, which is slightly bowed, indicates that the instrument is horizontal or vertical. Carpenters riding the techno-curve have switched to laser levels, which give truer readings.

staircase A flight of stairs. It's not unheard of for a home-owner, using stock parts, to build an eye-catching, eco-nomical staircase. Attaching the balustrade is the trickiest, most time-consuming part of the job.

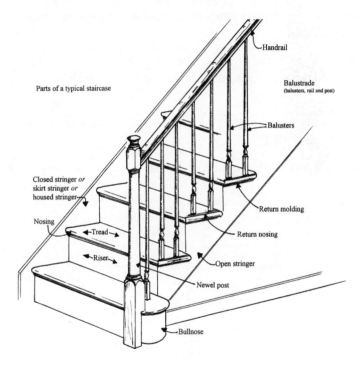

Parts of a typical staircase

Handrail

Balustrade
(balusters, rail and post)

Balusters

Closed stringer or
skirt stringer or
housed stringer

Return molding

Nosing

Tread

Return nosing

Riser

Open stringer

Newel post

Bullnose

step sheathing The type of roof deck on which to mount wood shingles. Made with one-by-three or one-by-four slats, step sheathing is installed with narrow gaps left be-tween each row. Air circulates through the gaps and under the shingles, preventing decay and allowing the shingles to "breathe"—that is, to expand and contract with atmos-pheric changes. As shingles alternately get wet and dry, cold and hot, they tend to push the nails out. That's why an old shingled roof may appear to be studded with nails. In the north country that's a plus, for the nails hold snow—

a good insulator—on the roof. Also called *open-deck sheathing* or *skip sheathing*.

stick-built A term that describes construction using two-by's. In contrast to the timbers in a post-and-beam structure, the pieces of a stick-built house are light enough for one person to lift and assemble alone. See *two-by's*.

stringers The main supporting beams on a set of stairs. See *staircase*.

stucco A mixture of cement, sand, and plaster slathered onto the exterior of a house in lieu of wood, vinyl, or another kind of siding.

stud The main supporting member of walls and partitions. See *stud wall*.

stud wall A wall framed with studs—usually two-by-sixes on exterior walls and on plumbing walls (those that encase drains and vents). Generally, two-by-four studs are used everywhere else.

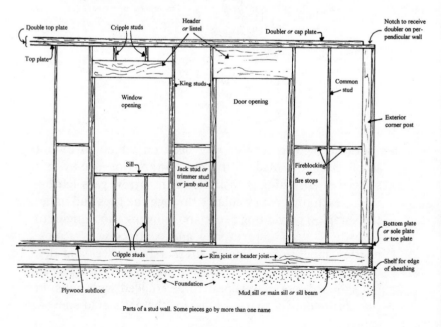

Parts of a stud wall. Some pieces go by more than one name

sub *or* **subcontractor**   A specialist in one of the building trades hired to do a job that an owner-builder declines to do himself. High on the list of subcontractors engaged by do-it-yourselfers are excavators, well diggers, masons, electricians, and plumbers.

subfloor   The first layer of wood attached to joists. A subfloor is usually made of plywood, wood planks or particle board. The finished floor is laid on top of it, often with a resinous building paper between the two layers to reduce squeaks.

sweating pipes   The process used to assemble copper pipes in a plumbing system. Intense heat applied to a joint with a propane torch melts the solder, which flows into the small opening between the pipe and its fitting, creating a permanent, leak-free seal. See *flux*.

table saw   A stationary, platform-mounted woodworking tool used for making straight, precise cuts. Stock is pushed into a rapidly spinning circular blade across a flat surface alongside an adjustable guide called a fence, or it can be guided by a miter attachment to make angled cuts. A furniture builder would be dead in the water without a reliable table saw.

taping   The process of concealing the gaps between sheets of drywall. Seams are covered with narrow strips of paper tape and smeared with several thin layers of joint compound until the seam is no longer visible. Sandpaper helps during the final stages. Taping is easier to describe than to do.

tenon   A projecting member of a piece of wood or timber for inserting into a mortise to form a joint. Tenons are used in timber framing and in furniture building. See *mortise and tenon*.

timber framing   A method of house framing featuring the use of large posts holding up large beams, the components joined by means of mortises and tenons. Before 1900, most houses and barns were timber framed. Now, the method is used to create a chic, country look. See *mortise and tenon*.

toenailing   Hammering a nail diagonally through one piece of wood into another. By toenailing, a vertical piece of the frame can be firmly attached to a horizontal piece.

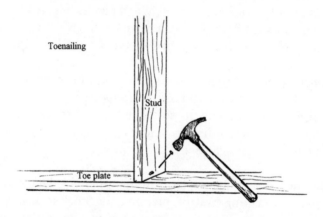

tongue and groove   A type of joint between parallel panels of wood. The edge of one panel has a protruding tongue that fits snugly into a groove cut into the next one.

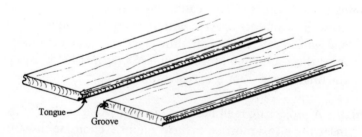

top plate   The horizontal member at the top of a wall frame. See *stud wall*.

tread   The horizontal surface of a step. See *staircase*.

truss A prefabricated assembly of boards used as the structural members of a roof. Trusses eliminate piece-by-piece roof framing. Instead, joists, rafters, and collar ties are nailed together in the factory and hoisted directly onto the walls. While saving a good deal of time and effort on the job site, trusses are too heavy and unwieldy for a builder working alone.

two-by's A term used to refer to common dimensional lumber: two-by-fours, two-by-sixes, etc. See also *dimensional lumber.*

Tyvek A resilient fibrous product used to wrap houses. Tyvek, which keeps out wind and rain, eliminates the need to install building paper, or felt, between the sheathing and the siding. Because it is light and hardy, Federal Express uses Tyvek for its FedEx Paks. An alternate product: Typar.

valley The area where two roof planes intersect. Cutting valley rafters and valley jack rafters is one of the more intricate framing tasks. Valleys need to be flashed with aluminum or other metal to keep them from leaking.

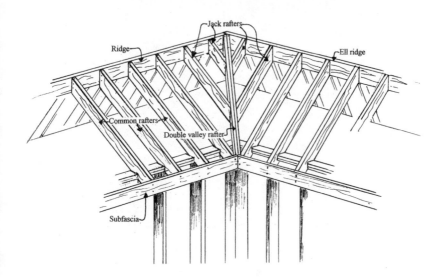

waferboard   A synthetic material made of wood chips and glue and often used as sheathing. A poor man's plywood, waferboard must be protected from water or it will swell and deteriorate.

wainscoting   Interior decorative wood paneling that covers part of a wall, ordinarily the lower third or half.

wallboard   See *drywall.*

wet saw   A water-cooled power saw that uses a diamond-studded blade to cut ceramic tile, marble, and other rock-hard materials.

References

Alexander, Christopher, et al. *A Pattern Language*. Oxford University Press, 1977.

Brann, Donald R. *How to Build an Addition*. Directions Simplified, Inc., 1974.

Gill, Eric. *A Holy Tradition of Working*, ed. Brian Keeble. Golgonooza Press, 1983.

Goldfrank, Janice. *Making Ourselves at Home*. Papier-Mâché Press, 1995.

Marcus, Clare Cooper. *House as a Mirror of Self*. Conari Press, 1995.

Nash, George. "Hinges." *This Old House* (July/August 1997).

Do-It-Yourself Housebuilding. Sterling Publishing Co., 1995.

Wooden Fences. Taunton Press, 1997.

Old Houses: A Rebuilder's Manual. Prentice-Hall, 1980.

Renovating Old Houses. Taunton Press, 1992.

Shope, Allan. "Raising a House Addition." *Fine Homebuilding*
  (Spring 1990).

Tetrault, Jean, and Sherry Thomas. *Country Women: Handbook for the New Farmer.* Anchor/Doubleday, 1976.

Thoreau, Henry David. *Walden.* Houghton Mifflin Co., 1957.

Vila, Bob. *This Old House.* Little, Brown & Co., 1980.

Index